KATE EDGER

Kate Edger

The life of a pioneering feminist

DIANA MORROW

OTAGO UNIVERSITY PRESS
Te Whare Tā o Te Wānanga o Ōtākou

Published by Otago University Press
Te Whare Tā o Te Wānanga o Ōtākou
Level 1, 398 Cumberland Street
Dunedin, New Zealand
university.press@otago.ac.nz
www.otago.ac.nz/press

First published 2021
Copyright © Diana Morrow
The moral rights of the author have been asserted.

ISBN 978-1-98-859264-0

Published with the assistance of Creative New Zealand

Editor: Anna Rogers
Index: Lee Slater
Design/layout: Fiona Moffat

Front cover: Kate Edger, image courtesy of Nelson College for Girls

Printed in New Zealand by Caxton

The higher ideal you place before yourself the more likely you are to reach it.
KATE EDGER, 1889

The woman who is a good citizen cannot be contented with things as they are.
KATE SHEPPARD, 1899

Contents

Preface and Acknowledgements

Kate Edger was a 'first-wave' New Zealand feminist, celebrated for her role in advancing the cause of higher education for women. Her achievements in that field were significant and far-reaching, but she was also involved in a wide range of influential social reform causes. As Kate Evans, after her marriage in 1890, she undertook decades of unpaid social work and campaigned for legislative change on behalf of vulnerable women and children, an aspect of her life's work that has been relatively unheralded. In doing so, she confronted physical, sexual and emotional abuse that social workers and feminist reformers in the twenty-first century are still striving to eradicate. Her religious beliefs, and the mid-Victorian evangelical impulses that underpinned them, were crucial in shaping and directing her social and feminist activism.

Few letters and private papers have survived to throw light on Kate's personality and intimate relationships. The available evidence suggests that she was blessed with an affectionate, supportive family, though her personal life had its share of grief, disappointment and drama. Her social activism has left richer sources in the historical record, including parliamentary papers, newspaper accounts, articles and letters by Kate and her fellow feminists, as well as the papers and publications generated by the major New Zealand women's groups of the time.

I have received help and assistance from a wide range of people and organisations. A Ministry for Culture and Heritage New Zealand History Research Trust Fund Award in 2016–17 helped to finance research for what was then intended to be a history of the whole Edger family. I soon decided to focus on Kate's life and work and am very grateful to Kate's granddaughter, Jill Smith, for allowing me access to the few family papers that remain, and to some wonderful photographs. In

Auckland, my research has been assisted by Jo Birks, cultural collections adviser, and Katherine Pawley, archivist, cultural collections, University of Auckland Library. Peter Marsh, manager/curator of the Albertland Heritage Centre, Wellsford, and David Verran of the Auckland Libraries Research Centre, answered queries online. During a research trip to Nelson I was grateful for the assistance of Jeanette Ware, research assistant, and Helen Pannett, curator, Archives and Research, at Nelson Provincial Museum, Pupuri Taonga o Te Tai Ao. Libby MacCreadie, archivist at Nelson College for Girls, and Cathy Ewing, principal of Nelson College for Girls, and Bruce Harding, curator/archivist at Christchurch Boys' High School, provided online assistance, as did Scott Campbell, Hocken Collections assistant at the University of Otago Library. Linda McGregor and David Retter, research librarians at the Alexander Turnbull Library, were unfailingly helpful during a research trip to Wellington. Linda has, since then, answered my various queries about sources with impressive efficiency and courteous forbearance.

I am also grateful to the historians Margaret Tennant and Margaret Lovell-Smith, both for their published works and for their help with sources, and to Richard Boast, not only for information about Frank Edger but for his enthusiasm about the project when I was starting out. It has been a pleasure working with Rachel Scott and Vanessa Manhire of Otago University Press, and I am grateful to Anna Rogers for her skilful and meticulous editing.

Finally, I would like to thank my husband John Morrow for his unflagging help and support throughout the writing of this book. He has read numerous drafts, each of which benefited from his sympathetic but sharp editorial input, and managed, with no uncertain diplomatic skill, to provide just the right balance of advice and encouragement.

Equal Rights, Superior Morals

In 1901 the *Free Lance*'s 'All Sorts of People' column described Kate Evans as 'one of the cleverest of New Zealand women' who, in addition to running an 'advanced academy' for young ladies, was the 'affectionate mother of a small family'. The article went on to paint a charming picture: 'Mrs. Evans is often seen in town doing her shopping per medium of her bicycle, upon which she trundles home a well-filled Maori kit [kete]. In her busy useful life she finds sufficient leisure to go into and about the slums of the city doing much good for the deserving poor.'[1] This evocative image of a busy, middle-aged professional woman, cycling around town and shopping for the family, has a curiously modern air. Most notable, in the context of the times, is the admiring tone. A bicycle-riding, middle-class female professional in the early twentieth century might well have fallen into that much vilified contemporary category, a 'New Woman'. These modern feminists, with their call for women's rights, were fair game for many journalists. According to one popular American columnist, much quoted in the New Zealand press, feminism drew its support from the 'unattractive and unloved'. 'New Women' were ugly, old maids or 'disappointed wives'.[2]

The other noteworthy thing about the piece is its lack of reference to Kate's pioneering role in women's higher education. Twenty-three years earlier, in 1877, aged 20, she became the first female university graduate in New Zealand, and the first woman in the British Empire to receive a Bachelor of Arts degree.[3] This one symbolic moment came to represent her claim to fame, and the landmark degree her most significant achievement. As a result, she is almost always known, in the scholarly accounts and commemorations of her life to date, by her maiden name, Kate Edger. But the BA was only the beginning.

Barbara Brookes, in *A History of New Zealand Women*, cites Kate Edger's life as a counter-example to all those many contemporaries who feared that the impact of higher education would 'unsex' women, place them in competition with men, rob them of their womanly virtues and make them unfit for traditional female roles as wives and mothers.[4] Anxieties about the combined impacts of first-wave feminism, higher education and expanding employment opportunities for women intensified in the early twentieth century.

An entry in the 1966 *Encyclopaedia of New Zealand* described Kate's main contribution to New Zealand as her influence on the feminist movement, adding: 'Her successful university career gave encouragement to future women students and served as a proof of women's capabilities, not only in higher education, but also in all other spheres previously debarred them.' The entry also noted that 'Any reform movement engaged her active support.'[5] Yet Beryl Hughes' 1993 account of Kate's life and work in the *Dictionary of New Zealand Biography* describes her as 'not strongly feminist in outlook', citing as evidence an article she wrote in 1923. In considering whether higher education for women had justified itself, Kate said: 'It is too soon yet for a complete answer to be given to this question, but thousands of university women are proving by their lives that it has not unfitted them for home-making, the noblest sphere of women's work.' Megan Hutching, in *Leading the Way: How New Zealand women won the vote* (2010), cites the same sentence and observes that, given the few records she left behind, 'it is impossible to know why Kate thought this way'. She conjectures that Kate was attempting to counter the popular perception that higher education and home-making were mutually exclusive.[6]

In common with most leading first-wave feminists, Kate was an evangelical Christian, whose belief in the 'noblest sphere' could and did go hand in hand with liberal progressive views and energetic campaigning to improve women's legal rights, education and employment opportunities. Religion, notably liberal nonconformism, and a pervasive evangelical domestic ideal that was seen to transcend religious and class divides, was central to the thinking of New Zealand's early feminists. Fifty-seven percent of the British-born feminists in the *Dictionary of New Zealand Biography* characterised as 'active in reform' came from nonconformist denominations.[7] But what those women believed, and how those beliefs shaped their activism, has received relatively little scholarly attention.[8]

John Stenhouse has examined this neglect within the context of a broader argument that New Zealand historians have generally marginalised religion in favour of a secular nationalist progression 'away from the darkness'. Religious nonconformists especially have been caricatured and vilified as sex-hating killjoys, who for decades wrapped a heavy cloak of stultifying puritanism around New Zealand culture. Yet, as Stenhouse observes, 'Enlightened Protestantism – politically liberal, religiously tolerant, socially inclusive, scientifically-oriented and intellectually progressive – constituted one of colonial New Zealand's most central cultural traditions.' He cites Kate Sheppard, a Congregationalist, and Kate Edger, whom he categorises as Baptist but who was Congregationalist as an adult, as high-profile examples of women who 'feminised' this liberal Protestant tradition.[9]

First-wave feminism in New Zealand, as elsewhere in the world, was a complex, evolving movement, incorporating many diverse and not always laudable points of view, including those from the fashionable pseudo-science of eugenics. But the religiously tolerant and liberal brand of feminism that Stenhouse describes was a dominant strain, especially among the nonconformist women who led the suffrage campaign. Both before and after acquiring the vote, these feminists campaigned for a wide range of social reforms that shaped New Zealand's wider culture for decades to come.

From the 1880s Kate Edger moved in a tightly knit circle of like-minded progressive liberal reformers and feminists, male and female, who exerted a significant impact and influence on legislation and national culture, especially during the Liberal government of 1891 to 1912. During that time, New Zealand earned international kudos as 'the world's social laboratory'. Kate's liberalism and her evangelical religious beliefs were inextricable from her feminism and from her efforts to introduce supportive legislation on behalf of women and children.

Dissent, liberty and social justice

Kate Edger came from a long line of Baptists and Congregationalists. These denominations, along with Presbyterians and a number of smaller radical Protestant religious groups, were known as 'Old Dissent', and had their roots in the sixteenth and seventeenth centuries. They were often collectively called Puritans, especially by their detractors, because they sought a more pure form of Protestantism, that is, purified from any vestige of Catholicism and more extensively reformed to enable freedom of conscience.[10] Congregationalists did not have a set creed and ran their own chapels, with members of each congregation administering chapel affairs and choosing their ministers. Baptists rejected infant baptism, believing instead in adult baptism for professing believers. They, too, had no set creed, no central controlling structure and were a diverse group, fiercely protective of freedom of conscience.

During the English Civil War of 1642–51 various dissenting groups, despite many differences of belief, fought together on the parliamentary side led by Oliver Cromwell against the Royalist supporters of King Charles I. When Charles II was restored as king and head of the Church of England in 1660, he implemented the Clarendon Code, a series of four legal statutes passed between 1661 and 1665 that ended toleration for dissenting or nonconforming religions, that is, those who refused to conform to the Church of England. The 1661 Corporation Act, for example, made it illegal for anyone not receiving communion in the Church of England to hold office in municipal corporations, while the 1662 Act of Uniformity required clergymen to accept the Book of Common Prayer. As a result of this latter act, some 1000 dissenting or nonconformist clergy lost their livings. Later, in 1673, the Test Act barred dissenters from holding public office or from being MPs. From the mid-eighteenth century 'New Dissenters', the followers of John Wesley, a Church of England clergyman who advocated a more enthusiastic and emotionally expressive or evangelical form of worship, joined the tradition of dissent from the established church and founded Methodism.[11] Dissenting denominations both old and new attended chapel rather than church.

However zealously they guarded their denominational differences, non-conformists shared many political and social attitudes and values. Church of England clergy were often conservative politically; many were connected to the traditional landed elite and related by marriage or association to the patrons of their livings. By contrast, dissenting ministers came from middle-, lower middle-or skilled working-class families. Most nonconformist congregations in Victorian Britain were predominantly working or lower middle class but dominated by a middle-class elite. Leading nonconformist families such as the Cadburys and the Colmans presided over lucrative businesses and factories, and generally played a significant role in advancing Britain's booming industrial revolution. They took pride in the fact that their success stemmed from hands-on hard work and initiative, in contrast to the inherited privilege of the landed elite. Nonconformists from all walks of life had a strong sense of social justice, and worked zealously for numerous social reform causes, from temperance and women's rights to vegetarianism, penal reform and animal rights. Female nonconformists were actively involved, gaining valuable experience in setting up meetings, public speaking, launching petitions and effective lobbying.[12] Although the Test and Corporation Acts were repealed in 1828, nonconformists continued to fight legal discrimination in five areas: they resented having to pay church rates to the Church of England, and not being able to marry in chapels, attend the ancient universities of Oxford and Cambridge, register births and deaths by civil means and conduct burials outside Church of England churchyards. These rights were achieved incrementally: legislation in 1837 enabled dissenters to marry in their own chapels and to register births, deaths and marriages civilly, but they did not obtain full access to degrees and fellowships at Oxford and Cambridge until 1871.[13]

From 1840, propaganda enticing settlers to New Zealand with the promise of a better life therefore held a special appeal to nonconformists. The new colony offered them equal rights as citizens, no state church and no powerful entrenched landed class.[14] New Zealand represented a relatively blank slate on which they could try to write their version of the ideal society. By 1871 Anglicans made up 42.5 percent of the total New Zealand population, Presbyterians 25.12, Roman Catholics 18.92, Wesleyan Methodists 7.62, Congregationalists 1.94 and Baptists 1.90. Twenty years later, in 1891, the proportions remained largely unchanged.[15] Collectively, nonconformists made up some 37 percent of the New Zealand population, just behind the Anglicans.

From the early 1860s most British nonconformists threw their political support behind William Gladstone's Liberal Party. Although Wesleyan Methodists were generally more conservative politically than the older dissenting groups they too, by the 1890s, had largely moved into the Liberal Party camp.[16] The dissenters were attracted to a political party that aimed to integrate and harmonise different groups within the nation and used its power to strengthen particular moral values in society. They perceived themselves as standard-bearers of a progressive liberalism that valued hard work, self-help, respectability and equality under the law.

Nonconformists placed great stock on liberty of conscience and of action. The philosophical expression of these values was provided by the influential liberal thinker John Stuart Mill, in arguments that were echoed by New Zealand feminists. Mill's *On Liberty*, published in 1859, three years before the Edger family emigrated to New Zealand, set out the importance of individual liberty and the need for citizens to be insulated from legislative and social pressures that compromised liberty. In 1869 his *The Subjection of Women* advocated equal rights and suffrage for women. Mill argued that women's supposed intellectual inferiority to men was not innate but due largely to poor education, and that their lower legal and social status represented a major impediment to progress.[17]

New Zealand feminists' push for suffrage used both these ideas and enlightenment arguments based on natural justice and equal rights of citizenship. Appeals to the 'rights of men' were more properly appeals to the rights of human beings, and justice required that claims to political and social rights should be recognised in all adult members of civilised communities. But feminists, influenced by evangelicalism and its accompanying domestic ideal, also claimed that allowing women to vote would benefit the nation, making it purer and more moral.

Evangelicalism and the domestic ideal

The dissenting denominations, most notably Congregationalists, Methodists and Baptists, as well as many members of the Church of England, were swept up in an enthusiastic, hugely influential evangelical spiritual revival that began in the late eighteenth century.[18] This placed great emphasis on salvation by faith. Individuals carried the responsibility for their own salvation, which was a matter of moral choice or individual conscience. Having undergone a conversion experience – in some sense having been born anew – they would then be certain of salvation. Evangelicals energetically spread the gospel of salvation at home and abroad and pushed for state reform on a range of moral issues and righteous causes, most famously and triumphantly the abolition of the slave trade and eventually slavery itself in all British territories.[19] They aimed to lead morally exemplary lives of service and self-sacrifice. Their high seriousness and earnest pursuit of social reform left them vulnerable to satire and mockery. Victorian literature abounds in sombrely attired evangelical hypocrites.

Evangelicalism was also a religion of the home, one that idealised and sanctified family life.[20] The evangelical domestic ideal invoked 'separate spheres'. While men worked in commerce or the professions, middle-class wives and mothers did not work outside the home but provided their husbands with a peaceful enclave, a haven from the cold realities of a competitive, materialistic society. The saving grace of domestic life was ordained by nature and religion. Home ties were believed to inspire in adults and children a wholesome, moral life. In all evangelical homes, whether Church of England or Dissenting, members prayed together and enforced certain common disciplines. Gender roles were unambiguous. Husbands governed, informed and provided; women managed, distributed and nurtured.[21] The ideal marriage relationship was monogamous, respectful and based on mutual responsibility.

Families in which members behaved dutifully, affectionately and responsibly towards one other represented a blueprint for society as a whole. Women were the moral linchpins of the home, their high moral status resting on the enhanced prestige of motherhood. By virtue of their natural role as wives and mothers, they were perceived to be sensitive, compassionate, benevolent, nurturing, self-renouncing and sexually pure. This middle-class model of domesticity, with its focus on clear-cut gender roles and emphasis on moral respectability, permeated Victorian society, sifting down through church and chapel, tracts and improving literature to the working classes, where the distinction between 'respectable' and 'rough' amounted almost to a class distinction.[22]

Moral influence and the feminist mission

Some advocates of the evangelical domestic ideal argued against extending women's purported moral influence. The influential public intellectual John Ruskin, for example, in his 1864 lecture 'Sesame and Lilies', opposed equal education for women on the grounds that their redemptive and gentle guiding powers found best expression in the 'sacred place' of home.[23] For many women, however, that role as moral protector gave the sense of spiritual worth and mission to become involved in philanthropic works and to morally protect others' homes (more often than not those of the working classes). This moralising role has been described as 'a crucial component both in the inspiration of many women *into* feminism, and also into the very nature of their feminist mission'. They 'stretched various family roles precisely to ratify their public activism'.[24]

Although the term 'feminist' was not used until the early 1890s, in America evangelical women had been radicalised as early as the 1820s and 1830s through the anti-slavery movement, which threw into relief the question of male ownership of women's bodies. They began lobbying state legislatures about the rights and vulnerabilities of women within marriage and the need to improve women's education.[25] Women's rights advocates became increasingly vocal in Victorian Britain from the mid-nineteenth century onwards, led predominantly by middle-class women from liberal nonconformist families. But from 1869, Josephine Butler, a middle-class Anglican evangelical, helped to galvanise the nascent women's movement when, along with Elizabeth Wolstenholme, she founded the Ladies National Association for the Repeal of the Contagious Diseases Act. Butler and her followers vehemently objected to this legislation, first passed in 1864, which enabled compulsory police checks of prostitutes for venereal disease while their male clients walked free. As a result of Butler's high-profile crusade, the act was repealed in 1886.

This was the first victorious battle in what became a series of social purity campaigns against sexual behaviour that fell short of the evangelical domestic ideal. Significantly, Butler's campaign inverted the prevailing view of 'fallen women', defending them both as citizens whose human rights had been violated, and as victims of male pollution.[26] Her high-profile campaign, articulated in impassioned language charged with evangelical moral indignation and reforming zeal, inspired women's rights activists throughout Britain, America and the British colonies, who endorsed the demand that male sexuality be subject to the same moral standard expected of women. To admit otherwise would, as Barbara Brookes has observed, involve sanctioning a belief in an 'ungovernable male sexuality which sanctioned unlimited child-bearing for wives, and prostitution, adultery and seduction'.[27]

Women's religious beliefs, and their strong sense of their role as moral arbiters of the family, empowered them to enter the male world of political debate and to criticise male sexual behaviour, especially the double standard – expecting women to be chaste but accepting a more lax standard of moral conduct in sexual matters for men. Kate Sheppard, writing in 1896, noted, 'If the tone of morality is to be raised, there must be only one standard of morality by which it is measured.' Fifteen years later, commenting on the impact of women's suffrage in New Zealand, she described its greatest benefit as 'a perceptible rise in the moral and humanitarian tone of the country'.[28]

For Kate Edger, as for many other first-wave feminists in New Zealand, the evangelical ideal of women as moral exemplars was a vital motivation for public activism and social reform. Spreading morally sound, sympathetic, compassionate womanly values into spheres outside the home represented a powerful and progressive force for good. To release this, women needed access to education and training, voting rights and involvement in public institutions and organisations.

Womanly values, education and social reform

When arguing the case for enhanced women's rights, Kate and her fellow feminists drew on the rhetoric of evangelical religion, but also used liberal enlightenment arguments based on natural justice and equal rights of citizenship. Progressive evolutionism was also invoked: women's increasing influence beyond the home was seen as part of an 'inevitable movement forward', away 'from natural selection to conscious moral selection'.[29] There was an element of millenarianism about this future feminised world, made peaceful and compassionate by womanly values. The trans-national element of this uplifting mission was expressed by international women's organisations such as the International Council of Women and the Women's Christian Temperance Union.

In New Zealand, Kate and her circle advocated a form of 'new liberalism'. This placed a strong emphasis on education and social reform, to improve the health and welfare of communities and enhance the lives of those most in need. The state must create an environment that would enable each individual to meet his or her potential and, to that end, pass laws to improve the health and welfare of the whole population. The first-wave feminists worked hard to initiate and promote legislation that would safeguard the family and restrain those aspects of male (and female) behaviour that threatened it. From the early 1890s, Kate was increasingly involved in pioneering social work, campaigning for legislation to protect women and children from physical and sexual violence and for a more rehabilitative prison system. Later in life she became a committed advocate of peaceful international arbitration through the League of Nations, which embodied the key female values of co-operation, compassion and conciliation among a family of nations.

The nature and significance of her ideas and achievements in social activism and reform have received little attention from historians. Beryl Hughes' biographical entry about Kate, and Katrina Ford's brief, lucidly written biography, *Unpretending Excellence*, published in 2017, both focus primarily on her achievements as a pioneer of women's higher education.[30] This is understandable, since opening up secondary and tertiary educational opportunities for women had profound long-term impacts. Women's higher education was not, however, only a vital precursor to suffrage: it expanded the intellectual and professional opportunities available to young women and gave them the confidence to proceed in life as men's intellectual equals.

This book, too, follows the story of Kate's life and considers her personality, with its mixture of calmness, equable courtesy, kindliness, energetic determination and high idealism. Contemporary descriptions of her in the press frequently used words such as 'gentle', 'modest', 'unassuming' and 'unpretending', but great strength of will and perseverance existed alongside an unthreatening manner. In her seemingly tireless activism she had a prodigious and impressive capacity for sustained hard work and was an expert at what would today be called multi-tasking.

Kate's life intersected with several key social reform movements of the nineteenth and twentieth centuries, and her long-term involvement in various causes highlights the often overlooked fact that she and many like her continued to work long and hard to strengthen women's welfare and interests during decades when organised feminism in New Zealand had more or less atrophied.[31]

By the early years of the twentieth century, older feminists such as Kate were coming into contact with a younger generation of women's rights activists who shared neither their unflinching emphasis on moral purity nor their liberal predilection for interclass harmony as opposed to class solidarity. These sorts of generational differences grew more marked during World War I and its aftermath, as New Zealand's political economic and cultural landscape became increasingly complex. Arguments reliant on women's morally elevating influence as wives and mothers could strain against notions of equal rights between the sexes; growing fears of racial degeneration and national and imperial decline, along with falling birth rates, were often invoked by those who wanted to bolster women's maternal and domestic roles and curtail their education and employment choices.

But though the evangelical domestic ideal could and often did find common cause with conservative policies that restricted women's opportunities, Kate and her colleagues remained committed to upholding women's equal rights under the law and improving their lives. In old age she continued to indignantly oppose the sexual double standard, and supported broadening women's educational and professional opportunities. Her brand of feminism encouraged women to use their purported special moral qualities to help elevate society and benefit those in need. Active citizenship was, in her view, a corollary of the suffrage, a duty and a privilege.

These reforming women believed themselves to be the moral guardians of the future, part of an inexorable, civilising, feminine force.[32] This empowering and inspiring responsibility transcended selfish motives and national boundaries. All her life Kate believed that with enough hard work and diligent nurture, womanly values could flourish, and a more just, caring society take root, both in New Zealand and around the globe.

1

To the Promised Land

Over the nineteenth century the most prominent image of New Zealand was as an ideal society for European settlers … The single most common allusion to New Zealand calls it 'a land of milk and honey' …

MILES FAIRBURN, *The Ideal Society and its Enemies*, 1989[1]

It was the unblushing doctrine then, Get people out to New Zealand; when there, let them shift for themselves.

SAMUEL EDGER, *Autobiographical Notes and Lectures*, 1886[2]

On 29 May 1862 Samuel and Louisa Edger and their five children embarked from London's East India docks, bound for New Zealand. They were travelling as part of a planned settlement of religious nonconformists destined for Albertland in the Kaipara region, north of Auckland. Farewell gatherings took place from Monday 26 May onwards, including a valedictory service in Newington and a fete at Bromley, with afternoon tea, music and other entertainments. On the departure day, Thursday 29th, there was a grand send-off at the docks, with hymn singing, brass bands and stirring farewell speeches. The ship was then towed to Gravesend where more speeches and 'reluctant good byes were said' before the long journey to the other side of the world began.[3]

Emigrating to New Zealand in the early 1860s was stepping into the unknown. The voyage was long, hazardous, even potentially fatal. Starting a new life thousands of miles away from familiar landscapes, family and friends was daunting, but most people did so because they wanted a better standard of living. New Zealand had a growing reputation as a place where bettering one's economic and social condition appeared likely. Land grants and assisted passages were an added incentive. When gold was discovered in Otago in 1861 many people, mostly from Australia and China, moved to the country to prospect and some ended up settling permanently. Other migrants had loftier goals: to realise religious and political dreams. The Edgers were just such a family: New Zealand was their promised land.

The Albertland prospectus announced that the community would comprise 'Christian men, united by common sympathies and aspirations', who wanted to see their children 'grow up amidst all the influence of a preached gospel and a practical religion'. Named after the recently deceased husband of Queen Victoria, Albertland was made up predominantly of farm labourers and craftsmen from the Midlands, Yorkshire and Lancashire.[4] It aimed to incorporate co-operative principles that would foster mutual assistance and brotherhood between fellow Christians of various social classes. The vast majority of migrants came from nonconformist denominations. In New Zealand, they would not face the legal and educational barriers that still confronted them in the old world because of their religious beliefs.

New Zealand has probably had more intentional communities than any other country in the world and occupies 'a special place in the history of utopianism'.[5] Albertland, one of the early special settlements and perhaps the best known, did not live up to the dreams of its founders, but it influenced many lives and careers and helped to shape national culture and politics. Kate's four years in Albertland, and her later childhood experiences in Auckland as the daughter of a crusading father, laid the groundwork for a lifelong dedication to progressive social reform.

Albertland: Co-operation in Kaipara

The Reverend Edger first heard about Albertland through a chance meeting with one of its organisers early in 1862, when he was feeling discouraged by sectarian rifts within his Baptist congregation in Abingdon, Berkshire. When told about the proposed settlement, he exclaimed, 'Why, that is just the thing for me!' The reply was an encouraging: 'And you are just the man for it.'[6] He was soon appointed pastor for the 688 emigrants who had signed up to sail on the first two ships to New Zealand. To the hiring committee, his anti-sectarian views seemed a bonus, because the intended settlers were a mixture of Baptists, Congregationalists, Methodists, Presbyterians and a small number of Anglicans and Quakers.

For Edger the scheme seemed a providential opportunity to build the kind of non-sectarian brotherhood of true Christians of which he had always dreamt. As he explained in his memoirs, 'Nothing whatever but the pressure of religious conviction brought about the change.'[7] Most Victorian clergymen would have counted themselves fortunate to raise a growing family in Abingdon, then a picturesque town of some 7000 inhabitants nestled beside the Thames, but for Edger factionalism in his congregation made it a hell on earth.[8] He and Louisa had married in 1846 and moved to Abingdon in 1853. At that point they had three children: Marion, Gertrude Evangeline (or Eva, as she was invariably known) and Herbert Frank (always called Frank). Kate Milligan, their third daughter, was born in Abingdon on 6 January 1857. Milligan was the name of a fellow preacher whom Samuel and Louisa liked and admired.[9] In 1861, Margaret Lilian, known by her second name, was born. When the Edgers emigrated a year later, Marion was 13, Eva 11, Frank nine, Kate five and Lilian a baby of one.

The Edger children descended from a long line of religious nonconformists, on both sides of the family. Samuel's parents belonged to the middle-class elite that dominated the chapels of the various dissenting denominations and set standards of behaviour and lifestyle for aspirational 'chapel folk'. His mother was a Congregationalist, and his father, John, a strict Particular Baptist.[10] They lived in Pickstone or Pixton Hill House, an imposing country residence in East Grinstead, Sussex. John Edger – the name is pronounced Edgar – was originally a silk manufacturer from Spitalfields in Middlesex, who retired from business to live the life of a gentleman farmer.[11] He owned the local chapel on their East Grinstead property and financed it entirely.

From the age of 15 Samuel wanted to be a preacher, but perhaps in reaction to his father's strict religious sectarianism, was vehemently anti-sectarian. He studied at Stepney Baptist College, part of the University of London, as a young man and earned a BA, and though he enjoyed the academic side of his studies, was disillusioned by what he saw as his fellow students' worldliness and sectarian prejudice.[12] A true mid-Victorian liberal evangelical, he believed in high standards of personal morality, the sanctity of the family and the ethos of self-sufficiency and self-help. He also felt deeply sympathetic towards the plight of the English working classes and was scathing about what he saw as the selfish materialism of the times. Instead of rampant laissez-faire profit-seeking, he endorsed a form of Christian Socialism, as advocated by theologian F.D. Maurice, priest and novelist Charles Kingsley and lawyer John Ludlow.[13]

Christian Socialists wanted a more just society based on Christian brotherhood: a co-operative community achieved by voluntary effort, in which individuals would be able to develop their inherent potential. Socialism would be 'the necessary result of a sound Christianity'.[14] For Samuel Edger, improved education, co-operative businesses and profit sharing between social classes were important means of achieving that goal. Socialism, for him, did not entail opposition between social classes but, rather, mutual assistance and co-operative endeavour. He tried to

Samuel Edger, c. 1850s, in the sombre attire of a serious-minded Victorian evangelical.

Jill Smith Collection

help working people to achieve their potential by advocating what he believed to be worthy causes, but never engaged in party politics. A religious man first and foremost, his uncompromising anti-sectarianism and liberal views placed him at the more radical end of the English theological spectrum.[15]

Slight, with a high, cerebral forehead, and always sombrely attired, Samuel looked exactly what he was: a pious evangelical intellectual. Later in life, long grey locks and an apostolic beard gave him an other-worldly look. Much of his writing reveals a visionary, even utopian cast of thought. In his memoirs, for example, he expressed 'immovable confidence' in the perpetual endurance of Christianity's 'transcendent power to transform all human life till the kingdom of heaven shall come on earth'.[16]

How did Louisa (née Harwood), some four years older than her husband, greet the decision to emigrate? Samuel's memoirs make no mention of her views on this or, indeed, on any other matter. She remains an elusive, shadowy figure, who, like many women of her time, left little to document her life. By contrast, her husband wrote a memoir, numerous essays and a multitude of irate letters to the press, which together help to establish both his views and personality. Louisa's uncle was pastor of the Bond Street Baptist Church in Birmingham, where Samuel had worked for a time as a co-pastor in the 1840s. This church, like that at Abingdon, had feuding factions. When Samuel resigned in characteristic high dudgeon, Louisa's denominational connections got him a position in Kimbolton, Huntingdonshire, a rural community of some 1700 people. He and Louisa spent seven happy years there, before the small salary of only £100 per annum and the prospect of more children induced Samuel to take the Abingdon post.

Albertland was a well-organised enterprise supported by some of England's leading nonconformist ministers and laymen. The scheme's mastermind, William Rawson Brame, was a young journalist and novelist and the son of a Baptist minister from Birmingham. The bicentenary of the 1662 expulsion of nonconformist clergy from the Church of England seemed a suitable time to found a community of nonconformists in the new world. Auckland's provincial government, hoping to offset a recent outflow of population to Australia's newly discovered goldfields, was offering free land under a 40-acre (16ha) scheme. Provided they could pay their own passage, anyone over 18 was entitled to 40 acres of land; each family member between the ages of five and 18 received a further 20. To obtain the freehold, settlers had to stay on the land for five years.[17]

Early in August 1861 Brame advertised in a Birmingham newspaper for prospective settlers. The response was enthusiastic. The Association for the Establishment of a Colony of Nonconformists in New Zealand opened an office in Birmingham, with Brame as secretary and general manager and the appealingly named Harper Twelvetrees as treasurer. Also in 1861, two agents travelled to New Zealand and selected three blocks, Paparoa, Matakohe and Ōruawharo, totalling some 70,000 acres (28,000ha), in the Kaipara district. In true booster fashion, their ensuing report waxed eloquent about the beauty and suitability of the chosen site. Back in England, momentum built. Twenty-seven local committees helped to organise the drive for colonists.[18]

A Shipping Subcommittee, tasked with finding seaworthy vessels for the prospective colonists, eventually signed a contract with the reputable firm Shaw, Savill and Co. After the first two ships departed in May 1862, there were four more sailings to Auckland, each in a different ship, over the next 15 months. In total, some 3000 Albertland emigrants sailed to New Zealand: a considerable number, given that in 1862 New Zealand's European population was 125,812.[19]

Port Albert, a proposed town at the junction of the Ōruawharo River and the Wharehine Creek, was to be Albertland's heart. Here, merchants, tradesmen and artisans would offer a range of services answering the needs of the surrounding farming community. To ensure the right types of settlers, the association published a list of relevant trades and occupations. They wanted hard-working nonconformists from the middle and labouring classes: morally upright and devout. There was to be a school, a library, newspaper, sawmill, flour mill and church. It all looked plausible on paper.

The Edgers sailed to New Zealand aboard the *Matilda Wattenbach*; the second ship, which left on 29 May, was the *Hanover*. The *Albertland Gazette*, started by the passengers en route, provides an insight into their serious-minded shipboard pastimes. Any day between 9.30 and 10.30am, for example, the Reverend Edger received the names of passengers wishing to become members of the Total Abstinence Society for the Prevention and Suppression of Drunkenness.[20] When not spreading the temperance message, Samuel complained in his journal about the behaviour of fellow passengers. On 26 July, for instance, some men were cruelly shooting seabirds while others, who in England 'would have been *loud* in their talk of the religious character of this emigration movement, are *here* the greatest promoters of an irreligious feeling etc.'[21]

Growing disaffection with Brame might well have stirred these irreligious feelings and misbehaviour. Relations between leader and led deteriorated during the voyage. Brame's aloof, superior manner apparently alienated the rank and file. Rumours swirled that many intending colonists had no intention of proceeding to the settlement at all. Suspicions about Brame's lack of interest had set in before the first ships sailed because his remuneration from the Auckland Provincial Government depended on numbers in the scheme: he received 10 shillings for each adult and 5 shillings for each child travelling to New Zealand. In addition, Shaw, Savill and Co. paid him 5 percent commission on all the passage money and freight of the settlers and offered him and his wife a free cabin and passage.[22]

From Auckland to Kaipara

The *Matilda Wattenbach* docked safely in Auckland on 8 September 1862. The *Hanover,* with another 336 prospective settlers, arrived nine days later.[23] Auckland in 1862 was the nation's capital, but not its most populous city. Pastoralism and gold made Otago the preferred destination. Auckland province had an estimated popu-

The Albertland settlers about to depart from London aboard the *Matilda Wattenbach*, from a 1912 illustration in the *Auckland Weekly News*.

Auckland Libraries Heritage Collections, AWNS-19120502-3-2

lation of 27,644 compared with Otago's 45,588. Farming development was limited and most people lived in Auckland city.[24] A notoriously speculative business community, engaged primarily in the kauri trade or in finance, dominated the economy. (Aucklanders, as Samuel Edger noted in his memoirs, were 'proverbial for their moral laxity in all matters of business and commerce'.)[25] The Bank of New Zealand, set up in 1861, helped to channel Auckland money to pastoralists in other parts of the county. The city was also, as residents were all too aware, close to Waikato, where tensions between the Māori King Movement and government forces were intensifying.[26] None of this entered into Marion Edger's impressions upon arrival. She later remembered Auckland as serenely bucolic and friendly: 'many friends

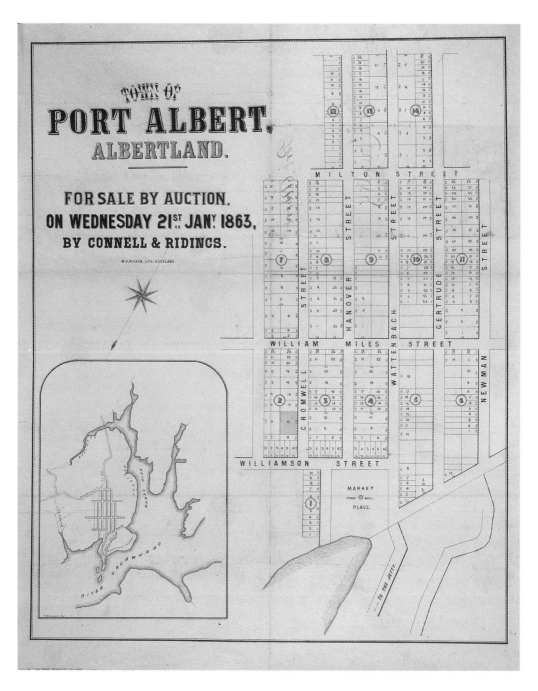

Poster advertising allotments for sale in Port Albert, 1863.
Auckland Libraries Heritage Collections, New Zealand Map 4498-30

came on board to welcome the new arrivals, and two days later a public welcome was given us ashore. I remember walking up Queen Street and seeing a gully full of arum lilies, just where the Town hall now stands, and picking watercress at the bottom of Shortland Street.'[27]

The Edgers and their shipmates now faced the daunting task of getting to Albertland. The lack of an efficient plan for transporting settlers from Auckland critically weakened Brame's scheme. The land chosen for the settlement was a remote wilderness, and roads marked on maps perused in England turned out to be surveyors' lines. The Great North Road between Albertland and Auckland was no more than a perilous track in places, and wheels for agricultural carts, transported across the globe, proved unusable. Moreover, the blocks of land, spread out along the shores of the Kaipara Harbour, covered an area of over 50 kilometres. Most settlers would be far apart from their neighbours, largely precluding the kind of co-operative close-knit community dreamt about in England. The land was generally poor. Even that of better quality was still hilly and covered in bush, requiring sustained hard work before it could be farmed profitably. Port Albert, so far removed from any sizeable market, was an unlikely spot for a thriving town. Shipping in supplies was frequently impossible in bad weather.

Before these dispiriting factors became evident, just getting to the land proved a major hurdle. Writing home in November 1862 Samuel lamented: 'It is eleven weeks today since we first set foot on land in Auckland, and it is three weeks today since I arrived here [Port Albert] with the last detachment of settlers from the first two ships, eight weeks having been occupied in the transit over sixty miles, eight weeks of anxiety, care, toil and vexation …'[28] When tales of other settlers' journeys to Albertland got back to migrants still in the city, many opted to stay put. Only about half of the Albertland colonists who arrived in Auckland ventured to the Kaipara. Of those who went, only half stayed.[29]

The Edgers' journey was a protracted nightmare. A cold, tiring trip to Riverhead in a barge was followed by a harrowing journey by bullock dray to Helensville, and two fraught boat journeys across the Kaipara Harbour, both of which involved being stranded on mudflats.[30] When, in late October, the rest of the family (with the exception of Louisa, Kate and Lilian, who remained at Waitematā) finally arrived at their destination, a tent settlement at the Ōruawharo River landing, it was an anti-climax: 'the ground was soaking wet with recent rain, and there was nothing to do but sit on a damp log watching the firelight, and waiting until it was possible to pitch our tent. Such was our arrival at our new home. Romance had faded into reality.'[31]

Louisa, Kate and Lilian arrived on New Year's morning 1863. A hot summer added to the Edgers' discomfort; mosquitoes blackened the walls of their tent by day. They enjoyed building their wooden home, however, which they named Cypress Lodge, and Samuel's letters now expressed exhilaration rather than despair: 'Not one regret at coming has ever crossed my mind … To feel that one is doing a little to bring this lovely country into a cultural garden, that our great great grandchildren will a century hence traverse with hearts full of grateful love is worth doing it.'[32]

Idealism and adversity

Initial hopes for the settlement were high. The *Albertland Gazette* operated in Port Albert for a time and a reading room opened in town; there was also a post office, a weekly mail service, a Mutual Improvement Society, a library and a Port Albert Music Society. This met in the Edger home, which possessed a 'fine organ'. The town soon boasted a co-operative store, a drapery store, a boarding house and a market square. Marion fondly remembered the regular, always friendly contact with Māori on the opposite side of the Ōruawharo River, and the 'beautiful ripe peaches' in kete that their neighbours would sell for 'the modest sum of one shilling'.[33]

Meanwhile Samuel was farming co-operatively with his nephews Frederick and Edward Judson and six farm labourers who had travelled from England for the purpose. They worked for Edger and Company as fellow shareholders rather than employees. Samuel's aim was to apply principles of non-competitive co-operation, Christian brotherhood and mutual help to farming. In Britain, many nonconformists strongly endorsed the co-operative movement, as advocated by Robert Owen, the founder of New Lanark, a co-operatively run mill in Scotland that operated from 1800 to 1825. In 1844 the Rochdale Pioneers, a consumer co-operative, was the first group to pay a dividend to consumers and the forerunner of the co-operative stores that still thrive in Britain today. Samuel, like many other nonconformists, approved of the co-operative movement's ethos of thrift, and its ability to strengthen rather than polarise relations between the middle and working classes.[34]

Edger wrote an article in the *Port Albert Gazette* chronicling the advances of his farming co-operative. In his letters he described the friendly withdrawal of two former members, observing that all those still involved were working 'in the truest harmony and brotherhood'. He felt liberated from old-world conventions and class constraints: 'I do not see how any but the most base slave could after a few years here, tolerate the laughable and often mournful restrictions of English society.'

While acknowledging that the co-operative's 'only rule in our everyday work' was 'the advantage of our whole little band', he noted that 'we field a little for the principle of self', as each family had their own garden, and Samuel had 129 hectares in wheat and an orchard of some 90 fruit trees.[35] Louisa and the children were settling in and enjoying their new house. Made of weatherboard and measuring 60 square metres, it boasted one large room and two smaller ones. Three tents acted as outhouses.

Although Edger and Company appeared to have made a promising start, the settlement itself began to founder. Many allotment holders had to forfeit their land because of a requirement that they live on their section, or build on it a house worth £20 within six months. These measures were designed to preclude speculation. But employment was scarce, the few established businesses struggled and residents started to leave. In 1864 a small wooden church was built in Port Albert near Market Street, where Samuel preached. Because so few migrants actually settled in the district and those who did were in no position to remunerate him, he worked constantly for no pay, apart from a small sum raised by some friends who had stayed in Auckland.[36] Meanwhile, the anti-sectarian message did not flourish as hoped.

In 1865 Samuel was asked to preach at the Albert Street Congregational Church in Auckland for eight weeks while the congregation awaited a new minister from England. He consented, grateful for the opportunity to add a little to the family's 'extremely scanty means'. Edger made several friends there, and received the congregation's 'affection, gratitude, and regret' at parting.[37] He returned to Port Albert with no expectation of further work in the city but felt that his religious message had not fallen on stony ground.

A message from God

At noon on Sunday 6 August 1866, just after the morning service, Edger was seated in the house of a Port Albert settler when the door suddenly opened and Frank appeared, wearing a strange expression. He then announced, with quivering lips, 'Papa – we have just met David Becroft [the child of a neighbour] and he says the house is burned down.' Samuel accepted the news impassively, then 'walked mechanically to the scene of ruin'. Viewing the charred remnants of Cypress Lodge, he remained unmoved until expressions of sympathy from others 'dissolved the ice' and his emotions burst forth. Eight days later, still overcome, he wrote: 'Not a shred remains, except my gold watch which I had on, and some silver spoons that were picked out of the ashes … Books, music, musical instruments, documents, deeds, M.S.S.; the result of twenty years' labour, swept away in an hour.' He went on to observe that fires in England were rarely so disastrous as those in the wooden homes of New Zealand. This particular home had been the focus of all his hopes: 'We stand on the shore of life's broad sea, and the vessel has gone down.'[38]

Samuel regarded the fire as a message from God about the future direction his life should take. He decided to move to Auckland where 'the retirement of Paradise' would be exchanged for 'perhaps, the more honourable field of battle'.[39] But Albertland had been a significant experience for the Edger children. They had experienced the hardships of a hard-working pioneering existence, enjoyed the compensations of a life lived close to nature, and seen their parents and neighbours trying to create a community where tolerance, harmony and mutual understanding would prevail.

Auckland: Cultural crusades

By late August 1866 the Edgers were in a comfortable rented house in Parnell,[40] found for them by the same friends who had urged Samuel to move to the city during his stint at the Albert Street Congregational Church. They even secured a lease on the Parnell Hall for three months, with an option to purchase, so he would have somewhere to preach.

Auckland had changed considerably since the *Matilda Wattenbach* arrived there in 1862. The imperial troops garrisoned in the city to fight in the Waikato war had mostly been withdrawn. Despite losing its status as the nation's capital in 1865, Auckland was entering an expansive period. The discovery of gold in the Coromandel in 1867, and a thriving timber trade, helped to attract new residents and filled the business community's coffers. In the 1870s the immigration policies of Colonial Treasurer Julius Vogel would bring in many more people. Auckland's reputation as crass and uncultured gradually diminished as some wealthier citizens began to support various intellectual and artistic enterprises.

The Edgers played a prominent role in the city's cultural scene. When not writing letters to the papers or provoking indignant editorials, Samuel chaired various soirées and concerts. His talks and sermons featured regularly in the entertainment and social columns. Kate and her siblings, who were all very talented musically, often found themselves on stage, performing in entertainments that aimed to promote causes their father espoused.

Queen Street, Auckland, in the mid-1860s.
Auckland Libraries Heritage Collections, 4-3147

By 1866 Marion was 17, Eva 15, Frank 12, Kate nine and Lilian five. In Parnell they were, their father noted in his diary, 'enough out of the city to enjoy the country and enough in it to secure its advantages'. He intended the Albertland farm to go on as usual – indeed 'perhaps more vigorously', as his nephews and Frank would manage it for a time – and observed that the children would have the option, if they wished, to resume rural life at a later date. Louisa and her companion, Miss Carpenter, who lived with the Edgers, would be 'more at home in town life'.[41] The family retained links with Albertland, building a modest residence called Linden Cottage on their land there, which they visited frequently. Indeed, it was described as 'the centre of social life' in Port Albert during the 1870s.[42]

Samuel began preaching in the Parnell Hall in August 1866 and spent the remaining 16 years of his life as the spiritual leader of a nameless churchless congregation. He became a well-known personality in Auckland. His sermons were learned and idealistic, with a strong sense of compassion for the poor and weak. Audiences at the various halls where he preached waxed and waned over the years, but his core congregation remained devoted. He also delivered lectures on varied subjects, from social issues to literary figures. These were usually free, with donations collected at the door for such causes as prohibition, prison reform and women's rights.

Samuel's feminism introduced his daughters to the outspoken early feminist teacher and journalist Mary Ann Colclough, or 'Polly Plum' (her nom de plume). As her biographer notes, Colclough likely took an interest in the education of Kate and Lilian.[43] Both sisters often performed music before her public lectures and would have frequently heard her speak. As 'Polly Plum' she advocated for women's rights and engaged in combative newspaper correspondence on the subject. She argued against the current situation, which offered married women no independent legal status and no control over their property or even over custody of their children. Husbands held all the cards. She had experienced the repercussions of this vulnerable legal situation when her husband's peculations and ill-health left her in the position of breadwinner, with debt collectors frequently at the door. Colclough also railed against the sexual double standard, argued for compassionate rehabilitation of 'fallen women', called for the improvement of the shocking conditions in Auckland's women's prison and eloquently urged for improvement to the quality of female education. Many women, she protested, would need to earn a living at some time in their lives: a sound education would facilitate financial independence and self-sufficiency.

Colclough believed that God had made men and women for different purposes and held that marriage and motherhood were central elements of female lives. But when women were forced to accept the duties and responsibilities of men, she wanted them to have a fair chance and equality of opportunity. She received support for her stance from international women's rights movements and corresponded with leading British feminists such as Millicent Fawcett and Isabella Tod.[44] Colclough's views about improving women's rights evoked scathing responses in the local correspondence columns. Appearing in public and lecturing, let alone defending her arguments with intelligence and flair in the press, provoked fierce attacks and personal abuse.

Samuel, too, engaged in protracted skirmishes with various clerics, newspaper editors and other correspondents, indignantly defending his radical views. Like Colcough, he 'continually challenged gendered and class-based social and economic hierarchies in favour of radical solutions'.[45] He, too, came under vehement attack. But he relished the gladiatorial combat. His sermons and lectures expressed lofty faith in humankind's ultimate regeneration; in the profane world he suffered neither fools nor opponents gladly.

Frank Edger.

Miss E. Edger.
(Mrs Hemus)

Miss Lillian Edger.

Rev Samuel Edger. Mrs S. Edger.

Miss M. Edger.
(Mrs F. Judson)

Miss K. Edger.
(Mrs Evans)

©Albertland Heritage LS1195

Frederick Judson.

A photo montage of the Edger family created for the 1927 book *The Albertlanders*.
This image is from a magic lantern slide taken from the original plate glass negative.
Albertland Heritage Centre, 2004-2-2007 1/95

Despite often feeling deeply hurt by his critics, Samuel flourished in the city. His health was indifferent, and he suffered periodic depression, but he led an active, busy, purposeful life. When the Parnell Hall proved too far removed from the city, he preached in more central locations, such as the Oddfellows Hall, the Choral Hall, City Hall and, finally, the Lorne Street Hall. The family moved to a rented house in Wynyard Street, which they eventually purchased.

Marion had a 'sweet, pure mezzo soprano' voice. She and her sister Eva, an accomplished pianist, were among the youngest members of the Auckland Choral Society. Frank, their handsome, personable brother, had a 'fine bass' voice, and was also a talented cellist.[46] In 1873 Frank and Marion went to England to further their musical training. Marion studied voice at the Royal Academy of Music and Frank cello.

In his memoirs, Samuel noted that moving to Auckland opened up 'a path of something like colonial prosperity', which explains the Edgers' ability to finance this overseas musical training.[47] Since his father's death in the late 1840s, Samuel's mother Susannah had provided her children with an annuity. When this modest inheritance was combined with financial contributions from his devoted congregation, and the proceeds from the sale of the Albertland property, sold incrementally between 1866 and 1880,[48] eventually the family enjoyed a comfortable lifestyle. A lavish or luxurious one would have been entirely uncharacteristic.

When Frank and Marion returned to Auckland in 1876, Marion continued to sing in concerts and soon earned respect as 'one of the best music teachers in Auckland', a status she enjoyed for some 20 years.[49] She married her cousin Frederick Judson in 1879, and their one child, Dora, became a celebrated concert pianist. Frank began working in the Native Land Department in 1879. Ten years later he was a barrister and solicitor of the Supreme Court. In 1894 he became a Native Land Court judge, then in 1906 served a short stint as under-secretary to Minister of Native Affairs James Carroll. His musical interests did not founder during this busy career. Together with his wife Augusta (née Langsford), a singer, he played in various concerts while on circuit and was a founder of the Auckland Orchestral Society in 1889. For many years he played in a celebrated Auckland quartet with his brother-in-law Charles Hemus, a talented amateur violinist. Hemus, a successful painter and photographer, also from a nonconformist, prohibitionist family, married Eva Edger in 1875. They had four children: two girls and two boys.

Kate Edger's public musical debut took place on 21 May 1872 when she was 15.

She and Eva performed what was described as 'Piano Duet (Beethoven Symphony) – "The Storm"' (possibly a transcription of the fourth movement of the Pastoral Symphony), at Mr and Madame Winter's 'Monster Concert' at City Hall.[50] The Winters ran a music school which the Edger children attended. Kate soon began playing regularly in public, often in piano duets with her younger sister Lilian who, like Kate, also played the violin.

One notable public appearance in October 1875 reveals much about Kate's character: her ability to remain calm under pressure, her determination and persistence and her sense of fairness. After playing a piano duet, a violin duet and a piano solo before the Lorne Street Hall congregation, and following her father's paper on spelling bees, she took part in one.[51] A dozen contestants battled away for over half an hour, leaving Kate and James Geddes alone on the platform. The two finalists proceeded to cope with 'polysyllabic' words until, at 10pm, it remained a tense draw. As the *New Zealand Herald* reported, 'Mr. Geddes gallantly offered to resign in favour of the lady, and the lady, not willing to be out-done in generosity, made the same offer to Mr. Geddes. Subsequently, they agreed that the prize should be given as a prize in a New Zealand Geographical Bee, which it is proposed to hold at an early date. Both competitors deserve the highest credit for the correctness and extensiveness of their orthographical knowledge.' Competing in an intellectual pursuit with the opposite sex, Kate held her own, quietly but effectively, and admirably declined to accept a victory that resulted from a gesture of male gallantry.[52]

In August 1876, at one of those 'pleasant social re-unions which occur every few months in connection with the Rev. S. Edger's congregation and friends', Kate and Lilian played a pianoforte duet from Gounod's *Faust* in what the *Daily Southern Cross* reviewer described as 'a brilliant manner'. They also appeared in a number of other musical items. After the concert, Samuel delivered a short paper on 'Culture and Religion': 'How much genius had been lost to the world simply for want of culture! It requires culture to appreciate good music, and religion can only yield happiness in proportion to the culture of those talents and capacities with which we are gifted.'[53]

Many of the soirées and musical evenings in which the Edgers participated during the 1860s and 1870s aimed to entice people away from the temptation to drink alcohol. More than any other issue, opposition to the 'demon drink' has shaped popular perceptions of nonconformists as joyless, repressive Puritans. Certainly, some were self-righteous and dauntingly strait-laced, but others, like the

Edgers, fostered public entertainments and cultural pursuits, partly to prove they could be enjoyed without alcohol but also out of a conviction that these activities enhanced the quality of both life and religion. To that end, Samuel campaigned for opening the Auckland Institute and Museum on Sundays, and gave lectures on popular authors such as Dickens, whose sympathy for the poor and powerless he believed embodied the best kind of religious compassion.

He defended the rights of Māori as citizens, and between 1879 and 1881 engaged in a fierce war of words with Auckland newspapers, defending the Chinese in New Zealand against a recent upsurge in racism. The Chinese were not newcomers to the country. In 1865 a few dozen had been brought into Otago, at the invitation of the Dunedin Chamber of Commerce and the Otago Provincial Council, to rework the goldfields. By 1872 there were some 4200 Chinese men in New Zealand,[54] who sent the lion's share of their wages home to their wives and children in China. Most lived in marginal mining areas in Otago, Westland and Southland and largely kept to themselves. Settler prejudice towards them began immediately, but was heightened in the late 1870s as the economy worsened and fears grew that European workers would be swamped by an influx of cheap Chinese labour. Edger eloquently supported the Chinese as hard-working and law-abiding, views that were met with heated rebukes from the Auckland press. His pleas for tolerance and acceptance did not prevail; in 1881 the Chinese Immigration Act introduced a £10 poll tax on all Chinese immigrants.[55] Throughout his life, Samuel remained a committed pacifist, internationalist and anti-imperialist, at one point delivering an optimistic, idealistic paper entitled 'The Possible Pacification of the World by Means of a Rational International Policy'.[56] These were causes that Kate would later advocate.

Spiritualism

Edger's contempt for what he saw as the selfish materialism of the age led to his involvement, throughout the 1870s, with spiritualism, then well into its controversial heyday. Although Kate never took part in seances, she often took aim at society's selfish materialism and the need for a more spiritual, less competitive society. Samuel, although sceptical about what he called the 'infinite amount of nonsense' the term spiritualism embraced, defended aspects of the movement in Auckland newspapers. A belief in the possibility of communicating with the spirits of the dead through mediums and seances was, in his view, a belief in something beyond the empirical and crassly material, and therefore potentially beneficial. If even one of spiritualism's claims were proven, it would, he hoped, 'rescue the age from the withering blight of this blank Materialism'.[57]

Some spiritualists were conservative pillars of the Anglican establishment, but a high proportion criticised religious sectarianism. Many remained Christian but urged that the Bible be examined critically and reinterpreted to accord with current scientific and social reality. Several distinguished scientists also believed in communing with the spirits of the dead: the evolutionary biologist Alfred Russel Wallace and the chemist and physicist Sir William Crookes, for example, were both convinced spiritualists, which gave the movement added credence in many people's minds.[58]

It was Samuel who almost invariably introduced visiting spiritualist speakers to the Auckland public. Although several of these lecturers had already been exposed as frauds, he somehow found himself able to explain away or ignore that fact. The trance medium Thomas Walker, for example, who visited in 1877, had been charged with 'causing felonious death' in 1874 after having accidentally burned a believer with phosphorus during a seance in Toronto.[59]

Towards the end of his life, Samuel assessed the impact of spiritualism on his reputation. With rare self-reproach, he accepted that his support for it probably created a certain popular prejudice towards him. Yet, partly out of advocacy for freedom of expression and a liberal toleration of views, he did not repent: 'the advantages in the shape of a broader and more catholic public feeling, a more pronounced dislike of bigotry, with some awakening of thought towards the more spiritual aspects of Christianity, fully outweigh any disadvantages that may be supposed to be involved in those events.'[60]

Many nonconformists were attracted to spiritualism for similar reasons. Anna Stout (née Logan), who would later work beside Kate in various women's causes and social reforms, also grew up with parents who were involved in the movement. Her father John, a deacon of Knox Presbyterian church in Dunedin, was excommunicated for appearing on stage with two visiting American spiritualists in 1873. Anti-sectarian freethinker Robert Stout, a young Scottish-born lawyer and journalist and Anna Logan's future husband, wrote an editorial in his newspaper the *Echo* entitled 'A Heresy Hunt in Otago', attacking the expulsion. After their banishment, the Logans embraced spiritualism; Anna's mother Jessie even became a medium.[61]

Samuel and Louisa's legacy

Kate grew up in a deeply religious nonconformist household that was more pro-gressive, liberal and even iconoclastic than those of many other dissenters. She witnessed her father's concern for social justice and for extending co-operative principles and compassion towards those less fortunate, and as an adult she worked for similar causes.

In contrast to other early New Zealand feminists, such as Mary Anne Muller ('Femina') and Mary Anne Colclough, Kate did not come to feminism and women's rights later in life after experiencing an unhappy, difficult or oppressive marriage. Rather she grew up with ideas that honoured women, strove to improve their rights as citizens and expand their influence within society. Her parents played a vital role in inculcating these beliefs and ideals.

2

'A Lady Admitted'

The Chief distinction in the intellectual powers of the two sexes is shewn by man attaining to a higher eminence, in whatever he takes up, than woman can attain – whether requiring deep thought, reason, or imagination, or merely the use of the sense and the hands.

CHARLES DARWIN, *The Descent of Man*, 1871[1]

Let us hear no more of the intellectual inferiority of women.

Newspaper editorial on Kate Edger's BA graduation, 11 July 1877[2]

Kate Edger was 20 years old when she became New Zealand's first female university graduate and the first woman in the British Empire to be awarded a Bachelor of Arts degree. This accomplishment earned her fame, both in her lifetime and posthumously. Achieving equal educational opportunities for girls and women from primary school through to university was one of the major goals of nineteenth-century feminism. Kate's graduation represented a milestone for women's rights, and New Zealanders proudly recognised it as such.

A year after Kate's graduation, in 1878, University College London received a charter to allow degrees to women, and the first four female BA students graduated from that institution in 1880. In 1892 all four Scottish universities admitted women to degrees. By 1895, only Cambridge and Oxford were not doing so. (Women could demonstrate their ability through examination but were denied the right to graduate or take on any role in university governance.) The number of British women attending university, however, remained significantly lower than in New Zealand. By 1893 more than half of university students in New Zealand were women; as late as 1914, women made up just over 20 percent of university students in Britain.[3]

The atmosphere on campuses of higher education in Britain and New Zealand also differed considerably. In Britain several separate women's colleges founded from the late 1860s onwards provided a domestic and sheltered environment in which standards of feminine decorum were strictly enforced: 'Women's colleges tried to act as substitute families and homes, shelters from the outside world; college heads tried to reassure parents and critical onlookers that students would act correctly and retain their femininity.'[4] When these colleges merged with universities, as many did in the 1890s, there was often tension and segregation between the sexes.[5]

By contrast, university education in New Zealand was from the outset co-educational, with a freer and easier atmosphere. When William Steadman Aldis arrived in the early 1880s to take up the chair of mathematics at Auckland University College, he was astounded by the casual mixing of the sexes. Whereas in England he would find a few women huddled at the back of the room, in New Zealand he encountered 'a cheerful bevy of colonial damsels' facing him from the front benches, with the men sitting modestly at the back.[6]

The fact that Kate sailed through her academic courses with flying colours was also significant. In addition to traditional religious views about women's subservient role within patriarchal families, male scholars from various disciplines wrote learned treatises about women's lack of reasoning and their intellectual inferiority to men. This was often attributed to purported biological factors, such as smaller brain size and hormonally induced emotionalism and hysteria. Charles Darwin claimed that the process of sexual selection had left women less highly evolved than men. In the latter half of the nineteenth century, the comparison of women and children and 'lower races' was widespread. Many writers with claims to scientific credibility asserted that these groups shared not only physical characteristics such as narrow, child-like skulls, but also mental ones: 'lack of willpower, emotionality, dependence, imitativeness, and little capacity for abstract thought.'[7]

In this context, Kate's academic achievement was not an isolated case. Rather, it opened the door for New Zealand women to earn university degrees alongside men. Many went on to enjoy the status of well-educated, financially independent professionals. Nevertheless, ideas about female intellectual inferiority did not disappear, either in New Zealand or around the world. Nor did concerns about the impact of higher education on women.

Kate and other contemporary feminists justified higher education for women by invoking liberal ideas about equal rights with men and arguments based on enlightenment principles of natural justice. It was a right to which both women and men should have access. It was a good in itself, elevating and enriching individual women, but also an important means of enabling women to further feminise the public sphere, bringing their special moral attributes, born in the home, into society for the common good.

The story of how and why Kate achieved her university degree began during her teenage years. It owed much to her parents' feminist views and to her own intellectual interests and capacity for self-disciplined study. Her admission into university was part of a crusade for women's education that had its roots in America and England, but the peculiar competitive and parochial nature of university politics within New Zealand in the 1870s also played a vital part.

Towards 'a system of perfect equality'

During their teenage years, Kate and Lilian, when not performing in musical concerts and triumphing in spelling bees, were taught at home by their father. They were keen, able students. Kate excelled at mathematics and languages, particularly Latin, and throughout her life read widely and enthusiastically in English literature. Lilian, equally adept in mathematics and languages, had a more philosophical, spiritual bent.

The two younger Edger sisters were fortunate to be taught by a father who took women's education seriously. In 1871, when Kate was 14, an Auckland newspaper published extracts from Mill's *The Subjection of Women*. Samuel found this essay so brilliant and far-sighted that he purchased all the copies he could find in Auckland so he could lend them to anyone interested in reading the full work.[8] Mill argued, 'The principle which regulates the existing social relationships between the two sexes – the legal subordination of one sex to the other – is wrong in itself, and now one of the chief hindrances to human improvement; and … it ought to be replaced by a system of perfect equality, admitting no power or privilege on the one side, nor disability on the other.' He also noted that 'The claim of women to be educated as solidly, and in the same branches of knowledge, as men, is urged with growing intensity, and with a great prospect of success; while the demand for their admission into professions and occupations hitherto closed to them, becomes every year more urgent.'[9]

In England, from the late 1850s, Emily Davies had led a campaign for the higher education of women. One of the Langham Place group of early feminists, who also began campaigning for women's suffrage and expanding employment opportunities, she is now primarily associated with the foundation in 1869 of Girton College, Cambridge, which, though not acknowledged as part of the university, was a recognised institution for the higher education of women. Davies also actively campaigned for women's educational equality with men. She pushed for women to be allowed to matriculate with men at the University of London and resisted differentiated university courses for women, believing that they perpetuated ideas about female intellectual inferiority and would be of little use in the campaign to open professional occupations to women.[10]

In America, colleges, seminaries and academies for women began in the 1830s, due partly to the powerful evangelical influences in that country but also to a strong belief that, with equal opportunities, women would prove themselves as capable as men. Some enthusiastic women reformers framed their demands for higher education in terms of the eighteenth-century American Revolution – as a battle for liberty against tyrants denying them access to human rights. The idea that women were intellectually equal to men existed alongside the concept of their special moral and educative mission and the desirability of their active citizenship outside the home. By the 1850s there were more than 45 degree-granting colleges open to American women.[11]

Many American institutions of higher education for women offered a gendered curriculum with a focus on domestic economy. Some, like Davies in Britain, opposed this. Feminist Susan B. Anthony, for example, argued that 'there was no more need for a special education for mothers than there was a need for a special education for fathers'. Only in the last quarter of the nineteenth century did women's colleges in America begin insisting on the same curriculum and the same entry standards for women as for men. Martha Carey Thomas, the founder of Bryn Mawr in Pennsylvania, famously disagreed with all courses designed for women only. But many women's colleges continued to follow a curriculum that largely perceived women's education in terms of their vocation as wives and mothers.[12]

Girls' schooling at the secondary level was also a matter of concern. From the late 1850s two British pioneers of women's secondary education, Frances Buss of the North London Collegiate School for Ladies and later the Camden School for Girls, and Dorothea Beale of Cheltenham Ladies' College, led a drive to improve girls' secondary schools. Like Davies, they campaigned for young women's right to sit public examinations and study in universities. In 1868 both women gave evidence before the Schools Inquiry Commission. Its subsequent report gave great impetus to improving girls' education in Britain from primary school upwards. It strongly condemned the existing state of girls' schools, denouncing their 'want of thoroughness and foundation; want of system, slovenliness and showy superficiality', to say nothing of their inattention to the rudiments of real learning, 'undue time

Learmonth White
Dalrymple, founder of
Otago Girls' High School
and a pioneer of higher
education for New
Zealand women.

Collection of Toitū Otago Settlers
Museum

given to accomplishments and those not taught intelligently or in any scientific manner' and lack of organisation.[13]

Secondary education for girls in New Zealand in the 1860s and 1870s would have been equally abysmal had Learmonth White Dalrymple not launched a seven-year campaign to improve it. Although her own education at Madras College in St Andrews, Scotland, was relatively extensive by contemporary standards, she found it frustratingly inadequate, especially with regard to mathematics. In 1853 her father, a prosperous, recently widowed merchant, emigrated to New Zealand with Dalrymple and three of her seven younger siblings in tow. Upon arrival he purchased a farm at Kaihiku, South Otago. No longer able to pursue further education, Dalrymple instead kept house for the family and started the area's first Sunday school. In 1863 a suggestion in the *Otago Daily Times*, likely written by Julius Vogel,[14] that a school for Dunedin girls should follow the recently opened Otago Boys' High School, galvanised her. She soon teamed up with her friend and neighbour Major J.L.C. Richardson, then Speaker of the Otago Provincial Council, to pursue this cause.

She wrote to Frances Buss in the late 1860s and received, in return, a response with ideas about curriculum. Buss believed this should 'in all essential points … be assimilated to that of boys'.[15] Dalrymple swung into action, writing letters, lobbying and organising petitions. Finally, with Richardson's active assistance in government circles, she achieved her goal. Otago Girls' High School opened on 6 February 1871 with 78 pupils. Dunedin now boasted the first public girls' high school in the southern hemisphere.

Auckland at this time had several privately run secondary schools for girls but they were not academically rigorous. Rather, they emphasised the kind of middle-class, lady-like 'accomplishments' lampooned 60 years before by Jane Austen and recently derided by Britain's Schools Inquiry Commission. For decades to come, Auckland lagged behind other New Zealand cities in not having a public girls' secondary school.[16] It was little wonder that Samuel decided to teach his two youngest daughters at home, and he was not unhappy at the prospect. In his essay 'A Contribution towards Elucidating the Ideal Education', he wrote that 'the parent is the true teacher, at least through the earlier stages, and that where other circumstances render it possible, no education can compare with home education'. In Samuel's view education comprised three intertwined branches, physical, intellectual and moral, and 'No education can be complete or ideal that does not embrace them all'. He opposed cramming for exams, advocating instead 'that well-balanced composure which is entirely dependent on moral training and is essential to all rightly developed character'. His criticism of 'cramming' extended to the competitive spirit in education generally:

> The desire to get beyond another, and the satisfaction of having secured from another the prize, is so essentially immoral that to attempt to incorporate that with any true moral training could only injure the individual by its incongruity and unreason … Knowledge is placed at a great disadvantage by being made a matter of mercenary calculation. Its best fruits must be reaped from a pure love of it for its own sake, which can never be when it is made the ladder of ambition.

Knowledge was 'tributary to virtue' and came with a responsibility to use it to benefit others.[17]

These views greatly influenced Kate and Lilian. The sisters' outstanding academic achievements owed much to the solid foundation they received at home. Learning and study in the Edger household was combined with a healthy daily routine and physical exercise, a regime that stood them both in good stead as students. Later, as teachers, they emphasised the equal importance of the intellectual, physical and moral aspects of education, and endorsed their father's reservations about competition and competitive prizes for learning.

Higher education for
New Zealand women: The Dunedin pioneers

Kate's acceptance into university built on, but in a significant sense leap-frogged, pioneering developments in women's tertiary education that had occurred a few years before in Dunedin. After her success with the creation of Otago Girls' High School, Dalrymple began a new campaign in the early 1870s. Working once again with Major Richardson, she pursued women's access to the newly created University of Otago, where it was hoped they could earn degrees on an equal footing with men. This cause gained steady momentum but faltered at the last hurdle. Dalrymple and Richardson's ideas, and the different roles they each assumed while campaigning for this cause, throw light on contemporary perceptions about women's role, and why female education was deemed important.

Major John Richardson is an attractive if slightly old-world figure in the political landscape of nineteenth-century New Zealand.[18] Born in Bengal, India, in 1810, the son of a civil servant in the East India Company, he became a soldier, serving with distinction in Afghanistan and India before retiring in 1851. By this time a widower with three children, he took up farming in New Zealand, eventually settling in 1856 on 60 hectares by the Puerua River in South Otago. A devout evangelical Anglican with a courteous, patrician manner, he was soon drawn into politics. Though generally conservative, he held liberal views on women's education and social welfare.

In 1870 Richardson gave a well-attended lecture entitled 'Thoughts on Female Education' at Knox Church in Dunedin. It began with a rambling historical survey of various ideas about women and education through the ages. When he arrived at the present 'age of progress', Richardson pulled out all the stops, describing women's education as 'the foundation of all human happiness and human progress', enhancing women's ability to intelligently and effectively undertake their crucial responsibilities within their 'natural sphere':

It has been said, and to my mind rightly said, that the 'sphere of a woman is her home'. Such a cultivation of mind as will make a really good wife, sister or daughter to an educated man, is the thing to be aimed at, and this must be something which recognizes woman, not as a *fair relict of nature* – something which may be brought up to the same point as man by education, and taught to be his rival – but rather as the complement of man, perfect in herself and intended to hold an entirely different place in the world.

As wives and mothers were 'in a sense the mainspring of the character of society', who moulded the characters of children and husbands, they should be able to instil a love of scholarship and correct thinking. There were, however, spheres outside the home in which educated women could make a valuable contribution, although 'it is our duty to see that, in acquiescing, the peculiar duties and character of women are not neglected or obliterated'.

Richardson certainly never threatened to up-end traditional gender roles, but he did express some potentially radical views about women's intellectual abilities. He argued, for example, against notions that 'the feminine mind is not adapted for abstract studies', saying, 'I am not sure that there is any great difference in capacity' between men and women. At America's Oberlin College, which had accepted women students since the 1830s, 'The girls on the whole are quite as advanced as the boys, and quite as capable of continued mental exertion, and … in Mathematics even, the proficiency of female students is commended.' He also praised positive British precedents.

The sort of women he saw benefiting from higher education were schoolteachers and governesses, who had to earn their living, and young middle-class women who would be better fitted to fulfil their future roles as wives and mothers if they were educated and aware of the benefits education bestowed. Arguing for a fixed standard of examination that did not differentiate between the sexes, he nevertheless warned against anything that led to 'the destruction of those feminine qualities which add a charm to beauty and a grace to intelligence'. He criticised parents who instilled in their daughters the idea that men 'dread clever women', which led to young girls fixing only on matrimony and superficialities, devoid of the kind of 'refined mental and moral emotions' so essential to a truly valuable wife and mother. The lecture ended with an emotional paean to Florence Nightingale, that 'relieving angel',[19] whose earnest, painstaking acquisition of practical knowledge and professional work outside the home had done so much to relieve sickness and sorrow.

John Larkins Cheese Richardson, the prominent Otago political
figure and Chancellor of the University of Otago, who worked with
Learmonth Dalrymple to foster women's educational opportunities.

Alexander Turnbull Library, Wellington, MNZ-0435-1/4F

In 1871, when Dalrymple started her campaign for promoting women's tertiary education, Richardson was both speaker of the Legislative Council (the upper House of Parliament) and first chancellor of the newly opened University of Otago. As he had been with Otago Girls' High School, he was the key figure promoting the cause in the public sphere. Dalrymple organised women's committees and petitions and wrote copious letters but generally stayed in the background. As a gesture to contemporary notions of propriety, she always found a married woman to preside over any committees or public meetings she set up.

In his inaugural address as university chancellor, Richardson praised Otago Girls' High School and hoped that 'in due time, a still higher education will be conferred through the instrumentality of colleges; and then woman, having at length attained to her rightful position, and moving in the sphere she is so well qualified to adorn, will add to the charms of a delicate sensibility and natural grace those other charms which only a refined and cultivated intellect can give.'[20]

The same day Robert Stout made a more pointed suggestion in the *Southern League* newspaper, advocating women's right to 'equal educational advantages with men'. Days later the newly appointed classics professor, G.S. Sale, in his first address, informally invited women to attend his lectures. Given Sale's later open opposition to women's higher education, he probably did so 'with some reluctance', having been directed by leading university figures such as Richardson.[21]

At this stage Dalrymple circulated a petition among Dunedin women. She quickly gained 140 signatures, including many from the wives of the city's leading citizens, a smaller number from shopkeepers and skilled tradespeople and a group of 10 women teachers. Much of the petition mirrored Richardson's 1870 lecture, seeking education for 'ladies, governesses, and schoolmistresses' and referring to the 'now well tried system of examinations for women by the Cambridge and other Universities'. The petition argued that 'the value of competition for a degree would be, to women intending to become teachers, far greater indirectly than directly. Few probably would pass, but inasmuch as a process of preparation is almost equal to a result, the higher culture would inevitably be attained, and thence shed its influence throughout every school and family in which they taught.'

This seemingly self-defeating reference to low passing rates was possibly included to assuage male fears of women outshining men. Dalrymple's petition argued that 'On all sides it is admitted that the standard of education for women should be raised; and this in no way can be more effectually furthered than by affording to them a participation in the many privileges which well-appointed Universities are calculated to bestow.' But it went further than any English universities had yet ventured, requesting 'that not only those ladies … who are regular students of your University be allowed to become candidates, but that the boon be further extended; and, on the plan of the University of London, ladies who may have studied at home or elsewhere be admitted as candidates for matriculation and degrees.'[22] This latter wording is significant: Dalrymple was fully aware that the University of London offered *certificates* to women rather than *degrees*. Her petition also asked that scholarships be made available to women in competition with men.

The petition was presented to the University Council at a special meeting on 8 August 1871. On the same day, the council unanimously resolved that women be admitted to all university classes and allowed to compete for 'all certificates equivalent to degrees'.[23] Women could not, however, take degrees or compete for scholarships with men. This decision might have been influenced by legal considerations. Any challenge in court to prevent a colonial university from admitting women to degrees would almost certainly have been sustained on the grounds of English precedent.[24]

Not everyone agreed with the council's view regarding scholarships for women. As a June 1872 editorial in the *Otago Witness* lamented,

> It may safely be predicted that unless some such assistance as a scholarship affords to be held out for competition, full effect will not be given to the general wish for a better education for women. Moreover, considering that the system of embracing both sexes in a University course is still, at least in this country, upon its trial, it is obviously desirable that a thoroughly fair opportunity should be given to what we had nearly called the weaker sex. This cannot be done so long as they are weighted in the race, not merely with the obstacles that arise from want of habit, but also with the absence of the same assistance and stimulant that is granted to men.[25]

How Dalrymple felt about the council's decision is not clear. In a privately circulated 1872 pamphlet, she wrote that 'the petition was received with favour' but made no comment on the failure to allow women to take degrees. She argued for a scholarship for women, and also for a course of study designed to help them be 'useful and good' rather than 'clever or learned', as the world seemed to require. Since 'Goodness is the talisman of a woman's power', she advocated the initiation of 'a scheme of Education' that would not seek 'an impossible equality with man … as if the laws of God and nature could be set aside' but one that would enable women to 'realise the path of duty' and 'tend to the culture of the understanding and affections, that with knowledge, might also come wisdom'. Courses offered to women students elsewhere were conservative and traditional and failed 'to develop the higher powers and faculties of human nature'.[26] Seemingly unconcerned that only certificates rather than degrees were being granted, she wrote to Richardson complaining about women's apparent reluctance to respond to the university's invitation to attend classes.

Dalrymple's belief that 'goodness is the talisman of women's power' was widespread during the late nineteenth and early twentieth centuries and firmly held by feminists and non-feminists alike. The women who later campaigned for the suffrage and equality of education thought, however, like Mill, that those rights were the corollary of women's right to equal citizenship under the law, and looked forward to the elevating moral and humanitarian tone of society once those rights had been bestowed. For them, the emphasis on equality and the force of domestic ideology were in no way at odds.

Richardson, in replying to Dalrymple, made it clear that as far as he was concerned, their campaign had achieved its goal:

> Don't worry and don't over exert yourself. We have gained three points: University sanction, acquiescence of professors, acceptance of opportunity by ladies. That is something; if we repine we may be challenged as ungrateful. We are planting strange seed in a strange soil. I am well pleased that it has germinated and is growing. Better fine deep, fibrous roots than too much foliage.[27]

Dalrymple, like her friend and ally, saw education as a means of assisting women to take part in 'the educational, domestic and social duties of life'. She had no desire for education that would make women 'clever, restless and unfeminine', and lamented 'the wild cry … for an impossible equality with man'.[28]

New Zealand's first female university student

In 1874 the University of Otago, with reluctance and after much tortuous negotiation, joined the University of New Zealand, a federally structured institution that had been created in September 1870. Canterbury College had been established in 1873; Auckland University College would follow in 1883 and then Wellington's Victoria University College in 1897.

The University of New Zealand's existence owed much to Canterbury's efforts to prevent Otago from monopolising tertiary education. The provincial era might have been over – since 1876 – but rivalries remained. It was no coincidence that the University of New Zealand's first headquarters were in Christchurch. From 1874, Canterbury College became the sole degree-granting institution in the country. The University of New Zealand Senate examined students; teaching took place at the University of Otago and Canterbury College, as well as at several affiliated secondary schools.

Auckland, with its poor record in promoting secondary schooling for girls, let alone tertiary education for women, seemed an unlikely place to produce the colony's first woman university graduate. It owed this distinction not to any protracted campaign but to a certain amount of audacious individual initiative and to the needs and aspirations of the University of New Zealand. Kate Edger's intellectual ability and capacity for self-disciplined academic work were also vital factors.

Farquhar Macrae, headmaster of Auckland College and Grammar, encouraged Kate Edger's ground-breaking university enrolment.

Auckland Libraries Heritage Collections, 4-2823A

By 1874 Kate was 17 and wanting to pursue her education. Home teaching was no longer sufficient, so Samuel contacted his friend Farquhar Macrae, headmaster of Auckland College and Grammar School, and asked if Kate might be allowed to study with the top class at the school. Macrae agreed to let her learn alongside 12 boys. Being the only girl in a boys' school could have been daunting, but Kate appears to have taken it in her stride. She later recalled being advised to enter the classroom with downcast eyes. Quiet-mannered and serious-minded, not given to outspokenness or attention seeking, she handled the situation well, and remembered being treated with courtesy by her fellow students.

Auckland College and Grammar, affiliated to the University of New Zealand, from 1872 offered evening classes in university subjects for local students interested in completing a degree course. As an ardent feminist, Samuel was familiar with recent developments in Britain concerning women and higher education, and as a University of London graduate, was also familiar with how a federal, non-teaching university operated. After discussion, he and Macrae could not find anything explicitly preventing a woman from sitting the university degree examinations. In May 1874, to test their theory, one K. Edger, gender unspecified, applied to the senate of the University of New Zealand to sit a university mathematical scholarship examination. It is not clear at what stage the senate realised Kate's gender, but it accepted the application without comment. Scholarships were intended to assist potential university graduates. Kate won the scholarship and then quietly but determinedly proceeded to obtain her degree. The whole episode of her acceptance into tertiary study has been described as 'virtually a non-event'.[29]

Several factors influenced the senate's decision to grant the scholarship. The University of New Zealand, then attempting to get both the University of Otago and Canterbury College to affiliate, was keen to attract more students, and perhaps reasoned that 'What the Colonial Office did not know about officially, it was not compelled to oppose'.[30] It was desperate to gain numbers and credibility; increased enrolments, whether male or female, were vital. They might have reasoned, too, that an outspoken public figure like Samuel Edger might make unwanted waves if Kate's request were denied.[31]

Their decision, born of expediency and practical economic considerations, had far-reaching impacts for New Zealand women. In contrast with British universities offering certificates rather than degrees, or American colleges with a gender-differentiated curriculum, Kate's acceptance into a degree programme on an equal footing with men constituted a huge step forward for women's rights. From the outset, women enrolled in New Zealand universities studied the same curriculum as their fellow male students, and welcomed the opportunity to expand their minds, their independence and their professional and occupational opportunities.

Hard work and 'indomitable perseverance'

Kate's experience as New Zealand's first female university student was unique and a far cry from that of her successors. She attended evening classes in university subjects at Auckland College and Grammar, but there were no clubs or social events to enliven or punctuate her course of study. She had to draw on considerable reserves of self-discipline, a propensity for hard work and what Macrae described as her 'indomitable perseverance'.[32]

The school building itself was far from prepossessing, and even potentially perilous. Hugh Hart Lusk, chairman of the Education Board for the Auckland district and later the member of the House of Representatives for Franklin, described it as 'a disused military hut, the floor of which is not quite safe to tread on, the roof of which is open to the sky, and which, as a residence, would be simply uninhabitable'. He went on to commend her for roughing it uncomplainingly and for persevering 'from day to day against all difficulties and discouragements'.[33] It is unlikely that Kate, having spent her early years in pioneering conditions in the Kaipara, would have been disconcerted by her surroundings. She had learnt how to work independently while being educated by Samuel and she did most of her studying at home, where she enjoyed the companionship and support of her parents and siblings. She obviously earned the respect of her fellow students, who turned out to applaud her graduation.

The university career leading to her achievement of a BA majoring in Latin and mathematics was smooth and distinguished. Having obtained the trail-blazing mathematical scholarship in May 1874, she won further scholarships in chemistry and physics in May 1875. She passed college examinations in Latin, mathematics and French in 1874, Latin, mathematics and chemistry in 1875, and English language and literature, constitutional history and chemistry in 1876. In all her subjects she took a first class, gaining more than 75 percent of the marks available. She passed the compulsory section of the BA examination in May 1876 and the optional section in November. The University of New Zealand Senate awarded her a senior scholarship for mathematics in May 1876.

A proud milestone

If 'K. Edger's' acceptance into university was something of a non-event, the same could certainly not be said of her graduation. In March 1877 the *Auckland Star* crowed about her achievements: 'A [sic] Auckland young lady of 20 years, Miss Kate Milligan Edger, third daughter of Rev. Samuel Edger, B.A., has eclipsed all other young ladies of this city in winning the highest position as a lady-student in the records of Great Britain and the colonies.' It went on to quote the official announcement, which would have been made in the *New Zealand Gazette*, of the senior scholarship and the degree, which would be 'publicly conferred in Auckland'. The paper also noted that 'Miss Kate Edger studied at the Auckland College and Grammar School, and at the December examination this persevering scholar obtained nearly the highest marks possible. We congratulate the young lady and her parents on the distinguished success of their daughter.'[34]

In April the *New Zealand Herald* cited Kate's achievement as proof of women's high intellectual ability. The author of this progressive piece, like Mill, attributed females' oft-proclaimed inferiority to restricted educational opportunity: 'it has been repeatedly cited that women are less capable of educational accomplishment than men, – the fact being that they have been denied the means and opportunities of culture, which would have enabled them to show their capacity.'[35]

Kate was proof that women possessed a 'capacity for intellectual attainment far beyond which our forefathers were disposed to credit them'. The article expressed pride that 'of all places within the broad British dominions' this colony 'at the uttermost end of the earth in relation to home' had acquired 'the lofty distinction of producing within the pale of scholarship the first "sweet girl graduate"' who had ever received the 'somewhat incongruous distinction of Bachelor of Arts'.[36] This reference to a 'sweet girl graduate', which recurred several times in the press coverage of Kate's graduation, is from Alfred Tennyson's 'The Princess' (1847). One of the heroines of this feminist poem, Lilia, laments women's lack of higher education and ruminates about a women-only college. The 'sweet girl graduates' phrase is a comment made by a patronising male: 'Pretty were the sight/If our old halls could change their sex and flaunt/With prudes for proctors, dowagers for deans/And sweet girl-graduates in their golden hair.'[37]

When Kate Edger graduated on 11 July 1877, such pillars of the Auckland community as Dr John Logan Campbell and J.C. Firth, along with an extensive list of clergymen, attended the ceremony with a large crowd, drawn by the novel spectacle of a woman receiving a university degree. Many of the spectators, as the *Herald* reported the following day, were women – 'three-fourths of the space of the large hall was occupied by ladies, for whom sufficient sitting accommodation could scarcely be found' – but the 'remaining space … was occupied by male spectators of all classes'. Up in the gallery were Kate's fellow students, who 'were not a little demonstrative of their satisfaction that a lady fellow student should be the recipient of competitive honour. They clapped their hands, and cheered heartily when the lady was observed.'[38] The venue, the Choral Hall in Symonds Street, would have been familiar to Kate as Samuel regularly preached there, and she and Lilian had performed on its stage.

The *Herald* had already praised Kate's high intellectual ability, noted her numerous scholarships and stressed the magnitude of her achievement. 'Much might be made out of this' – and Tennyson could, again, be quoted:

Kate Edger, New Zealand's first female university graduate,
photographed in 1877 by Hemus and Hanna.

Macmillan Brown Library, Christchurch, University of Canterbury
research photographs MB 1448, Ref 4804

But we prefer to treat the affair as the important thing it is; an event showing that in this new land of ours, female intellect and female studiousness have scope in which to display themselves, and that these are regarded and rewarded in proportion to their deserts [sic]. Many will, we think, be present to-day, not only out of regard to the spirit of chivalry which makes much of every good deed done by a woman, but also out of acknowledgement to the industry and accomplishments of one who has set an example which may be, and we hope will be, followed by many of her sex.[39]

This theme featured in various speeches during the graduation ceremony. Dr William Cowie, the Anglican Bishop of Auckland, noted that in Britain women could not take a BA degree, and disparaged old-world arguments based on lack of precedent and on derisive attitudes towards 'blue-stockings'. Acquiring higher education did not mitigate 'tenderness', which was one of women's 'principal charms'. By way of proving his point, he cited the example of Sara Coleridge, the distinguished daughter of poet Samuel Taylor Coleridge, who was recognised as both educated and scholarly but also 'one of the most tender and refined' of women. Studying for a university degree would help women to become fitting help-meets for 'these fellow mortals with whom they look forward to share the joys and halve the sorrows of life'.[40] The next speaker, the Reverend David Bruce, a member of the University of New Zealand Senate, hoped that Kate's achievement would stimulate other women to follow her example, and encourage 'gentlemen of wealth' to establish competitive bursaries and endow some professorial chairs.

Farquhar Macrae then conducted Kate to the table on the platform and presented her to Lusk, who was representing the University of New Zealand, 'for admission to the degree of Bachelor of Arts'. In the words of the *Auckland Star* reporter, 'The young lady was greeted with cheers, all the gentlemen on the platform rising to receive her.' After Lusk had bestowed Kate's degree diploma, the bishop presented her with what one reporter described as 'a white camellia of considerable size and beauty'. This flower symbolised 'unpretending excellence' and Kate received it 'with becoming modesty'.[41] The 'newly admitted Bachelor of Arts made no reply that was audible' and afterwards 'descended into the body of the hall and took her seat amongst her friends'.[42]

The next day the tributes continued. The *Herald* praised Kate's achievement as one that would give 'lasting impetus' to the cause of higher education. Aucklanders felt proud of this 'modest maid' and of New Zealand.

Let us hear no more of the intellectual inferiority of women. For generations their education has been neglected. They have not obtained their fair share of culture

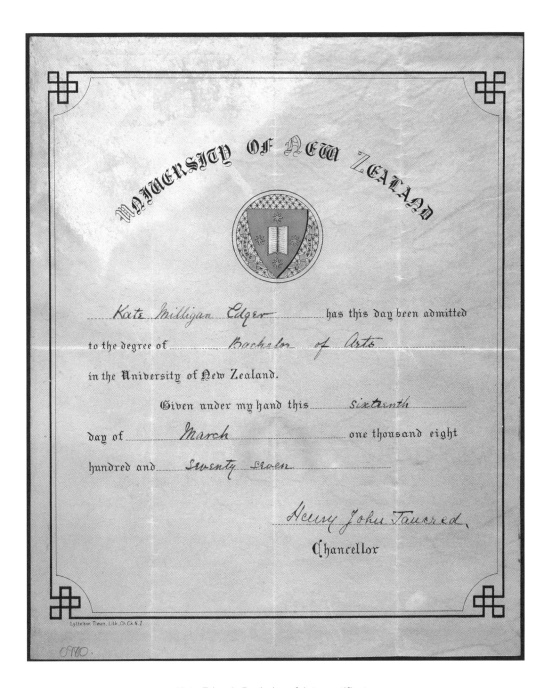

Kate Edger's Bachelor of Arts certificate.

University of Auckland Historical Collection Part 1, Mss and Archives E-8, Box 2, Folder 2, Special Collections, University of Auckland Libraries and Learning Services

… The true measure of a woman's right to knowledge is her capacity of receiving it; and we know of no influence more beneficial to society, to the training of children, the teaching of manliness to boys and of true pure womanliness to their sisters, than the influence of cultured women, whose powers of mind have been thoroughly trained and who are embued with a true conception of the duties they are called upon to discharge … [W]e believe a brighter day is dawning, and the first rays of the rising sun of female intellectual advancement are now being reflected from this remote dependency of the British Empire.

The *Herald* could 'scarcely imagine a more pleasing sight than the eager interest displayed in the faces of the several hundreds of young girls, most of them students, who witnessed the ceremony': this was surely 'an augury of future success'. Now it was up to their parents to 'keep aglow that interest and feed the flame which creates a thirst for knowledge in the minds of their children'.[43]

An influential achievement

Over the next few years this small, remote country would achieve various firsts, from votes for women to old age pensions, but Kate's graduation was one of the earliest occasions when the self-congratulatory bell was rung. It would later emerge that she was not, in fact, the first woman in the British Empire to receive a university degree; she was the first to receive a BA. A Canadian woman, Grace Lockhart – like Kate, the daughter of a nonconformist minister – had graduated with a bachelor's degree in science and English literature from Mount Allison University in Sackville, New Brunswick, on 25 May 1875. This fact remained unknown in New Zealand for some considerable time, and Kate went to her deathbed in 1935 believing she was the first woman in the empire to have earned a university degree.

Boasting about Kate's achievement did not end with her graduation. In 1891, for example, the *Auckland Star* commemorated the event, observing with unabashed smugness:

Here we were in what our English friends are pleased to term 'a corner of the earth' actually leading the van of educational reform, and shocking European Professors and legislators by the boldness with which we solved a problem over which they were still shaking their learned heads … In a young country, where everything is new, and where changes are rapid, the spirit of freedom and disregard of conventional usage always have freer play than in a land where the customs and habits of past ages surround society like an atmosphere.

The fact that Oxford and Cambridge still did not allow women to take degrees was held up as out of step with a changed appreciation of women's intellectual ability and the benefits of higher education. In the past, 'lady "bachelors" were hard hit by the shafts of wits and satirists, and "sweet girl graduates" constantly figured in cartoon and caricature. It was steadily maintained that women as a body were intellectually inferior to men, and that if in a few cases they distinguished themselves by winning academical honours, their very success would unfit them for the duties of domestic life.' The best riposte to this, 'even in England', lay in a 'series of startling successes, which are brilliant enough to convince the most sceptical'. At the University of Cambridge women had 'carried off the highest honours in some of the most important tripos examinations', and in a variety of subjects: 'history, mediaeval and modern languages, moral science and classics [and] mathematics'. All too clear was 'the urgent necessity that exists for a change in the statutes that regulate the procedure of the older English Universities'.[44]

In 1929, when the *Herald* ran a series of articles paying tribute to 'The Makers of Auckland', Kate's degree was referred to as long 'a matter of pride' to the city; the University of New Zealand had given 'a lead to the rest of the British in putting the fair sex on an equality with men in respect to academic qualifications'.[45] Two years later the *Herald* again praised Kate and her degree and paid tribute to the 'enlightened' part that New Zealand played in 'the sweeping advance' made in women's education during the past half century.[46]

The fact that, unlike Britain and the United States, New Zealand had offered university education to women on the same terms as men was also a cause for pride, as was the fact that in future the country's universities were without exception co-educational. Contemporary coverage of Kate's graduation often stressed the hope that her educational achievement would induce more women to take advantage of higher education. This hope was fulfilled. By 1890 there were 211 females among the 575 students on the University of New Zealand roll and the percentage of females attending university far exceeded that of Britain for several decades.[47]

The opening up of university education to New Zealand women arguably helped to pave the way for the future success of the suffrage campaign, by providing ammunition against all those who claimed women were intellectually lesser beings and therefore precluded from equality with men under the law. However, anxieties about higher education for women, and arguments about its negative physical and mental impacts on women remained, as did scientific pontifications about their supposedly inferior brains.[48]

The argument that degrees like Kate's would enhance rather than restrict women's ability to fulfil their natural roles as wives and mothers helped to convince many people that higher education did not pose a threat to the 'natural' female sphere. Not unrelated to that reassuring thought, Kate's unselfconsciously modest manner and gentle personality were several times commended in accounts of the graduation ceremony. She clearly did not conform to stereotypes of brittle, assertively competitive blue-stockings. Kate, like Sara Coleridge, combined scholarly pursuits with a pleasingly unthreatening manner. The fact that she was about to embark on a career in teaching also fitted perfectly with expectations about middle-class femininity and women's natural role as carers and nurturers of the young. At the same time, for a 20-year-old university-educated middle-class woman to move to a distant city, live independently of her family and begin a rewarding, meaningful, well-remunerated professional life was, in 1877, a notable feminist achievement in itself.

3

'Eminent Success in her Profession'

These women [Kate and Lilian Edger] are examples of what women's abilities can accomplish, and we hope others of their sex, seeing what they have done, will strike out and do likewise.

New Zealand Herald, 22 May 1878

[T]hey were like the ancient athletes who won victory more for their city than themselves. When their own course was finished they turned with equal or even greater enthusiasm to the training of other girls.

Edith Searle Grossmann, 'The Woman Movement in New Zealand', *Westminster Review*, 1908

In September 1877, not long after the excitement of her highly publicised graduation ceremony, Kate left Auckland to teach in Christchurch. For the next five years as a founding teacher at Canterbury College Girls' High School (soon more commonly known as Christchurch Girls' High School[1]) and as a postgraduate student at Canterbury College, she once again played a leading role in advancing the cause of secondary and tertiary education for women. Christchurch Girls' High, which was managed by Christchurch College's board of governors, quickly became New Zealand's leading source of future female university students.

Her experiences teaching there, and as one of the country's first female postgraduates, offer a rare insight into the origins and development of women's education in New Zealand. She was among the vanguard of a new, still tiny, group of female secondary school teachers. Along with her sister Lilian and their mutual friend and fellow teacher Helen Connon, she not only helped students to qualify for university studies but served as a new kind of role model for them. Her ideas about women's education influenced what and how her students were taught.

The creation of girls' secondary schools in nineteenth-century New Zealand, and the attitudes towards women's education and achievement they inculcated in their pupils, had an incalculable impact both on women's higher education and their rights and potential roles within society. These institutions took female learning and academic achievement seriously, enhanced their students' sense of solidarity and increased their ability to contribute positively to society both within and outside the domestic sphere.[2]

Kate entered secondary school teaching at a crucial point. During the provincial period, education had been expensive, badly and inconsistently resourced and very low on the list of regional priorities. In 1877 a national Education Act made education free, secular and compulsory between the ages of seven and 13. Although secondary schools were publicly endowed, they charged fees and were, and long remained, almost exclusively middle-class preserves providing pathways into university education. With the expansion of district high schools – by 1890 there were 14 of these for boys and seven for girls – the secondary school population steadily rose. But even as late as 1917, only 37 percent of primary school leavers in New Zealand proceeded to secondary school.[3] The syllabus for secondary students was highly academic and classically oriented: Latin, French, English, Euclid (geometry) and algebra featured prominently.

Male university students were destined for careers in teaching, business or the professions. Female university students who went on to paid employment usually became teachers: almost three-quarters of those who graduated from the University of New Zealand between 1878 and 1920 did so, mainly at secondary schools.[4] Their professional efforts enabled subsequent generations of young women both to attend university and to cope with its requirements. Many of their students, in turn, became admired and emulated secondary school teachers.

The common career destination of female graduates had a marked impact on public perceptions of women's education. Early societal unease at the advent of young women graduates earning an independent living outside the home did not lessen as the nineteenth century progressed, but it was tempered by the prevalent belief that teaching, like nursing, represented a natural extension of women's traditional domestic role.

Parents who could afford it increasingly came to consider university education as a desirable attribute, even a status symbol, for their daughters, who could thus become more cultured and better able to fulfil their roles as educated wives and effective mothers of high-achieving offspring. Teaching's connotations of domesticity and public service made it attractive to many women, and it did not threaten male employment.

First female university-educated teacher

Kate Edger applied successfully for the position of first assistant at Christchurch Girls' High School in June 1876, before that institution had opened its doors. In a fulsome letter of reference accompanying her job application, Farquhar Macrae sang Kate's praises, pointing to her various scholarships, unprecedented achievement at university and the fact that she was an accomplished musician. He even paid tribute to the academic promise of her younger sister Lilian, who had recently left all rivals, male and female, far behind in the Auckland Education Board Open Scholarships competition.[5]

Macrae pointed out that Kate already had teaching experience. For the past two years she had tutored both his children and those of David Bruce, to the great satisfaction of both sets of parents. Her charges entertained 'a warm affection' for their teacher and, thanks to her sterling efforts, now took 'intelligent interest' in their academic work. He confidently predicted a successful professional career:

> Although Miss Edger has had no experience in the conducting of large classes, I have no hesitation in expressing my conviction that she will prove a good Public Teacher. Her educational attainments, her love of teaching, her power of winning the affection of the young, her indomitable perseverance and her strong sense of duty afford the promise of eminent success in her profession.[6]

Kate started on a salary of £300 per annum.[7] Those sceptical about the benefits of women's university education might have revised their opinions somewhat given the clear economic advantages a degree bestowed. At a young age, Kate had quickly found permanent employment on a relatively high salary.[8] In 1874 only 20 percent of women over 15 worked for wages. (By 1891 that figure had risen only to 24 percent.) Sixty percent of wage-earning women were domestic servants, usually earning between 10 and 12s a week (about £25–30 a year) plus full board, but as late as 1890 an underhousemaid could earn as little as 7s 6d per week.[9] Student teachers working under the apprentice-certificate system in the primary school sector earned £20 per year. Middle-class women rarely worked, but if necessity demanded it, could become governesses or music teachers, or they might set up a private school, usually in their own homes. For a young, single, middle-class woman like Kate to be a well-paid professional was remarkable.

Christchurch in the late 1870s

The years Kate spent in Christchurch were extremely busy but also, as she later recalled with some nostalgia, deeply rewarding. Unlike Auckland, Canterbury was a planned Anglican settlement designed to mirror the social hierarchies of the old world. Although its development did not run entirely to plan, thanks to difficulties over land sales, it was a more stratified society. A wealthy landed elite played a leading role socially and politically, along with a growing number of well-heeled professionals and businessmen in the city.

The early 1870s were buoyant times for the province. Wool and wheat farming thrived and population boomed. In 1871 Canterbury's population was 46,801 and Auckland province's 62,335. Between 1874 and 1878 Canterbury's population increased by 33,147 to 91,922 while Auckland's rose by a mere 15,210 to 82,661.[10] By 1878 Christchurch boasted a museum, a hospital, several imposing banks and two daily newspapers. Wealthy male pastoralists belonged to the prestigious Christchurch Club, established in 1856; merchants and financiers joined the Canterbury Club, opened in 1874. The architect Benjamin Mountfort designed several of the city's early public buildings in Gothic Revival style, including the Provincial Council Buildings (1865), Canterbury Museum (1870) and parts of Canterbury (University) College (1877). He was also, from 1873, supervising architect on Christ Church Cathedral, which would, from the 1880s, become a symbol of the city. In the last two decades of the nineteenth century, the spreading suburbs became linked to the city centre by steam and horse-drawn trams.[11]

Canterbury College and Christchurch Girls' High School

Christchurch's landed gentry and well-off businessmen and professionals sent their sons to Christ's College. Established in 1850 in Lyttelton and occupying its present site on Rolleston Avenue from 1856, the school was closely modelled on prestigious English public schools. Initially, however, pupils who wished to advance to university education had to go to Britain.

William Rolleston, Canterbury's last provincial superintendent, was an active advocate of higher education for girls. After putting aside, in the provincial estimates, £3000 to build a girls' high school, on 25 May 1876 he wrote to William Montgomery, the chairman of the Canterbury College Board of Governors, asking to talk with him and other board members about such a school. Time was of the

Part of the Wheeler Brothers' 1881 photographic panorama of Christchurch, showing the view from the partially completed cathedral spire, looking west along Worcester Street. At the far end is Canterbury Museum, with Canterbury College on the left and Christ's College on the right.

Museum of New Zealand Te Papa Tongarewa, AL.000 608

essence since the designated money would lapse at the end of September; after that, thanks to the abolition of the provincial system, finance would have to be negotiated with the central government in Wellington. When Rolleston met the board on 3 June 1876, he proposed that Canterbury College should manage the school because its educational standing, and 'especially the advantages it possesses through its professorial staff', would offer both status and efficiency. The board accepted responsibility promptly, with the proviso that it would receive 'adequate funds' to run the school until it was self-supporting, and purchased a quarter-acre site (1000m²) on the corner of Hereford and Antigua streets. (The part of Antigua Street from Cambridge Terrace to Armagh Street later became Rolleston Avenue.) With the help of some extra money, building began in October.[12]

Canterbury College has been described as 'the first practical co-educational university institute in the British world'.[13] A shortfall in expected male enrolments had encouraged this welcoming approach, which was supported by John Macmillan Brown, one of the college's most energetic and influential founding professors. The Canterbury University College Board of Governors ran the high school with the aim of preparing students for the Matriculation (university entrance) and University Scholarship examinations. Parents were aware of this when they sent their daughters to the new school,[14] which quickly became a rich source of future female tertiary students. By the time Otago had produced its first woman graduate, Caroline Freeman, in 1885, Canterbury University College boasted eight women graduates. Seven had master's degrees and all were employed as teachers. It also had about 100 females enrolled in its programmes.

At the outset, however, it was not all plain sailing. In 1927 Kate wrote an article for the school's jubilee celebrations aptly entitled 'Early Months: Aims and difficulties'. Clearly no one had given much thought to the organisation of classes, a task compounded by the students' varied ages and educational backgrounds. As Kate observed, 'to the first appointed teachers it seemed somewhat unwise to have anticipated by two or three months the completion of the most indispensable preparation for the successful carrying out of so important a prospect. The high school building was not ready for occupation, the third member of the staff was unable to take up her duties for two months, books were not available in sufficient numbers, – so that in every way temporary arrangements had to be entered into.' As if aware that her comments came close to criticism, Kate added, with characteristic diplomacy, 'No doubt, however, there was a great deal to be said for hurrying the opening. It was a great advantage to have one term for making experiments, so to speak, thus enabling a good beginning to be made the following year, and ensuring a complete year's work being done on a well-established basis.'[15]

Initially, the school staff consisted only of Kate and the 'Lady Principal', Georgiana Ingle, a widow with three children who had, like many others of her age and class, been educated at a dame school, a small private school with a female teacher. She had a thorough knowledge of secondary schools, because both her father, Richard Poulett-Harris, and her late husband had been headmasters of boys' high schools in Australia. The first students, 74 girls aged between seven and 17, were housed temporarily in part of the newly completed initial block of Canterbury College, which was being used for lectures. In Kate's view this accommodation was 'most unsuitable' for a school, with two lecture rooms arranged as a gallery that had to be entered from only one side.

Kate and the principal began by grouping the girls into classes based on age and educational attainments. Ingle wanted to admit very young children, so that the school could better 'train them from the beginning in our own methods'.[16] Parents were willing to pay for their primary school-aged daughters to receive what they perceived to be a better education than that offered in state primary schools. Although Kate acknowledged there was much to be said for this, it greatly added to the initial difficulties because of the range in the students' ages and differences in scholastic attainments. Eventually the board hired two temporary teachers, to enable staff to cope. Numbers quickly reached 90. To add to the travails, one of the new teachers got whooping cough and was absent for three weeks. According to Kate, by the time the holidays began on 13 December Ingle had been brought 'almost to breaking point', a situation exacerbated by illness in her own family.

By February 1878 the new school building was ready for use. There were now four good classrooms. The largest, divided by a heavy curtain, could hold 100 pupils and was used for two classes. Now 'the real work of a High School could be undertaken'.[17] The enrolment in 1878 reached 115 girls, and the staff included Georgiana Ingle, Kate, Martha Hamilton, the second assistant teacher and two assistant teachers: Frances Dunnage, whose father was the Reverend George Dunnage of Papanui Road, and 21-year-old Helen Connon, who had passed the examinations for a teacher's certificate but needed practical experience before she could be certified.

Setting the tone: Aims and standards

As the first term of 1878 loomed, the staff considered what Kate later described as 'the most important' question of all, namely the definite aim of the school:

> Was it to be mainly for preparing girls to pass the various examinations, and District Scholarships (which in Canterbury were open to children as young as 10) or was it to be for giving a good general education, without special thought of examinations? There were pros and cons on both sides. Examinations tended to 'cram' and to confining the curriculum within definite limits, which, unless fairly elastic, were likely to crush individual initiative and to produce *types* of mind instead of fostering free growth of individual belief. On the other hand, the avowed intention in establishing the High School was to prepare students for the University, so that Matriculation and University Scholarship had to be regarded as the standard aimed at.[18]

69

Following full discussions among the staff and with the board of governors, the five women decided to aim for a middle course. Matriculation and University Scholarship exams were the goal, but all work merely for the sake of a good showing in examinations would be discouraged because 'the true purpose of education [was] the building up of a well-balanced character'. The scheme of work drawn up would see matriculation and entrance into university as the 'natural climax': at the end of five years, they hoped that a girl of average ability would be 'fairly well educated and ready for a university course'. Cramming was to be avoided. Only those girls ready to sit an examination without undue strain or overwork would do so.[19] The school's ethos, which bore a marked similarity to some of Samuel's key views on the ideal education,[20] stood it in good stead and endured. To this day the school motto, 'Sapientia et Veritas' (Wisdom and Truth), refers to a kind of learning that embraces 'a holistic approach to education', in which academic development 'must be balanced with the development of the whole person'.[21]

Ingle deferred to her more educated staff members when it came to matters of curriculum and style of teaching, and this helped to build a strong, unified sense of loyalty among the staff. Kate and Helen Connon, who quickly developed a lasting friendship, played a key role in setting the tone and standards of the school. They shared a great many interests, not least a love of learning and teaching, and a prodigious capacity for sustained hard work.

Helen was a statuesque young woman with a serene, dignified manner. She came from a relatively humble background. Her father was a carpenter who, after working in goldfield towns in Australia, took his wife and children to Dunedin in 1862, where Helen was taught by Robert Stout. In 1865 the family moved to New Zealand's West Coast, before settling in Christchurch in 1874. She entered Canterbury University College to study for a BA not long after Kate enrolled at Auckland, finishing her studies late in 1879 and graduating in 1880. In 1881 she completed a master's degree in English and Latin with first-class honours, the first woman in the British Empire to earn a degree with honours.

At university or in the classroom, associates and friends, teachers and students praised Helen as a person of great character; the word 'worship' was frequently used. Her first biographer, for example, novelist Edith Searle Grossmann, a former pupil of Helen at Christchurch Girls' and then a fellow student at Canterbury College, described her as 'the idol of the College; many of the old students who knew her then still treasure their early recollections of her. The women loved her, the men all admired and not a few worshipped her.' At school, Grossmann remembered, 'I would have walked through raging flames to please her.'[22] To Grossmann, and to many others, Helen Connon seemed to be 'the embodiment of womanly dignity and beautiful wisdom.'[23] In a more recent biography, Margaret Lovell-Smith has observed that if such remarks about Connon now seem 'somewhat overstated', it is important to bear in mind that she embodied 'a completely new and exciting way of living. For both middle-class and working-class girls she represented a world of possibilities for women: the opportunity to train their minds for work that was intellectually satisfying and could lead to economic independence.'[24]

This was also true of Kate. Although she never inspired the ardent response that Helen evoked, former Christchurch Girls' High students remembered her with warm admiration. In 1927, for example, Margaret Lorimer MA recalled her as 'a splendid mistress, whom we all admired and respected. Sound in her knowledge, clear and lucid in her presentation of matter, easy in her discipline, and encouraging in her manner, she did very solid work, and especially in Mathematics, Latin, Roman History and Antiquities.'[25] Another former student, Elizabeth Whyte (née Milsom) MA, noted that 'Miss Edger and Miss Connon were the two who left the strongest impression on the minds of their scholars … the fact that Christchurch Girls' soon took a high place in educational circles was due to them.'[26]

All the staff, including Ingle, had a heavy teaching workload, with only a free lunch period in the course of the school day. Each woman taught at all levels. Kate's subjects were English, Latin and Mathematics. She had a reputation 'for being absolutely thorough, and also as taking a great interest in the girls'.[27]

Official reports on the school, undertaken annually by Inspector General of Schools the Reverend W.J. Habens, tell a story of rapid improvement. The first, in June 1878, noted that the standard of achievement was 'low' but that 'this is to be accounted for by the necessity of laying a good foundation where it has not before been laid, and that the present staff is quite competent to do much higher work when the pupils are ready for it'. By 1881 he could write, 'The work now being done in it is of a high order, very thorough, and altogether worthy of a good secondary school preparing pupils for a course of University study.' By 1882 Habens could describe it as 'one of the best schools I know'.[28] In July 1881, at the beginning of the third term, due to overcrowding and because Canterbury College needed the old building for its School of Art, Christchurch Girls' moved to a new site in Cranmer Square, on the corner of Armagh and Montreal streets.

Photographs of Christchurch educational buildings, from the *New Zealand Graphic*, 11 June 1898. Christchurch Girls' High School, bottom right, was originally temporarily housed in Canterbury College, top and bottom left.

Graduation photograph
of Lilian Edger, Helen
Connon and Kate Edger,
1881.

Macmillan Brown Library,
Christchurch, William James
Gardner Papers, MB234, Ref
499s56

Postgraduate study: For 'pleasure and advantage'

In 1878 Lilian joined Kate in Christchurch and worked towards her BA at Canterbury University College. With her sister and Helen Connon both enrolled, Kate initially began going along to lectures for 'the pleasure and advantage' they afforded.[29] Lilian graduated BA in 1881, at the same ceremony in which Helen Connon received her groundbreaking MA. Elizabeth Whyte was one of the Girls' High students who attended the occasion: 'The senior pupils were taken to the Provincial Chambers to see the ceremony in the beautiful Hall. The Chancellor of the University was there, and I remember so well him putting an MA hood over Miss Connon's head. The ladies were then presented with a bouquet of white camellias. Very proud of our teachers were we that day.'[30]

Earlier that year Lilian had become a teacher at Christchurch Girls' High, replacing Frances Dunnage. The two sisters flatted at 152 Salisbury Street, a 15-minute walk from the school. Both then studied together for an MA, receiving their respective degrees in 1882, Kate's in mathematics and Lilian's (a double first) in Latin and English. That Kate, Lilian and their intimate friend Helen Connon all managed to combine highly successful university study with full-time teaching is impressive. Most lectures were held in the mornings, from 7.45 to 8.45, allowing them just enough time to make it from the nearby college to their classrooms; they also attended evening classes.

The Edger sisters' academic achievement attracted both admiring comment and some critics. On the positive side, the *Herald* gave 'All praise to the training, the brains, and the perseverance which produce such results. These girls are examples of what women's abilities can accomplish, and we hope others of their sex, seeing what they have done, will strive to go and do likewise.'[31] On the negative side, as the author of 'Our Christchurch Letter' in the *Observer* drolly noted in 1882, some women believed that attracting academic distinction and attracting male suitors were mutually exclusive: 'Those very clever girls the Misses Edger appear to prosper well. I hear, on all sides, that they are models of energy, perseverance, application, and method. One extremely naughty girl told me she would rather be in the "Sweet bye-and-bye" than be them with never a lover and never a lark.'[32]

But academic achievement did not mean spinsterhood and a lack of fun. Despite a heavy teaching workload and demanding study, the five years Kate spent in Christchurch were full of interest and amusement, if not larks and lovers. In 1927 she described how 'a trio of girl student friends … entered with equal enjoyment into the serious intellectual activities of the college, and into the lighter recreations of boating and walking afforded by the Avon and the gardens that are in close proximity to the college. They met in the lecture room on equal terms with the men students, they attended the Dialectical Society, and took part in the debates …' For her, those years at Canterbury College

> were very happy times … when the students were numbered by the half dozen instead of the hundred, and were like one big family. Though the present generation enjoy many advantages which were not available for the small numbers of the early times, there were compensating features, chief among them the enthusiasm and inspiration with which the whole time of the college course was filled because professors and students alike were deeply impressed with the value of work for its own sake.[33]

In her biography of Helen Connon, Edith Grossmann mentioned 'abuse and ridicule' towards female students,[34] but this was not Kate's experience. Fellow student John Innes, later a teacher at Timaru Boys' High School, recalled looking over the new college buildings with Kate, Lilian and Helen in 1880 during the September holidays. On another occasion he walked with them and William Herbert from Sydenham to Governors Bay, a distance of some 11 kilometres, and then another 14 back to Lyttelton, to catch the train home into Christchurch.[35]

In lectures, female students sat together at the front of the room and the men sat behind them, though whether this happened naturally or was directed by the staff is unclear. Women could relax and talk or study together in the 'ladies' room', a 'dusty little place under the clocktower, furnished with a table, some chairs and a few bookshelves'.[36] Male students, by contrast, had no common room at all, just a couple of 'dens' under the French and English lecture rooms where they could wash their hands and hang up their academic gowns. Student numbers were small enough to justify Kate's reference to a happy family. In 1880 six students graduated with BA degrees and two with an MA. As part of the festivities afterwards, Lilian and a fellow student called Louis Cohen took turns playing the 'fiddle'.[37]

Socialising between professors and students was not uncommon, with Alexander William Bickerton, the unconventional science professor, playing a key role on that front. When Kate wrote about him in her 1927 reminiscences, his university career had been over for 21 years. He annoyed the university authorities for decades with his espousal of socialism, his creation of a 'Federative Home' (a kind of commune in the suburb of Wainoni) in the 1890s and his renunciation of conventional marriage. In 1902, after opposing the jingoism of the South African War and launching various public attacks on the Canterbury College Board of Governors, Bickerton was fired. As his biographer has observed, 'He was essentially one of those men whose opinions, actions and methods are a standing challenge to orthodoxy. Indeed, one is led to suspect that he often flouted convention purely for the fun of doing so.'[38]

Kate's tribute to Bickerton is warmly effusive and completely lacking in moral judgment. Having grown up with a father who was often more than happy to challenge orthodoxy, she took Bickerton's eccentricity in her stride and remembered him as 'a most versatile genius. Whether he was dealing with an ordinary scientific subject in a popular manner, or expatiating learnedly on his pet theory of partial impact, or carrying out some experiment requiring skilful manipulation, he was equally happy in his style and method.' She also recalled how his home 'became a sort of miniature fairyland, with lovely little conservatories reflected and multiplied by skilful arrangement of mirrors' and how he and his wife 'kept practically an open house to students who cared to avail themselves of the hearty general invitation that they gave. Many a pleasant Sunday evening was spent there … when the time passed all too quickly in genial chat, or in friendly argument on every kind of subject.' In summer students also sometimes visited the Bickertons at their Sumner seaside cottage. They would either go for 'delightful tramps' over the Port Hills or indulge in 'lazy basking on the hot sand while the larks sang overhead'.[39]

John Macmillan Brown and women's higher education

One of Bickerton's somewhat unlikely friends, and a frequent visitor, was Professor John Macmillan Brown. Born in Scotland, the son of a shipmaster, Brown took his first degree at the University of Glasgow and later studied at Oxford with the legendary classical scholar and tutor Benjamin Jowett. In 1874, despite a disappointing second-class degree due to the insomnia that plagued him all his life, Brown was appointed founding professor of classics and English at Canterbury College. An energetic, commanding, serious young man, he threw himself into the work, putting in 16-hour days of lecturing, marking and administrating. He worked hard to make the college a centre of academic excellence and was in the vanguard of co-education. Despite a lack of humour, his lectures were widely regarded as brilliant and inspiring. The adoring trio of Kate, Lilian and Helen Connon most enjoyed the times

> when the professor of English gave them help and advice in his private room; for Professor Macmillan Brown was always more than a professor to his students: he was friend, advisor and tutor all in one, and it would be difficult to overestimate the strength and permanence of his influence upon all who threw themselves into their work with enthusiasm. It was an inspiration to listen to his lectures, but to be admitted into his sanctum, with its overflowing shelves, to be allowed to use his books, and even at times to revel or make extracts from them in the ante-room to his study, was a privilege indeed. He would have no laggards there: a giant in work himself, he expected from his students the same energy and enthusiasm.[40]

It is easy to see how Brown, who considered himself at the forefront of a 'moral and cultural crusade' in which education played a key role, would appeal to Kate and Lilian.[41] Like their father, he denounced the vulgar materialism of the colony and he, too, had an evangelical mission – to spread the university's positive influence through society by means of educated, public-minded citizens. This message had a profound influence on Kate.

The warm relationship between Brown and the Edger sisters continued. In 1884, when she was the well-respected principal of Nelson Girls' College, Kate asked Brown to speak at the certificate of merit ceremony:

> Miss Bell has invited Mr. and Mrs. Andrew and Professor Sale for Saturday night to meet you, not understanding that we [Kate and Lilian] were so selfish we wanted you all to ourselves and nobody else! So do spare us another evening as well – do please …

> You see we are so anxious to have you, and are so much afraid of other people carrying you off, that we are obliged to suggest several nights, so as to ensure one. But I am sure you will spare us one of them. If you only knew what a treat it is to us to see and hear you – we could have stayed last night for hours only we knew it would not do. So please write and let us know which night.[42]

As he grew older, the object of this unguarded admiration became increasingly conservative and self-regarding. His memoirs, published posthumously in 1974, do not endear him to posterity, nor do his several unreadable eugenicist novels written later in life.[43] Even his marriage to Helen Connon, in 1886, has a depressing downwards arc. The distinguished couple, though ensconced in a house and gardens of some grandeur, were both increasingly plagued by sleeplessness. But as a young man in the late 1870s and early 1880s, Brown was doing the best, most important work of his life, actively encouraging and fostering the higher education of women. The idealistic tenor of his thought and the richness of his language shine through in his opening address to Canterbury College students in March 1878:

> The University teaches him [the student] the highest use of the liberty of manhood. It gives predominance to his higher faculties, and thus makes the task of life less mediated by the lower passions, and therefore easier … [H]e has not the faculty of wonder killed within him … what has happened is only the recession of the limit of wonder, the curtain of mystery that hides the universe has not been destroyed, only drawn further back.[44]

The Dialectic Society

After Brown suggested that a debating group would add to university life, the Dialectic Society was formed in 1878. The name, suggested by a student studying Greek, was endorsed by the founders on the grounds that 'theirs should be no common Debating Society'. Kate, Lilian and Helen were keen members. In 1879 they listened to debates on such matters as free trade versus protection, whether country or city life was 'more conducive to development of genius' and whether science or literature provided 'better training for the Imagination'. Free trade and literature romped home but country life won only on the casting vote of the chairman. Whether women should be admitted to the learned professions was favoured by eight votes to six. A motion deprecating 'the idea that barbarous nations could be dispossessed of their lands because more civilized nations may make better use of them' was lost by a resounding nine to three.[45]

In 1880, along with fellow student Charles Chiltern, Kate acted as secretary of the society. During that year Bickerton spoke on 'The Laws and Growth of Opinion' and a Mr Hay spoke on Gladstone vs Disraeli. (The former won by 12 votes to six; a victory of seriousness over frivolity.) In September, when a 'youthful naturalist' read a paper on Darwinism, the minutes record that only four members supported the speaker, 'a large number voted against it' and 'a few declined to vote at all'. On 25 September that year, Kate read a paper on the Chinese question.[46] This has not survived, but it is probable that, like her father, she opposed contemporary racist attitudes towards the Chinese.

By 1881, when Helen Connon took over from Kate as secretary, the society had steadily grown from attendances ranging from eight to 18 in the late 1870s to an average regular attendance of 28. The society also held a couple of concerts at Christchurch Girls' High School, during which Kate and Lilian played the piano duet from *Faust* they had perfected as teenagers. In December 1881 and again in June 1882, the society also put on Shakespeare's *Much Ado About Nothing*. Neither Kate nor Lilian acted in this, but Helen played Hero.[47]

One college contemporary later described Kate and Lilian as 'serious and staid', and Helen as 'stately'.[48] They were certainly, all three, earnest young women; not the sort to engage in anything even remotely risqué. When, in 1882, the society redrafted its constitution, setting out its aim as 'to promote the fellowship and mental culture of the students', Kate, Lilian and Helen were among the eight women signatories from a total of 30.[49]

Kate and Helen remained close friends for the rest of their lives. In 1881, when Georgiana Ingle was forced to reduce the salaries of her teaching staff, Kate suggested that her own salary be reduced further so that Helen's could be increased to the same amount. Her friend refused to accept the offer.[50]

Family grief and a new career path

By October 1882 Ingle was feeling the strain. Five months earlier she had asked for three months' leave on the grounds that she needed rest and a change of scenery. In December that year she resigned. As first assistant mistress, Kate would normally have succeeded her, but in May 1882 she had successfully applied for a position as founding lady principal of the newly created Nelson College for Girls. Aged only 25, she was assuming a leadership position of great responsibility, which came with a salary of £350. Lilian was appointed second mistress at a salary of £150. The two sisters had been chosen from fields, respectively, of 13 and 15 impressive applicants, all local.[51] The school governors did not, as anticipated, have to advertise in England. Helen Connon became a legendary headmistress of Christchurch Girls', working there until 1894, eight years after her marriage.[52]

Although Kate and Lilian's years in the 'one big family' of Canterbury College and high school were happy ones, they faced the loss of both parents during their time in Christchurch. On 21 September 1880 their mother Louisa died, aged 61. Her funeral was held two days later at the Edger home in Wynyard Street. The *Herald*, reporting on this event, observed that 'The deceased lady was of a retiring and unassuming disposition, and in accordance with her last wishes there was no mourning worn, and the arrangements of her interment were so conducted as to avoid needless display.' Samuel spoke briefly at the service in Wynyard Street on the afternoon of the 23rd, and also briefly at the cemetery, but as the paper noted, 'the whole proceedings were of a private character.'[53]

Following his wife's death, Samuel moved to a home in Ponsonby with a large garden and soon settled into life there.[54] Now about 60, he enjoyed preaching and working in his garden. He felt more accepted and less at odds with other ministers: 'For the most part, during my Ponsonby life, I have experienced only courtesy and kindness in that quarter from which, at one time, I received nothing but neglect and misrepresentation.' True to his anti-sectarian aspirations, he was 'on the best of terms' with Anglicans, Presbyterians, Primitive Methodists and United Free Methodists, and 'have rendered most of them more or less of service.'[55] His personality and presence had by this time become a part of the city and its culture; religious sectarianism had, he believed, mellowed and other ministers no longer perceived him as a threat.

But old health problems, later described by the *Herald* as a 'stone in the bladder', recurred and soon made daily life so unbearable that he resolved to go to England

Samuel Edger in the early 1880s, looking like a biblical
prophet. This portrait was taken by his son-in-law Charles
Hemus, of Hemus and Hanna Photographers.

Auckland Libraries Heritage Collections, 959-1

for an operation. He died in London on 30 September 1882, only a few days after arriving. Ironically, even in death he did not escape a sectarian label; his death certificate noted his religion as 'Congregationalist'. For Kate and Lilian, his death represented an enormous loss. Auckland, too, lamented his passing: 'The tidings of Mr. Edger's decease will be received by all classes in the community with regret, on account of his scholarly ability, and his earnest labours in connection with most of the institutions in the city for the social and moral improvement of the masses.'[56]

Opening the door

During her five years in Christchurch Kate had begun a well-paid professional career, established lasting friendships, helped to found and to shape the culture of a school that became the major conduit for girls to enter university education, and completed an MA in mathematics at Canterbury College. While studying there she enjoyed the kind of university experience that had not featured during her BA study in Auckland.

Kate's postgraduate degree, which she received on 29 August 1882 in the 'handsome new hall at Canterbury College', which was being used for the first time,[57] once again gave the lie to female intellectual inferiority, especially since mathematics was deemed a subject particularly unsuited to women with their purported deficiencies in logic and reasoning.

As the country's first female university-educated secondary school teacher, Kate was once more a trail-blazer. Secondary teaching rapidly became the major career destination for generations of university-educated women. In New Zealand, as in Britain and America, such female teachers experienced a dramatic rise in status during the last quarter of the nineteenth century. As Henrietta Barnett, an English clergyman's wife, observed in 1884, teaching had been looked upon in the past as 'the only bread-winning resource for poor ladies'. Now it was 'happily considered as a noble profession, not beneath the acceptance of any'.[58] Women could take up this role without challenging either class or gender expectations. Primary school teaching was also dominated by female teachers, but the vast majority did not study at prestigious secondary schools or have a university degree. Many trained as pupil–teachers in an apprenticeship system and were clustered in the lower grades of the profession. Their status, training and pay began to improve only in the early twentieth century.[59]

Kate's achievements, both as a university student and as a teaching professional, represented a great leap ahead for the kind of liberal feminist views, advocated by Mill and others, which attributed women's lack of intellectual achievement to environmental factors and regarded education as a right and a good in itself. At the same time, the profession of secondary teaching, in New Zealand as elsewhere, accorded with the Victorian ideal of womanhood. If women were well suited to guard the morality of their own children, it was only a small step to further assert that their natural abilities as nurturers and protectors of the young could be used to serve other people's children.

In Christchurch Kate experienced a sometimes remarkable degree of independence and freedom of movement and opportunity for a single middle-class woman in her early twenties. As one of a small cadre of educated women in a new profession, she forged strong friendships and, in their classrooms and by example, she and her fellow teachers redefined what young women might aspire to. Often, those who studied together remained in contact through old girls' associations, professional associations and women's organisations.[60] Although it was predominantly middle-class girls who entered secondary school and went on to study at university, a small number from working-class backgrounds also did so, often assisted by scholarships or by becoming pupil–teachers. Those who followed this path were sometimes criticised by other girls. Rhoda Barr recalled that, when she enrolled at Waitaki Girls' High School in 1892, her classmates 'thought it a very snobbish and unnecessary step to take, and even hinted that the money to be spent in fees could be spent more profitably'.[61] As late as 1909, the Department of Education complained in its annual report about the number of parents who placed little value on girls' education, even at the primary level, allowing them to start later and leave earlier, apparently thinking it 'sufficient for a girl to have little more than half the amount of schooling that a boy receives'.[62] The long-term impact of schools such as Otago Girls' and Christchurch Girls', in placing a high value on educating girls, taking their intellectual development seriously and preparing them for tertiary study on an equal basis with men, is incalculable.

4

Founding Headmistress

The girls could not have too much education, and the more they had, the better wives and mothers they would make.

JUDGE LOWTHER BROAD, Chairman, Nelson College Board of Governors, 1887

Mere intellectual attainments form but a part of what we ought to aim at ... the intellect is not the only or the noblest part of man, and to train that without training the heart and spirit cannot be truly called education.

KATE EDGER, 1887[1]

In February 1883 the citizens of Nelson celebrated the opening of a long-awaited girls' secondary school. In the role of founding headmistress of Nelson College for Girls, Kate acquired considerable status and authority, along with a lucrative salary. For the next seven years she capably undertook this testing, multi-faceted, rewarding job, encountering and overcoming problems and achieving some remarkable successes despite a severe economic downturn in the latter part of the decade. Both her capacity for hard work and her implacable determination proved invaluable assets.

In addition to teaching English grammar, composition and literature, physical science, Latin, geography, arithmetic, algebra, Euclid and sometimes singing, Kate liaised with the council of governors, strove to ensure that staff operated in an effective, harmonious fashion, communicated with parents, organised part-time teachers for elective subjects such as dancing and art, and oversaw myriad administrative matters. She also had the crucial responsibility for setting the new school's overall aims, tone and esprit de corps.

For someone so reputedly gentle, kindly and modest, she could show a will of steel on what constituted the ideal education for girls and women. Her graduates would be high-minded and earnest women, selflessly devoted to their husbands and children but also concerned to extend their elevating moral influence and values

Looking south-west across Nelson City from the 'Zigzag' track at the top of Botanical Hill, c. 1882–87. Nelson College for Girls is in the middle distance and Nelson College in the left background.

Nelson Provincial Museum/Pupuri Taonga o Te Tai Ao, Tyree Studio Collection, 176325

into the wider society. Unlike frivolous middle-class woman selfishly devoted to fashion and worldly materialism, her pupils would ideally become Christians with a social conscience, active on behalf of worthy causes and helping those in need. They would be self-disciplined and hard-working, able to fulfil their own potential while benefiting others. Those who did not marry could yet live worthy professional lives, but there was never any doubt in her mind that marriage and family represented a high and noble calling.

Nelson: Arrival and acquaintances

Immediately following the announcement of Kate's appointment in July 1882, Oswald Curtis, secretary of the Nelson College subcommittee responsible for setting up the new school, began seeking her advice. Drawing on her experience at Christchurch Girls', Kate diligently responded to his queries, which covered everything from lighting to furniture, books and maps. From the outset, however, she had reservations about overseeing the boarding establishment, a duty that had been presented as an option to the successful candidate.[2] She believed herself unsuited to this role both temperamentally and due to lack of experience, and for a time even considered withdrawing her application. However, the governors soon agreed to her request to appoint a matron. Elizabeth Bruce Bell, who won the position from a field of 46 applicants, appeared to be a suitably strong-minded, capable person. Kate was to exercise general supervision over the boarding establishment, but the lady matron would oversee its daily operations.[3]

By November 1882 Curtis's queries showed no signs of abating, so Kate offered to visit the school in person when travelling north with Lilian en route to a family Christmas in Ponsonby. Curtis eagerly accepted this offer: 'There are many matters of detail upon which they [the council of governors] are anxious to learn your views.'[4]

Kate and Lilian arrived by coastal steamer on 19 December 1882. Nelson in the early 1880s, though a relatively small city of 7500 people, was a prosperous place with its own special character and charm. The city centre had numerous churches, shops, gardens and impressive public buildings, most notably the Provincial Council Buildings, built in 1861 in a grand Jacobean style. Local industries included a cloth mill, a brewery and the recently opened Kirkpatrick and Co. factory, which turned locally grown fruit and vegetables into jams and preserves. The various entertainment and recreational options on offer included the Nelson Institute and Library, a Harmonic Society for singers, and rowing, chess and jockey clubs. There were also lectures, shows and the occasional visiting ballet or opera at the Theatre Royal. The Nelson Regatta on Boxing Day and sports activities and picnics at the Botanical Reserve on New Year's Day were popular annual events.[5]

Nelson society was dominated by the influential and ubiquitous Richmond–Atkinson clan. A group of Richmonds and Atkinsons had emigrated from England to Taranaki in the early 1850s, intermarried, prospered and became part of the colony's political and social élite. Charles Fell, the chairman of the councils of both

Jane Maria Atkinson in the 1880s.

Alexander Turnbull Library, Wellington, PAColl-1802-1-01

Nelson College and Nelson College for Girls and mayor of Nelson from 1882 to 1887, was a son-in-law of Arthur Atkinson, the well-respected lawyer and brother of Sir Harry Atkinson, who was New Zealand premier on four different occasions.

Arthur's wife Jane Maria (née Richmond), known as Maria, was an intelligent, well-read, warm-hearted woman with a fine sense of humour. She had long campaigned for a girls' secondary school. The Richmonds were Unitarians, committed to the kind of free thought and high principles that had formed part of Kate's nonconformist heritage. Unitarians had a strong allegiance to egalitarianism, notably the power to reason and a belief in natural rights, tolerance and freedom. They perceived intellectual and moral education as interdependent and an essential aspect of the progress of human goodness.[6]

Maria Atkinson soon came to admire the new lady principal and count her among her friends. Though from different generations – Atkinson was some 20 years Kate's senior – the two women were alike in many respects. Both advocated higher education for women but were also convinced of women's special place within the home and their important role as moral arbiters. Atkinson, like Kate, supported women's suffrage and the temperance movement. Her son A.R. Atkinson, or 'Arf' as he was affectionately known, also ardently espoused these causes and would later, with his outgoing and energetic wife Lily (née Kirk), become a lifelong friend of Kate's, serving on the same committees and working for the same causes in Wellington.

A long-awaited facility

Nelson College for Girls was an institution close to Maria Atkinson's heart. Nelson College, the colony's first state secondary school, had been founded in 1856. Acquiring a comparable school for girls took another 27 years, but not for want of trying. After moving to Nelson from Taranaki in 1868, Atkinson began a school in her home for her own children and those of relatives, but never stopped hoping and pushing for a public girls' secondary school. Writing to her friend Margaret Taylor in England in 1870 she observed:

> Whatever influence I might have in the world I should wish to use in the cause of education. I want my girls to have a boy's education because it is a better education than what is called a girl's, since it better exercises the faculties God has given girls as well as boys. I certainly approve of any woman studying medicine or anything else she selects provided she does it earnestly. I only wish I had studied medicine myself; the mental training would have made me an infinitely more valuable member of society …[7]

She formed a 'Committee of Ladies' that began pushing for a girls' school in the early 1870s, and which presented its case to the Nelson College board of governors on 21 December 1871. Finding sufficient funds proved difficult: a report by a sub-committee of the board on 11 January 1872 found that there was not enough funding to support such a costly venture, noting succinctly: 'So far only moral support has been possible.'[8] But in May 1882 the governors announced their intention to establish and preside over the management of the new secondary school for girls. They found themselves in a sufficiently healthy financial position to proceed because a Mrs Edwards had offered a loan of £5000 at 8 percent and the school commissioners, who received revenue from school reserves, made a substantial contribution of £650. They procured a 1.2-hectare site fronting Trafalgar Street South, formerly used for grazing, ensuring that the new institution would command a beautiful view of the town and bay.[9] C.E. Beatson, son of the architect who had designed the Nelson College building in 1861, won the competition to design the girls' school. Then came deliberation over a suitable name. Some of the more cumbersome suggestions included 'Advanced School for Young Ladies' and 'Superior School for Girls'. In the end they wisely opted for Nelson College for Girls.[10] (The school was often known as Nelson Girls' College.)

Building and fitting out the new school was rushed and ad hoc; it began in September 1882 and the doors were to open in early February 1883. When Kate and Lilian returned from Auckland on 18 January, construction was still under way and little seemed organised to cope with an influx of pupils. Maria and Arthur Atkinson kindly offered up their handsome home, Fairfield House, as a kind of 'open house' for the school staff.

As Lilian later described to her sister Eva,

> The architect told us again and again that we couldn't get in, but we declared we would and so we did. On Monday the furniture began to come up … There were only four little bedrooms that the workmen were out of, so the furniture had to be put anywhere. There were two other rooms ready, but we wanted hot water upstairs, so they had to be upset again. On Tuesday we had the desks up, the schoolroom was full of timber and all sorts of things, but when the desks came of course the room had to be cleared.
>
> On Wednesday we brought our own things. We just managed to get into our rooms … There was nothing whatever to use in the kitchen except one small stove; no table or anything. The dining room was crowded with furniture, so we had our first two meals on the desk in the schoolroom.[11]

Opening and early days

An official opening was considered somewhat belatedly in mid-January, but quietly abandoned. This was perhaps just as well. The school, though large and impressive, was still surrounded by piles of bricks and timber and set in a bare paddock. Nevertheless it opened, miraculously, on the scheduled day, Friday 2 February 1883, quietly and without formal fanfare. The *Nelson Evening Mail* proudly hailed the event:

Nelson College for Girls c. 1884.

Nelson Provincial Museum/Pupuri Taonga o Te Tai Ao, Tyree Studio Collection, 182153

The Girls College opened this morning with 67 pupils, which is regarded as a very favourable commencement. It is very satisfactory to know that Nelson possesses so excellent an institution, the advantages of which, by means of scholarships, are open to those attending Government schools. We have no doubt that with such excellent opportunities of educating the young of both sexes as are now offered by the two Colleges we shall have many families coming to reside in Nelson who would otherwise have sought homes for themselves elsewhere.[12]

The first girls to enter the school were 'upcountry' students, who travelled into Nelson together by train. After they knocked on the door, a uniformed maid took them to a room where the lady principal and first mistress sat behind a table. Kate asked who had knocked first. Fanny Malcolm, the oldest girl, stepped forward. With a sense of occasion, Kate advised her to always remember that she was the school's first pupil. Gradually more groups arrived. Some had travelled by steamer from Whanganui. When all the new students were gathered together, Kate delivered a short speech. A pupil from that first day later recalled her kind and welcoming manner. Then Kate and Lilian examined the girls, whose ages ranged from seven to 19, so that they could be put into suitable classes.[13] There was still a considerable degree of chaos, however, as Lilian told Eva:

> We began school on Friday. There is no cloakroom, so the girls have to put their hats on the floor beside them. There is no ink, as we have had to send to Wellington for inkwells. There is only one room – really two rooms, but the partition will not be up for a week or so. We shall have to use the dining room and the upstairs sitting room as schoolrooms. We had no blackboards on Friday, so we examined our girls rather under difficulties. However we managed it and have classified them roughly …
>
> It is a good beginning is it not? … We have begun our day in spite of everything. I think we shall have some very nice good girls.[14]

From the outset, Kate was aware that her sister's time in Nelson would be short-lived. A wry letter from John Macmillan Brown to his friend James Sclanders, a member of the Nelson Girls' College subcommittee, explains the reason:

> Fate and I have been laughing much at two criticisms you passed when down here in the winter: one was the unsuitability of Miss Hamilton for any such position as a teachership in a girls' school – she has just been appointed Lady Principal of Wellington G.H.S. at £350.0s.0d a year; the other was the sheer impossibility of either of the Miss Edgers, but especially of the younger, getting married. The younger, Miss Lilian, has just got engaged to a very nice young fellow, a master in the Boys' High School here and that brings me to the point on which I want to speak to you.[15]

Brown went on to explain that Lilian had not been engaged when she applied for the job but her fiancé had arrived from University College, London, some six weeks before and was pressing for them to marry sooner rather than later. She wanted the school to be aware of the engagement and was willing to work for a time as per her contract, but also wished to avoid being on a false footing and to make her position clear. She had sought Brown's advice on how best to proceed. The governors took up Lilian's offer. Although she left in 1884 and resumed teaching at Christchurch Girls' High under Helen Connon, the intended marriage never eventuated. Lilian remained single.[16]

Nelson College for Girls was extremely fortunate in its lady principal and first mistress. Both were academically rigorous, kindly teachers, who made a concerted effort to bring out their students' natural interests and abilities. Like Christchurch Girls', this school was seen by many as a pathway to university, usually Canterbury College. As historian W.J. Gardner observed, 'The general importance of public girls' high schools in the growth of New Zealand universities can hardly be overemphasised. In the period up to 1914, 65 per cent of Otago and Canterbury women graduates came from such schools.'[17]

Public schools' reputations rested largely on their scholarship record and it was hoped that some pupils would enter university in this way. During their first year in Nelson Kate and Lilian worked tirelessly, but not just with the intention of turning out scholarship winners. From the beginning they held decided views both about academic goals and the sort of school culture they were creating.

The ideal education

Somehow, in addition to their enormous workloads, Kate and Lilian found time to edit two editions of their late father's writings. In doing so they read his essay, 'A Contribution Towards Elucidating the Ideal Education', which advocated many of the ideas and practices they were currently implementing, both in the school's class-rooms and in its extra-curricular activities.[18] Samuel's main point, that education should combine intellectual learning with moral teaching and physical education, was not particularly unusual for the time. Yet his view that education should never be seen as a competitive stepping-stone to personal advancement at the expense of rivals was less common. Both sisters shared this belief. Kate was determined, for example, to replace school prizes with certificates of merit, which were distributed to students who worked steadily, industriously and conscientiously.

In an end-of-year speech delivered in 1887, Kate acknowledged the regret of 'a great many' that no prizes were awarded and explained her position:

> One reason for my objection is that I think it inadvisable to encourage that feeling, so rife at the present day, of wanting always to secure some personal gain in return for one's exertions. How comparatively rare are the men and women who will work for the sake of work itself, because it is of benefit to the world in general, or their country, or neighbours … now shall we carry this spirit into the training of our children? What else is it we are doing when we offer prizes for their work, declaring, as I have heard it said within the last fortnight, that they will work better for prizes than without? That is to say they will do for a bribe what they will not do for the sake of right.[19]

Competition in life was unavoidable, and it would be 'quixotic and absurd' to try to get on without it, but 'if the present tone of morality in society, in trade, in politics and even in the churches all over the world, shows at all accurately how the world has got on with it, you will perhaps agree with me that it might be well to try another principle.' She believed competition to be 'opposed to the spirit of Christianity'. Instead she wanted to foster 'perseverance and conscientious faithful work'. Work was 'the grandest thing in existence', and the education that 'fits every part of our nature to perform the work allotted to us in the noblest, most unselfish way, is the only perfect education'. To this day, the system of certificates of merit is maintained at Nelson College for Girls.[20] The way Kate stuck to her guns on this issue, despite subsequent attempts by the governors to introduce prizes, illustrates her underlying strength of will. She had no intention of letting others influence her vision of what was morally desirable for the school's culture.

Not all competition was discouraged, however. Kate enthusiastically endorsed school sports and physical fitness. In this she was achieving an important aim of Victorian feminists, as Ruth Fry has noted: 'Political emancipation, the chance to earn a living, better education and improved health (with clothing reform and improved physical exercise) were inseparable goals.'[21] That games and physical activity did not impede femininity was a progressive view. In London in the 1880s, Martina Bergman Österberg had pioneered the training of women teachers as specialists in girls' physical education, using a Swedish system. As well as helping to counter those who argued that too much physical education harmed young women, this emphasis accorded with Kate's views about the importance of a course of study in which mind, body and spirit achieved a sound balance. She pushed successfully for the construction of tennis courts at the school, a sport the girls took up with keen interest. An annual tennis tournament became a school tradition and there were spirited matches with Nelson College, in which the female players more often than not held their own. In 1887, for example, M. Armstrong was deemed a 'plucky little player' after winning three games against a male opponent in the singles, who had 'hard work to win'.[22]

For Kate, these occasions helped to build 'excellent spirit' among the girls. She took pride in 'how heartily all rejoice in the successes of their companions' and noted that 'it is not the least valuable part of school games that it helps us to do our best even when the odds are against us'. In an 1886 quarterly report to the governors, she noted that she had 'introduced among the Junior Pupils the use of Indian Clubs to supplement the instruction they receive from the Drill Sergeant' and added

Students at Nelson College for Girls playing tennis, 1889.

hopefully, 'I trust the day is not far distant when a Gymnasium will be provided for the use of the College.'[23] This call for better facilities for girls' physical education was ahead of its time: it was not until 1912 that a formal physical education syllabus, based on a British model, was introduced to New Zealand state schools.[24]

The college also boasted such cultural activities as musical concerts, drawing and dance classes. From the first year, the boarders set up a dramatic society, which gave small performances in a classroom. A thriving debating club involved staff and senior girls (the Nelson College equivalent waned and only once agreed to combat the girls, much to their scorn). The culture and ambience of the school was an important part of what Kate set out to achieve: 'as our College grows older we see with satisfaction the growth of that *esprit de corps* that is perhaps the feature most to be desired in an educational institution.'[25]

Triumphant success

The governors' end-of-year report for 1883 hailed the new school as a triumphant success, one that fulfilled their hopes 'to the fullest'. From an initial roll of 80 day girls and boarders in February, by December numbers had risen to 118, including 26 boarders. Nelson College, by comparison, had only 102 pupils. The governors lauded the lady principal and her assistants for their 'unremitting exertion', acknowledging that 'a very large measure of the signal success which has attended the opening year of the new institution' was due to their efforts. Already four pupils had passed the matriculation examination of the University of New Zealand. The governors resolved to pledge £30 from their fees to set up two new scholarships for scholars aged 17, in addition to the six scholarships granted from the college funds to pupils from Nelson and Marlborough government schools.[26]

The school's success prompted calls for the recognition and adequate remuneration of its leaders. 'Schoolgirl', writing to the *Nelson Evening Mail* in December 1883, wanted the Edgers to enjoy equal status as examiners with their male counterparts:

> I do not think it is quite fair that the masters of the Boys' College should examine the girls unless the mistresses of the Girls College examine the boys. Is not Miss Edger, M.A., quite as competent as Mr. Andrew, M.A.? and is not Miss Lilian Edger, M.A., able to hold her own with Mr. Fearnley, M.A.? Have not examinations of the Boys' College run too much in a narrow groove for years past? And if so, a little change in the direction of joining the gifted ladies, who are at the head of the Girls College, with the present Examiner and his work might not be amiss.[27]

This letter apparently gave the governors food for thought, because in December 1884, the *Nelson Evening Mail* reproduced Kate's examiner's 'Report on the English, Euclid, Algebra and Lower Latin of the Boys' College, Nelson'. Her assessment of the Upper School's English compositions was magisterially unenthusiastic: 'The composition is indifferent; there is a want of originality as regards the subject matter, and in style very few show much idea of arrangement, or paragraphing, whilst too many papers are marred by verbosity and the frequent introduction of the writer's personality'.[28]

Kate Edger in the 1880s, during her time as lady principal of Nelson College for Girls,

Nelson Provincial Museum/Pupuri Taonga o Te Tai Ao, Tyree Studio Collection, 31041

Women's higher education in dispute: Brown vs Sale

Strides were clearly being made in equalising the secondary education of boys and girls, and in recognising the ability of professional women to operate on an equal level with their male counterparts. Some, however, felt uneasy about this development. In February 1884 Nelson happened to be the venue for the annual meeting of the University of New Zealand Senate. Most of the leading (male) figures in tertiary education in the colony accepted an invitation to attend the Nelson Girls' College certificates of merit ceremony, which had been deferred from the end of 1883 as the certificates had not arrived, and was delayed to facilitate the men's attendance.

On the platform, along with the bishops of Nelson and Auckland, were Charles Fell and other school governors; William Rolleston, now Speaker of the House of Representatives, J.C. Tancred, the chancellor of the University of New Zealand, and several leading professors. Kate's mentor Professor John Macmillan Brown spoke extempore, as did Professor G.S. Sale, now professor of classics at Otago University.

Brown began by praising Kate, noting that he had long been acquainted with her and 'knew her abilities and energies perhaps better than anyone'. Having watched her in class and at Christchurch Girls' he 'felt perfectly satisfied that there was no one in New Zealand who could surpass her'. He then paid stirring tribute to the position she had attained, and to the forward march of women's education. The country, emerging from a state of 'barbarism', had long denied women equal educational opportunities, but was now rectifying that mistake. There were many women whom it was cruel to confine to the home, where they had 'no opportunity of bringing their intellect into play'. After citing the examples of Scottish science writer Mary Somerville, and novelists George Eliot and George Sand, he noted that, closer to home, two females had outstripped all male competitors in recent scholarship exams. He hoped to see the day when women would take their place in politics and art and literature, and when 'the same methods of culture would be as freely open to them as to men'.[29]

Unlike Brown and the bishop of Auckland, who 'had been able to congratulate themselves upon being, to some extent connected with the institution', in his speech Sale stated that he 'could not do this, nor could he agree with what had fallen from his friend Professor Brown'. The latter, he complained, 'would have a Parliament of women, and not only that, but arts, sciences, and professions were to be as full of women as of men, in fact, the world was to be turned topsyturvy'. He should be 'very sorry to see such a consummation'. When the bishop had read out the subjects in which one pupil receiving a certificate had distinguished herself, he considered the list 'appalling' and 'could not help wondering to himself what he should do if his little daughter were to bring home such a certificate and perhaps begin to submit him to a little examination in the multitudinous Subjects referred to'.

> The wise man had said, 'Be not righteous over much'. To this he would add 'Be not studious over much', for it was quite possible to learn too much, and he … would be extremely sorry indeed to see the grace and charm of Womanhood sacrificed to these advanced notions of the power of intellect. However, from the slight glance he had been able to cast round upon the faces of the young people by whom he was surrounded, he was glad to say that he did not think there was much danger of their persistently, striving after honours until they lost their position in the sphere for which they were originally intended.[30]

Sale was certainly not alone in his reservations. In numerous annual speeches at certificate presentations, Bishop of Nelson Andrew Suter often expressed the hope that women's 'special qualities' would not be marred or neglected as a result of academic learning. The vast majority of contemporary women, including Kate, shared this concern for and belief in women's special qualities and nurturing role. Like Brown, however, Kate had no doubt that education would enhance, not jeopardise, them.

The *Herald* reported that 'Judging from the applause the verdict of the larger portion of the audience was in favour of Professor Sale's theory'.[31] In closing the proceedings, Charles Fell felt compelled to 'break a lance' with Sale, noting that 'He had yet to learn that an educated woman had lost her charms'. He also expressed a sense of pride in the school and its achievements: 'with Miss Edger as Lady Principal, and with such a staff of teachers as she had under her, he felt that they could hold out attractions to parents of girls in other parts that could not be surpassed in New Zealand.'[32]

Daily challenges

Kate also had to contend with various practical daily challenges, some avoidable and others outside her control. The first involved the music teacher, Cecilia Summerhayes. Kate, who was very knowledgeable about music, apparently had decided views about how to teach it. In September 1883 Summerhayes resigned, decrying 'the constant supervision of your Lady Principal to teach me my duty towards my pupils'. She even denounced Kate's behaviour as 'unladylike'.[33] When

Summerhayes later changed her mind, the board refused to accept the withdrawal of her resignation.

Another, more protracted battle involved the matron, Elizabeth Bruce Bell. The exact nature of the dispute is not clear, but it almost certainly revolved around their respective responsibilities and differing temperaments. Relations between the two women rapidly deteriorated and by June 1884 both were required to attend a governors' meeting to discuss their differences. A draft letter from the governors to Bell, later diplomatically edited, made it clear that she had problems with other staff members as well as Kate. In a final letter the governors regretted that 'your valuable services have been unavoidably lost to the College'. Although the governors supported Kate throughout this 'unpleasant situation', it took a toll.[34] Then, in September 1884, Lilian departed for Christchurch, leaving Kate without her sister's practical and emotional support.

The school building added to Kate's headaches. Although the *Nelson Evening Mail* pronounced this complete by early July 1883,[35] there was still landscaping and fencing to do, and problems soon arose regarding the quality of the workmanship. By September these remained unresolved and final payments to the builder were withheld. Even after these defects were fixed, however, there were ongoing difficulties. Although Beatson's design had certainly resulted in an aesthetically pleasing school, spacious enough to house 150 pupils, some 40–50 boarders and the teaching staff, there were no fire escapes, the drains were faulty and the earth-closets (toilets were outside then) were so close to the building that unpleasant smells wafted into the classrooms, especially in summer.[36] The invariably cold dining room looked onto a south-facing quad and doubled as a passageway for girls changing classrooms.

One large classroom, located between the two wings, where Kate taught science, lacked a fireplace and she submitted heartfelt requests to the governors to install one. Two fireplaces were finally built but smoked so badly that windows had to be left open, thus lowering the temperature again. Kate's letters were usually models of politeness, but these fireplaces evoked an uncharacteristically vehement demand: 'I should be obliged if you could see to this matter today'. A month later, her patience having worn thin, she described the room as 'unbearable'.[37]

Economic depression and hard times

In addition to these trials, the deepening economic depression of the 1880s began to take a toll on school life. Rolls dropped dramatically at both boys' and girls' colleges. In late 1885, the former had 84 pupils compared with 102 the previous year. By the end of 1885 the Nelson Girls' total was 92; it, too, had boasted 102 in 1884. By 1886, the roll at the girls' school was down to 78, six of whom attended only for the special classes. When, in the middle of that year, one student had to be removed due to 'special circumstances', Kate expressed the hope that 'brighter days are in store for the College in this respect'.[38] The governors found ways to cut back expenses; in 1885, for instance, they severely pruned the number of external examiners. Writing in December that year to Ann Richmond, who intermittently taught French and German at the school, Maria Atkinson observed: 'The College is in the thick of exams and all the mistresses except Miss Edger, who revels in work, are nearly dead of it as there is no outside examiner or help this Christmas except Dr. Johansen in French and German.'[39]

There was a flurry of staff resignations in 1885, including one from Kate herself in September. Richmond considered that Kate's decision stemmed not from exhaustion or disaffection but from a desire to go to England,[40] but Kate stressed the continuing strain on all the teachers, and particularly the pressures arising from the boarding establishment. As Oswald Curtis noted, 'you fear that to continue in your present position would involve a complete breakdown in health'.[41] The governors were nonplussed by the staff's apparent exhaustion, given that there were four resident teachers and declining rolls. Similarly, they failed to understand why looking after the boarders produced such strain when boarder numbers had fallen from 25 to 11.[42]

Charles Fell liaised with Kate, who in mid-October agreed to stay on with the proviso that she no longer be expected to live at the college or be responsible for the boarders. Her salary, formerly £375, would now be £350. She proposed that it be reduced further, but the governors refused, though gratefully recording 'the liberal spirit and the earnest desire to promote the interests of the College, which lets you make the offer'.[43] At this point Kate received permission to build a stable on the school grounds for her horse.

The depression had an adverse effect on the school's finances. Staff salaries were often paid late. On 9 June 1886, for example, it was necessary to remind the governors that 'the cheques for the salaries for May have not arrived'.[44] By 1888 Kate was informed, with no consultation, that in six months' time her salary would be reduced to £300. All other staff salaries were reduced as well.

In 1886 Kate had offered two new annual Edger Scholarships, which she funded from her salary, of £50 each. This 'munificent gift', designed to enable girls from less wealthy households to attend the school, was a welcome offer in the financial climate.[45] The lady principal's personal generosity and kindness were also illustrated in a letter she wrote early in 1886 to Katie Thompson, who had just heard that she had failed an examination (probably Matriculation). Kate began by saying how sorry she had been about the result; she hoped that Katie would not regret having tried, and suggested she might try again in future. Katie should 'come up to the College and see me' if she was ever in town: 'If there is anything in which I can help you, I shall be very pleased to do so, I am your sincere friend, Kate M. Edger.'[46] Katie Thompson later had a long and successful career teaching primary school in Picton.

Fair treatment for teachers

Kate became involved with the Nelson District Teachers' Association, which was formed in 1885. The monthly meetings provided an opportunity for teachers to discuss educational issues and matters that affected their profession. In May 1887, as vice-president of the association, she and the president William Littlejohn MA, who was mathematics and science master at Nelson College, gave a demonstration for some 40 local association members in the girls' college, where they exhibited one of the school's sets of chemical apparatus designed by Alexander Bickerton.[47] In the brave new world of secondary education for girls, science had an important role to play, just as it did for the boys' curriculum. Kate taught this subject herself and had acquired the apparatus from Bickerton especially for the purpose.

In 1888 the New Zealand Educational Institute, which had been established in Christchurch in 1883 to represent the interests of teachers, protect them from unfair treatment and campaign for higher educational standards, held its sixth meeting and fifth conference in the Nelson College for Girls' hall. Representatives from almost every education district in the country attended. Kate, who had recently joined the NZEI, participated in the varied discussions on subjects ranging from technical colleges to more liberal provisions for secondary school education. With regard to the latter, she expressed the view that although she would like the poor to have easier access to secondary education, she believed that a free education was not as highly valued as when a small fee was paid. She also hoped that parents would allow their daughters to remain in secondary school from the ages of 14 to 18, rather than, as was often the case, removing them at 16, and thus denying them the benefits of a full secondary education and the chance to go on to university.

At a banquet in the Provincial Hall on the final evening of the conference, a toast was made to the college. The proposer, William Fitzgerald from Otago, a former institute president, said that the college governors 'had been particularly happy in their selection of a lady principal' – there were loud cheers at this point – and that 'He had been struck with the remarkable ability [Kate] had shown in the discussions over the last few days.' Responding 'with some emotion', Kate said,

> Had it been fifteen years ago she might have felt it necessary to apologise for the position she held, but the position of women now was very different to what it was then, and she believed the change had been brought about by higher education having been thrown open to women. There was, perhaps, a little danger of giving too great prominence to the intellectual training of women, but she trusted it would always be the aim of every girls' college to devote attention to the moral as well as to the intellectual training of the pupils. Intellectual training would not make blue stockings, but true women, when it was combined with the training of the heart and soul. They need not fear to give high intellectual training to women, as it would not unfit them for the home.[48]

Higher education and women's 'highest role'

At almost every certificate of merit ceremony that Kate attended as head of Nelson Girls', the male dignitaries stated that the girl students' 'highest role' would be as wives and mothers. Men who wholeheartedly endorsed improved educational opportunities for women were no exception. In 1887, for example, Judge Lowther Broad began his speech with a spirited defence of the situation in America, where women now worked as doctors, lawyers and divines. One woman had even risen to become a Supreme Court judge in Nebraska. There was no reason why women could not operate effectively and make important contributions in all these roles, as education made brains and ability the ultimate test of merit. He praised Queen Victoria as a prime contemporary example of a world leader and devoted mother who still found time to 'discharge many other womanly duties, and to employ herself in works of charity and humanity'. Students must keep learning after leaving school, because then 'they will find that they will make all the better wives and better mothers'.[49]

Like Broad, Kate commended America 'for the exalted position she grants to her women'. In 1885, helping to advertise a book that highlighted the achievements of leading American women, she hoped that it would 'inspire us with an earnest desire to follow the example set by our American sisters ... It breathes a lofty enthusiasm, a noble striving after right, a perseverance and a determination to overcome all obstacles that cannot but stir up any sincere nature to greater earnestness.'[50]

In her speech at the 1886 certificate of merit ceremony she urged parents to keep girls in school, arguing that teaching them domestic skills would be just as valid as further academic study. Kate believed that practical domestic economy was an important part of every girl's education, and would only be 'too glad' to see the subject taught at school, but not until the intellectual side of learning had been completed. It was even preferable to take a year or so from earlier girlhood education for inculcating domestic skills rather than cutting off the 'two most valuable years' of school life, from 16 to 18.[51]

In an 1888 speech she spoke about the 'urgency' of finding suitable professions or occupations for girls who were yearly leaving secondary schools and colleges throughout the country. Believing that the ranks of the teaching profession were nearly full, she urged the 'vital importance' of subjects such as dressmaking, cooking, bookkeeping and even the medical profession, though she acknowledged that the last was 'nearly impossible' for women in the colony.[52]

Her views on education were inseparable from her Christian faith, as her final speech at the 1889 certificate of merit ceremony illustrates:

> That teacher will never be successful who tries by brute force to drive knowledge into his pupils, but he will be who endeavours to create enthusiasm and a love of work. Just so it is with moral and religious training; the only influence that must be exercised is that of love and sympathy, not of fear. If religion is to run through secular education, the result will be conscientiousness and high principle in all you do ... Then there must be unselfishness. Put away from you the spirit of competition and false ambition – the desire to get above somebody else.

Citing the certificates as an example of this spirit – they were awarded 'to all who deserved them' – she hoped that if the girls 'went out into the world with some such ideal as this before them, then though the Nelson Girls' College is not large, and may not make a great name for itself, still I venture to say that it will be a power for good in the land'. The girls who were leaving should not regard their education as finished but consider that they had just gone through 'the elementary stage', and

Teachers at Nelson College for Girls taking tea outdoors, 1889.
Kate Edger is seated far right.

Nelson Provincial Museum/Pupuri Taonga o Te Tai Ao, Tyree Studio Collection, 179046

remember that 'the higher ideal you place before yourselves the more likely you are to reach it'.[53]

At that 1889 ceremony Charles Fell announced that 'Miss Edger as Miss Edger they would see no more'. The girls would have four more days of holiday to allow 'the Lady Principal to be a party to a transaction of the highest importance to herself and all connected with her in any way'. Fell could say, on behalf of everyone, governors and pupils, that 'there was no one in Nelson in whom they took a more kindly interest than herself, and he wished her God speed'.[54]

5

A Reforming Partnership – The Forward Movement

Let us then in the name of God and humanity, combine heartily to abolish Slavery, Drunkenness, Lust, Gambling, Ignorance, Pauperism, Mammonism and War.
Hugh Price Hughes, *Social Christianity*, 1889[1]

Faith, hope and love, which have triumphed in the past, yet abide, and are available to those that have the courage to embody and articulate them.
Forward Movement pamphlet, 'The Diamond Jubilee', 1897[2]

On 6 January 1890, her thirty-third birthday, Kate Milligan Edger married the Reverend William Albert Evans in Ponsonby. The *Observer's* 'Fashionable Marriages' column described this wedding as 'interesting', noting that the groom, having arrived from England only some three months before, 'promptly fell in love with the learned lady'.[3] Evans arrived in Nelson in August 1889, began preaching in the Nelson Congregational Church in September and by January 1890 had taken up the role as its minister.

Three years later the Evanses embarked on a remarkable project: to found, in Wellington, a branch of Britain's Forward Movement. Its aims were to encourage progressive social reform, bolster a sense of unity among social classes and extend Christian support and compassion towards those in need. So that William could work full time for this cause, Kate became the family breadwinner for the next 11 years. Even for a 'New Woman', this was a highly unusual role for a middle-class wife. In addition to supporting her growing family economically, she played an active role in all aspects of the Forward Movement, assisting with its clubs, programmes and various educational and cultural activities. She frequently gave 'lay sermons', a distinctive feature of advanced liberalism in the late Victorian period, and always filled in for her husband if he was too sick to deliver his sermon.

In undertaking this project together, and especially in reversing traditional gender roles, the Evanses had the kind of union of educated equals that Mill had advocated in *The Subjection of Women*. Like a number of contemporary married couples devoted to progressive social reform in Britain, such as the Fabian socialists Beatrice and Sidney Webb, or the prominent Independent Labour Party activists John and Katharine Glasier, Kate and William worked together as a team to achieve their goals.[4] They wanted to encourage a form of Christian social activism that advocated unity and co-operative assistance rather than polarisation of social classes. Wellington's Forward Movement attracted a number of individuals who went on to play important roles in the Liberal government. As an example of politically liberal, religiously tolerant, progressive Protestant activism, the movement added to the capital's philanthropic profile and provided a forum for discussing progressive social government policy. Elements of the Christian Socialist ideals espoused by the Forward Movement were also later prominent in the Labour Party. The movement attracted a group of like-minded people, many of them religious nonconformists, whose endeavours and beliefs had a lasting impact on New Zealand's social and political culture. Kate's professional earnings, her prodigious capacity for hard work and the idealism she shared with her husband enabled the Forward Movement to stride ahead.

Mr and Mrs Evans

Kate and William celebrated their wedding in the family home on Ponsonby Road which, according to Eva's daughter Geraldine, 'stood high in spacious grounds in the best part of Ponsonby and commanded exquisite views in all directions'. After moving back to Auckland from Christchurch in 1888, Lilian had lived there with her sister Marion, and run Ponsonby College, her own girls' secondary school, in the large, gracious house. She had had the upper-storey classrooms fitted with 'beautiful mouldings in wood, skilfully panelled and artistically decorated'. On the top floor, two 'charming little rooms with dormer windows' formed her own living quarters.[5]

The bridegroom was a handsome man, with deep-set blue eyes, a shock of red hair and a full beard. His interests seemed to make him an ideal partner for Kate. Hard-working, deeply devout, a fervent idealist with a strong sense of social duty, William Evans was keen to improve the lives of the less fortunate. He also, however, had a lighter side: he loved music and singing and was sociable and warmly convivial. A later newspaper piece, written in 1901, paid tribute to his combination of earnest high-mindedness and down-to-earth fun: 'he is a deeply read man who has made a special study of social economic and moral philosophy. Although a staunch prohibitionist he dearly loves to "blow a cloud" [smoke] and can play a good game of billiards.'[6]

William's origins were humble. His parental home was in Llangyfelach, a village some 6 kilometres north of Swansea, and early in life he worked as a shepherd boy in the hills of south Wales. He and his brother, who also became a Congregationalist minister, took turns at attending school and university, each working to support the other financially. Until well into their teens, both spoke only Welsh. Later in life Evans remarked that he 'still had to think in Welsh and translate his thoughts into English as he spoke'. This would have surprised those who heard 'the remarkable English vocabulary' of his eloquent sermons and lectures.[7] After graduating from the Congregational College of Spring Hill in Birmingham, he began preaching in Bradford. Health problems, possibly respiratory, caused him to emigrate to New Zealand in November 1888 in search of a more benign climate. His first position was a temporary one, as minister for the Moray Place Congregational Church in Dunedin in March 1889. In April he was asked, and agreed, to stay on permanently. However, his health again deteriorated in the severe Dunedin weather. In September of that year he visited Nelson, where the climate suited him better, and over the next few months delivered guest sermons and lectures. In December he was asked to become the permanent minister of the Nelson Congregationalist Church and started in this role in the New Year of 1890.[8]

Evans' evening lectures in Nelson dealt with various social and political and philosophical issues. It must have quickly become apparent to Kate that they shared a great many views and values, many of them from their nonconformist cultural heritage. Evans espoused 'the social gospel', the notion that it was time evangelical Christians moved beyond a focus on individual salvation towards the salvation of society. Like the new liberal philosopher T.H. Green in England, he saw evolutionary progress as moving away from self-interest towards self-sacrifice, altruism and active citizenship working for the common good.[9] Whereas formerly the evangelical conscience had focused primarily on inward faith, it now needed to move towards broader social objectives. Evans advocated a form of Christian socialism that envisioned education and incremental social and legislative reform as the key to a more just and equitable society. These views had much in common with Kate's father's idealistic social and religious vision and were consistent with her own educational ideals.

Initially Kate intended to return to work following the wedding. Just before her departure for Ponsonby she received, from some 85 old girls, a wedding present of an elegant tea and coffee service. As the *Nelson Evening Mail* reported, 'not only does [this gift] indicate the regard entertained for her as a personal friend by her old pupils, but she may fairly accept it as a proof of their appreciation of the faithful and able manner in which she discharged her duties as their teacher'.[10] Although the college was keen for her to continue as principal, Kate resigned in March 1890 after becoming pregnant with the first of her three sons. Edger James (always known as James) was born in 1890, Elwyn in 1891 and Eurfryn (or Vryn as he was usually known) in 1895.

During the next few years in Nelson, while raising a growing family, Kate kept busy outside the domestic sphere. She often preached lay sermons in the Congregational Church and energetically supported William in his role as minister. She also advertised her availability as a tutor for students who wanted to sit the university degree exams, acted as an examiner for the University of New Zealand and was involved in the suffrage and temperance campaigns. She stood for the Nelson Education Board at a time when women rarely attempted to stand for public office, but did not succeed. Not surprisingly, she advertised, in 1892, for a 'Lady Homehelp' to assist with 'the charge of children' and with needlework.[11]

In 1893 William resigned as Nelson's Congregational minister, relinquishing the financial security of a regular salary along with his ministerial duties. Kate's earnings alone now supported the family. The couple moved to Wellington where, with William's friend and fellow Congregational minister Charles Bradbury, who had also recently resigned his living in Christchurch, they devoted themselves to establishing a far-flung branch of the Forward Movement.

Origins of the Forward Movement

The Forward Movement originated in London in the public sensation that followed the 1883 publication of a pamphlet called *The Bitter Cry of Outcast London* and subtitled 'An Inquiry into the Conditions of the Abject Poor'. Sponsored by the Congregational Union to investigate slum life, it was originally anonymous, though Andrew Mearns, the secretary of the Congregationalist Union and a former Congregationalist minister, later came forward as its author. In the pamphlet he vividly described the poverty he had witnessed while walking in London's East End. His references to the 'heart-breaking misery' and 'absolute godlessness' he saw there generated much middle-class anxiety about the moral and physical deterioration that urban life was wreaking on the lowest classes of society. The sense that 'This terrible flood of misery and sin is gaining upon us' became more pressing and urgent.[12] In response, the Congregational Union called all the free-church denominations together for a conference. The Congregationalists began opening unused chapels throughout London, where the homeless could find shelter and sustenance; the Wesleyans set up a Central Mission, also using halls and chapels for religious activism and a range of social services.

In the same year the Reverend Samuel Barnett, an Anglican, and his wife Henrietta, purchased and renovated a building adjacent to St Jude's Church in Whitechapel, in London's East End, where Barnett was the vicar. They named this building Toynbee Hall, after their recently deceased friend Arnold Toynbee. An Oxford academic, student of T.H. Green and a dedicated social reformer, Toynbee dedicated much of his short life to assisting London's poor. In the past, Barnett had invited students from Oxford and Cambridge to visit Whitechapel during the holidays, to see first hand the impoverished conditions there. Now he planned to make Toynbee Hall a place of residence for Oxbridge graduates who would come to live for a two- to three-year 'settlement' period and help contribute to the local community. A number of wealthy supporters, including the Duke of Westminster and Arthur Balfour, a future prime minister, helped to fund this project.

Barnett envisioned a place where different social classes lived and worked together in Christian harmony; Toynbee Hall was open to all Christian denominations. Education was a key aim, since Barnett believed that learning would enrich and improve the lives of the local poor. The hall soon housed many practical courses, in home hygiene, nursing, shorthand, sewing and practical skills, but it was also a place of culture, where art exhibitions were encouraged and cultural life enhanced.[13] The settlement students worked to improve sanitation and housing conditions throughout the neighbourhood by working with landlords and local authorities. When they left the settlement and embarked upon careers it was hoped they would still strive to achieve these aims. The Barnetts wanted to inculcate in the poor of Whitechapel habits of industry, self-improvement, self-respect and civic responsibility, but the process of education was two-way, benefiting both the residents and the settlement students. Although philanthropy as practised at Toynbee Hall aimed to lessen social distance, there was, in the words of one historian, 'a decided middle-classness' about the place.[14] Nevertheless, the emphasis was on active Christianity, and active citizenship, to bring social classes together.

Barnett, a liberal, approved of trade unions, which he saw as an important self-help tool and a vital step on the road towards a more just industrial order. Toynbee Hall was highly influential. Eventually the university settlement movement, based on the Barnetts' aims and principles, flourished not only in England but around the globe.

One American settlement influenced by Barnett mirrored Kate's feminist approach to social amelioration. Hull House in Chicago, co-founded in 1889 by Jane Addams and Ellen Gates Starr, was an all-female endeavour. One of the first settlement houses in the United States, it was soon one of its best known. The wealthy Addams has been described as combining 'feminist sensibilities with an unwavering commitment to social improvement through co-operative efforts'. She believed that 'responsibility, care and obligation' were the source of women's power and encouraged female activism in municipal affairs as a matter of 'civic housekeeping'. She supported women's suffrage because it would enable women to clean up and organise their communities.[15] Community and social conditions had to be improved to keep families safe, and women were best suited to this cause. Addams, like Kate, was a pioneer of social work who later went on to become an advocate of peace – she was awarded the Nobel Peace Prize in 1931 – and a high-profile supporter of the League of Nations. For her the pursuit of peace was especially suited to women by virtue of their affinity for protecting the young, advancing community well-being and promoting general health and welfare. Like Kate, she was deeply religious, a Presbyterian Christian Socialist who believed that the old individualist outlook of the early Victorian era was not adequate in modern society. She compared the workings of government with the domestic household, and shared Kate's belief that women's activism and involvement in social reform would elevate and uplift the community and advance national and international relations.

Hull House was not part of the Forward Movement, which involved only nonconformist missions in Britain and, from 1893, Kate and William's offshoot in Wellington. The city missions set up by nonconformist denominations in London were, however, an expression of the settlement movement inspired by Barnett's example, and they developed a range of services to assist London's poor. The Methodist East End Mission, opened in 1885 under the Reverend Peter Thompson, for example, engaged in philanthropic work, and educated all those associated with the mission in the duties of 'active citizenship'. Thompson, following Green's example, became involved in local politics himself. The Reverend Hugh Price Hughes' West End Mission, established in 1887, offered innovative social services such as an 'enquiry office' and a 'Poor Man's Lawyer'. Hughes' wife Katherine set up the Sisters of the People, who visited the sick and hungry and attempted to both save 'fallen women' and encourage teetotalism.[16]

Hughes, soon recognised as the leader of the Forward Movement, wanted Christian compassion and activism to permeate all aspects of community life. Although it was initially a Methodist scheme, he extended the Forward Movement to include all nonconformist denominations. Instead of a focus on individual salvation, he wanted the church to become directly involved in the betterment of society as a whole. As he wrote in his popular book *Social Christianity* (1889), 'we have practically neglected the fact that Christ came to save the Nation as well as the Individual, and that it is an essential feature of His mission to reconstruct human society on a basis of Justice and Love.'[17]

In 1890 Salvation Army founder General William Booth's sensational exposé *In Darkest England and the Way Out* made improving the conditions of the urban poor seem more pressing than ever. More missions sprang up, in London and in other cities around England. The Congregationalists' Mansion House University Settlement, in Canning Town in London's East End, founded in 1890, was similar in outlook and ethos to Toynbee Hall. Percy Alden, its warden, was influenced by Green, Toynbee, F.D. Maurice and the Christian Socialists.

Bringing the social gospel to Wellington

William Evans' education and early experiences as a cleric had exposed him to England's settlement movement and to its ethos. His lectures in Nelson in the early 1890s are imbued with the sentiments and aspirations of the social gospel. On 7 September 1890, for example, his lecture, 'The Voice of the Past to the Men of the Present concerning Wealth', predicted that 'out of the breaking up of the old order there necessarily will arise a new order which will far outshine anything the world has ever seen in sympathy, co-operation, and righteousness … The capitalist will recognise that his capital is but a power to be used by him not for personal ends, but for the common weal, that the more he has, the greater his responsibility to humanity and to the Eternal Spirit who incarnates himself in man.'[18] On 21 September, in another lecture, he urged unions to be less autocratic and exclusive and more democratic. He also hoped they would rise above 'mere material welfare' and aim to 'achieve character'. While association was 'the watchword of the future' it 'must be based on moral laws and will succeed in producing a people as loyal to God as they are devoted to one another'.[19] The gospel of duty necessarily transcended class and sectional interest. Just a few days after delivering this lecture, William was elected one of the two vice-presidents of the Nelson Trades and Labour Union. He advocated unions as a progressive step towards a more just and equitable society, and like Barnett at Toynbee Hall, emphasised social unity rather than class antagonism.

Kate and William decided to set up a branch of the Forward Movement in Wellington because New Zealand seemed less and less like a 'Better Britain'. The colony's cities had not reached London's dire socio-economic inequalities, but in the so-called 'long depression' of the 1880s even middle-class families foundered. Parts of the nation's capital now had unemployed workers, ragged children playing in the streets, mean alleys and dark damp cottages. In these slum areas poverty, drunkenness, avoidable disease, gambling and prostitution were rife. As newly arrived settlers found it increasingly difficult to acquire good land in New Zealand, there was growing resentment of wealthy land-engrossing quasi-gentry.

Industrial working conditions deteriorated as hard-pressed employers cut costs. The results were graphically illustrated in the findings of a royal commission on sweating set up in 1890. Although the report concluded that 'London sweating' did not exist in New Zealand, an addendum by three commission members took issue with that finding, arguing 'there is abundant evidence of its existence', namely 'numerous overcrowded and insanitary workrooms, great number of workers [doing] long and irregular hours, and wages in many trades … at the lowest possible ebb'. They warned that the commission's conclusions created 'an impression that the duty of taking vigorous action to ward off the evils that oppress the industrial world in the older civilisations is not imperative'. Without 'aroused public opinion and prompt legislative action … these very evils will have struck deep their roots in our midst'.[20] Before the Liberal government's reforms of the 1890s, welfare measures were unevenly organised and insufficient for those who, through no fault of their own, found themselves jobless and destitute.

On 30 January 1893 Kate, James and Elwyn left William in Nelson and moved to Ponsonby, where Kate spent the ensuing school year teaching alongside Lilian at Ponsonby College. She preached a sermon the night before she left as William suddenly took ill on the 25th.[21] He resigned his living in April and by the beginning of May had moved to Wellington. He and Bradbury, 'conductors of the Congregational Mission which is to open at the Exchange Hall next Sunday [7 May], as the colonial counterpart of the English "forward movement"', published an explanatory leaflet: 'The basis of our mission is the Gospel of Christ as contained in that magnificent conception of the Kingdom of God – a conception which expresses His social ideal – the true co-ordination of the individual and society by common loyalty to the Father of all men. Our work, therefore, will be to translate that Truth into the terms of modern life in all the complexity of its manifestations.' They had chosen Wellington as their 'field of operation because it is the centre of our national life, and so offers facilities which none of the other cities afford'. They planned to preach, to give lectures and to run 'classes for the study of the economics of a Christian community'.[22]

The two men began their free weekly lectures on social, political and religious subjects at the Rechabite Hall in Manners Street. At this stage, the nascent enterprise was called the Wellington Congregational Mission, though it was not financially supported by that church. In July, however, they adopted the Forward Movement name and announced that the Rechabite Hall would be the centre or base of their future work.

During these formative months William delivered well-attended lectures on subjects such as Robert Owen, the pioneering socialist. The local press praised the lecture on Owen, noting that the audience reportedly enjoyed it so much they showed signs of breaking into applause throughout.[23] Kate's brother Frank, then based in Wellington as a barrister and solicitor of the Supreme Court, sometimes performed a musical interlude on his cello during these events.

On 27 August 1893 the Forward Movement held its first official meeting in Wellington. Its constitution set out four key aims:

a. to give practical expression to the Social spirit of Christianity
b. to foster the spirit of mutual helpfulness among all classes of the community
c. to expose vice and injustice to the light of truth and righteousness
d. to bring in the Social Ideal of Christ as the regulative standard of life – political, civic, domestic, and individual.[24]

The movement took Christ's Sermon on the Mount as the law of life and practice. This was the social gospel of love and selfless practical compassion, eschewing the vision of God as judge and enforcer which permeated much of the Old Testament. Accepting this text and signing a members' roll were the only conditions of membership. All members aimed to fulfil and encourage the duties of active citizenship, enhance equality of opportunity for those less fortunate and stimulate co-operative sympathy and understanding between social classes. At this first meeting, 38 individuals signed up and four women and 12 men were chosen as a committee of management. The Richmond–Atkinson clan made a strong showing. Among them were Arthur Richmond Atkinson (Arf) the lawyer, journalist and later MP; his wife Lily, the temperance campaigner and feminist; and Maurice Richmond, later a law professor at Victoria College.[25]

Fundraising was discussed and remained a constant concern. An early Forward Movement flyer asked potential supporters to contribute to a 'Building Fund' for a purpose-built hall; this never eventuated. Optimistic about society's progressive evolution, the writers fulsomely praised 'that noble man' Arnold Toynbee, whose name was 'intimately associated' with the Forward Movement, as well as the work of the Mansfield House University Settlement in Canning Town. They hoped that Wellington's Forward Movement would 'fulfil the same functions here as Toynbee Hall and Mansfield House have done, and are doing, in the Old Country'. Because the movement's aims were 'wide enough to appeal to the sympathies of those who desire the Social and Moral Welfare of their fellows', they felt they could confidently make a general appeal.[26] But in contrast to England and America, wealthy New Zealand patrons remained conspicuously unforthcoming. As a consequence, in 1895 Charles Bradbury, feeling the financial strain of no steady wage, left the movement for paid employment with the Congregationalist Church, first in Dunedin and a few years later in Melbourne. It would be Kate's financial support that enabled the survival of Wellington's Forward Movement.

A joint effort

After she returned to Wellington just before Christmas 1893, Kate began working from home, coaching students who aimed to sit the university entrance and teacher's certificate examinations. The Evanses bought a house in Porritt Avenue, Mount Victoria, in 1894 in Kate's name, perhaps because William was unwaged. In 1896 they bought, this time in William's name, a house with a double section in nearby Ellice Avenue.[27] They called their new home Dehra Dhoon, after a picturesque valley in Riwaka near Nelson.[28]

From there, Kate continued to do examination coaching in the evenings. From about June 1896, in the mornings, she ran a private secondary class for girls. This initially accepted 12–14 girls per annum and later took some 20–25.[29] It provided the income that facilitated William's Forward Movement work. In the afternoons, from February 1897, there were also private tuition classes offering coaching in preparation for Matriculation, the Civil Service exams and Teachers' Certificates.[30]

Kate was also involved in several key Forward Movement activities and programmes. On Sunday afternoons she regularly delivered lay sermons in an open-air site adjacent to the Harbour Board offices, and covered for William by preaching and chairing meetings when he fell ill, which happened frequently. The movement's programme of work for 1895 gives some sense of the busy schedule. On Sunday there were morning and evening services, Sunday school in the afternoon, open-air preaching in the city, and a social in the hall after 8pm. On Mondays there were Band of Hope and Penny Club meetings (temperance groups for children and teens) and in the evening reports from the movement's committees on social reform. There were evening continuation classes on Tuesdays for boys over 16 whose parents had taken them out of school, followed in the evening by a class on 'Socialism and other kindred topics'. On Wednesday evening continuation classes were held for boys under 16, followed by meetings of the Literary Society. On Thursday afternoons a Mutual Help Society brought together poorer citizens and those disposed to help them 'intellectually, morally and materially'. The 37 members of this society donated clothes and bedding and taught classes that advised on improving the character and health of the home. As Doris Williams Elliot has suggested, middle-class women's home management skills were perceived as 'one of the chief remedies of social ills'.[31] The practical classes offered at Toynbee Hall to working-class people of both sexes were absent in Wellington's Forward Movement, because the capital already had a well-respected Technical Art School, established in 1886 by Arthur Dewhurst Riley, a pioneer of technical and vocational education in New Zealand.[32] Early Thursday evening there was the Young Women's Guild, then 'Lectures on Current Questions'. On Friday evening a 'Pleasant Hour' for mothers was followed by a meeting of the Forward Movement Brotherhood. On Saturday there were more Penny Club readings and temperance concerts at varied times.[33] Because this was a movement to address the negative social impacts of urban living, it would have catered almost exclusively for Pākehā, since until 1900 98 percent of Māori lived in scattered rural communities.[34]

Wellington had no university to provide settlement students, but founding such an institution was something Forward Movement members pushed for throughout the early 1890s. In the meantime, members offered public lectures and educational programmes. The Wednesday night Literary Society, for example, soon proved enormously popular. After only four months it had attracted over 150 members and more joined each week. Its success was ascribed to fulfilling 'a real need in the City'. Kate, who had a lifelong love of literature, played a prominent role. Forward Movement members took turns with public lectures, for which a small fee was asked: Kate spoke on George Eliot, Justice C.W. Richmond on Robert Browning, John Findlay on John Ruskin and Robert Stout on the novelist Carl Emil François.[35] Kate's talk on George Eliot was offered in June 1895 to an overflowing audience, who listened 'with the greatest interest and pleasure. Mrs. Evans gave an admirable sketch of the life of George Eliot, and illustrated her development, intellectual and emotional, by well-chosen and well-rendered extracts from the novelist's works … It is a pity that a larger hall was not secured for the lecture. If the other public lectures of the society attract audiences of the same dimensions, it will be absolutely necessary to do so.'[36]

Ernest Beaglehole, an accounts clerk with Sharlands wholesale chemist in Dixon Street, greatly appreciated the society, which introduced him to the joys of literature and gave him a more fulfilling life.[37] Many of Wellington's Forward Movement members were middle class, but it also attracted working- and lower middle-class followers such as Beaglehole, who came to the first meeting and within six months was serving as secretary. For Beaglehole, whose sons Ernest and John Cawte went on to become distinguished academics, the intellectual stimulus the Forward Movement offered was its greatest reward.

In 1895 the movement launched a journal called *The Citizen*, financed through subscriptions and advertisers. Each issue featured a few literary reviews, articles and poems, but most articles grappled with political and social subjects. Socialist and feminist Louisa Blake wrote urging the state to create an industrial fund and compulsory work scheme to banish unemployment and make charitable aid redundant; male feminist Basil Stocker argued for 'co-operative housekeeping', which would involve several families cooking in one communal kitchen, the object being 'the emancipation of wives and mothers, women and girls, from their present deplorable slavery'. Anna Stout, in an article on the 'New Woman', urged women to lead a moral charge for sexual purity and a 'white life for two' – a monogamous marriage without any tolerance for the prevailing sexual double standard. Lilian Edger, who had recently embraced theosophy, wrote a piece arguing that because theosophy embraced the brotherhood of man regardless of race, creed or social rank, 'many of its teachings bear more or less directly on the question of social reform.'[38]

The Citizen

Vol. I.   OCTOBER, 1895.   No. 2.

W. A. EVANS

William Albert Evans, featured on the front page of the Forward Movement journal *The Citizen* in 1895.

Alexander Turnbull Library, Wellington

Anna Paterson Stout, Kate Edger's friend and fellow
feminist campaigner for social reform, c. 1880s.

Alexander Turnbull Library, Wellington, 1/2-0002687-F

Several future leading lights of the Liberal government contributed to *The Citizen*. George Fowlds, later minister of education and of health, wrote on 'The Ethics of the Land Question'. He was one of a small, vocal, persistent group of radical, often nonconformist liberals known as 'single taxers', who believed that taxing what American political economist Henry George called the 'unearned increment' on land (that is, increases in value that were not the result of investing productive labour), would solve a multitude of social ills and make all other taxes redundant. John Findlay, later attorney general, leader of the Legislative Council, colonial secretary and minister of justice, wrote a two-part article endorsing the view that society was moving progressively away from the era of selfish individualism to more state involvement in public welfare.[39] Robert Stout, who would become chief justice in 1899, wrote on reforming local government; J.H. Helliwell, secretary and chief executive officer of the Wellington Gas Company, urged the need for a 'gospel of civic duty', a cause dear to the Evanses' hearts, as was Arf Atkinson's catalogue of the evils of alcohol. Dr William Chapple wrote about the need for a strong association between universities and technical education. Universities were 'uplevelling' and 'the pride and glory of all democracies'; Wellington's lack of one was a 'pressing need'.[40]

William contributed several articles, infused with impassioned idealism and a strong belief in education's role in a progressive evolution towards 'the universal good'.[41] One later recruit to the Forward Movement, George Hogben, was well placed to help the cause of education. He had been at Canterbury College with Kate and, like her, worked as a teacher and active member of the New Zealand Educational Institute in the 1880s. By the early 1900s Hogben, a devout Congregationalist, was both a close friend of the Evanses and a power in the land: from 1899 he led the Department of Education and introduced several key pieces of legislation that helped to open up New Zealand secondary school education to all classes, promoted manual and technical education and improved pay and conditions for teachers.[42] Although technical schools in New Zealand aimed to teach practical skills and provide a good general education, they were 'stamped with the label of social inferiority given to them in British education'.[43] Kate and William sent their three boys to Wellington Technical School, a highly unusual move for a middle-class couple. In doing so, they were signalling support for a form of education that would not foster elitism and would be available to all.[44]

The Citizen ceased publication in 1896, probably for lack of finances or time. Nevertheless, the Forward Movement continued to produce some literature on topical issues. During the Diamond Jubilee, for example, a pamphlet took issue with a proposal by the Prince of Wales that the London poor be given a dinner to mark the occasion. The writer, anonymous but in all likelihood William, fulminated: 'the sooner the Royal Family realises that what the poor need is not occasional bursts of benevolence but a larger measure of justice, the sooner the difficulties their existence cause will be removed.'[45]

In Wellington William regularly visited the poor and attempted to improve conditions in the city slums, as well as helping to implement a more rational and effective system of charitable aid.[46] By the mid-1890s the Forward Movement was making progress and raising its profile. A flyer put out to advertise its work asked,

Kate and William Evans' three sons: Elwyn, James (standing)
and Eurfryn or Vryn, late 1890s.

Jill Smith Collection

'Why not help us in our efforts to put an end to Poverty, Ignorance, and Vice, and bring in the era of Plenty, Knowledge and Virtue?' and reproduced a quote from John Ruskin: 'Every noble life leaves the fibre of it interwoven in the work of the world.'[47]

Kate's energetic contributions to the movement were also attracting attention and receiving approving comment in the press. The *Observer* enthusiastically commended her efforts in November 1895:

> Wellington has a model minister's wife in Mrs W.A. Evans, whose husband is head of the religo-philanthropic Forward Movement. She is not only his right hand in all the philanthropic phases of the work, but during his illness is conducting some of the religious services. Mrs Evans was formerly Miss Kate Edger, of Auckland. She was, if we mistake not, New Zealand's first lady M.A., and is now an *ma* in another sense three or four times over.[48]

The writer was mistaken about Kate being the first 'lady M.A.', but she was indeed a 'ma' three times over, having given birth to her third son, Vryn, that year. Forward Movement members clearly appreciated Kate. In 1897 they gave her a Christmas present, for which she thanked them fulsomely, ending with characteristic modesty: 'I have always rejoiced that circumstances have allowed Mr. Evans to devote himself to the work he has most at heart, and the best reward that he or I can have is to know that his work is not without its results in helping to make clear the thoughts and ennoble the lives of even a few.'[49]

A union for domestic workers and for the unemployed

In July 1898 William and Kate encouraged the creation of a Domestic Workers' Union in Wellington to advance the well-being and working conditions of female domestic servants. Previous attempts to organise female domestics, in Dunedin in 1890 and in Christchurch in 1894, had been short-lived and unsuccessful. The women spearheading them had links to other unions: Harriet Morison, president of the New Zealand Domestic Servants' Union formed in Dunedin, was also head of the Dunedin Tailoresses' Union, and Aileen Garmson in Christchurch had a role in the New Zealand Workers' Union. New Zealand domestic servants, who usually worked for long hours and little pay, had been excluded from protection under the Liberals' Industrial Conciliation and Arbitration Act of 1894, on the grounds that employers did not profit from their work.[50]

Kate presided at the 'inaugural social' of the fledgling Wellington union because William was too ill to attend, reading out a speech he had written. The movement's aims were modest: to avoid unreasonable hours of labour, procure a weekly half-holiday guaranteed by legislation, and create a benefit fund and a social club. William praised the women involved for 'elevating not only themselves but their work'. Their aim, to provide the best relations between employer and employed in a 'moderate, reasonable and gradual manner', was commendable, but the women should 'never prostitute the purpose of their Union to the shibboleths of a Party'. Robert Stout praised domestic workers as a group not valued sufficiently by society and 'thought that all people would be delighted to know that the domestic workers had combined'. Minister of Public Works William Hall-Jones, standing in for the premier Richard Seddon, also spoke, wishing the new group every success.[51]

The union resolved to hold fortnightly social evenings, and in late June a deputation waited on Seddon to request a weekly half-holiday for domestic servants. Although he promised to 'submit the matter to the Labour Department', and to 'see what could be done', the matter was effectively mothballed.[52] The union carried on for some time but then lost momentum. In October 1899, when the outspoken feminist and former domestic servant Marianne Tasker advertised a Wellington Domestic Workers' Union, she was oblivious to the fact that an organisation with the same name already existed. Feathers were ruffled and an antagonistic correspondence between the two unions flared in the local press. The formidable Mrs Tasker got the upper hand in this exchange, dismissing the existing union as feeble and effectively 'moribund'.[53] Both unions eventually faded away, however, having achieved little for their members.

In 1906 Tasker tried again and had more success with the Wellington Domestic Workers' Union. Registered under the Arbitration Act, with 38 members and affiliated with the Wellington Trades Council, it managed to gain employers' agreement to a 68-hour week. But disputes over holiday pay and allocation of hours on particular days ended up in the Arbitration Court. In 1908 the union failed to submit an annual return and as a result had its registration cancelled. Although other domestic workers' unions formed in Auckland in 1907 and in Christchurch in 1908, these, too, followed a familiar pattern of falling membership and failure.[54] Domestic service was an employment choice of last resort for most New Zealand women. As clerical and other employment opportunities for women burgeoned, it became more and more difficult to hire servants. In time, however, new labour-saving household appliances reduced the need for domestic staff.

William also for a time supported the New Zealand Workers' Union. Originally the Shearers' Union, this group rebranded itself in 1893 and began to court urban workers. Throughout the 1890s, in the aftermath of the defeated 1890 Maritime Strike, most New Zealand unions were 'broken, flaccid and penniless'.[55] The new organisation, however, was something of an exception, attracting workers excluded from the more conservative craft unions. In 1896 William helped to press the New Zealand Workers' Union's case for a state farm for unemployed workers, liaising with Seddon on the matter. The Labour Department did set up a farm, in Johnsonville, which was a precursor to the government work schemes of the Great Depression, albeit on a smaller scale.[56] In June 1899, in one of his Forward Movement services, William addressed unemployment once again, urging the establishment of state farms where men weakened by poverty and crime might be brought back to a healthy moral and physical condition. In its 'Side-lights from Wellington' column, the *Press* expressed scepticism about a 'back to the land' panacea: 'Lord give some of us a little common sense, and teach us that a decayed apothecary or what not is not necessarily an agriculturalist!'[57]

A goal achieved and the end of the movement

In 1897 one of the Forward Movement's longstanding goals eventuated with the founding of Victoria University College. Four professors were appointed in 1899, and although it took until 1906 to settle on the Kelburn site and erect suitable buildings, for all intents and purposes the city now had a university. It is often claimed that Seddon, having for years turned a deaf ear to Stout's call to establish a university in Wellington, agreed to establish one after his delight at receiving an honorary doctorate from Cambridge when visiting England for Queen Victoria's Diamond Jubilee in 1897. Several other factors influenced his altered view: a newly buoyant economy, a desire to fortify the Liberals' grip on Wellington and a wish to keep up with Britain, where popular universities such as the University of London and various applied higher education facilities in Birmingham and elsewhere were rapidly increasing in number and enrolling students from a wider range of social classes.[58] After Victoria opened, the evening lectures and discussion groups formerly organised by the Forward Movement gradually ceased. However, both William Evans and Robert Stout played an active role in the new tertiary institution.[59]

Encouraging active citizenship among all sectors of the Wellington community remained a key endeavour for the Forward Movement. A meeting on the evening of 30 March 1898 moved to establish a Citizens' Union, to 'create and foster a civic spirit' and 'infuse the progressive spirit into the administration of civic affairs'.[60] The creation of the union was widely lauded in the press; the *Evening Post*, for example, noted that 'Anything … which will make for enlightenment and progress in national and civic affairs must be hailed as a means of breathing a soul into the dry bones of our public life.'[61] In early April an executive was formed, consisting of F.H.D. Bell as president and William, John Findlay and Wellington MP John Hutcheson as vice-presidents. These were high-profile public men. Bell, for example, had a successful law career, had been mayor of Wellington twice in the 1890s and later became a minister in the Reform Party and briefly prime minister in 1925. Over the next few months various Citizens' Union speakers delivered talks in the Forward Movement Hall. Stout spoke on the need for wider streets and more parks in Wellington, and Bell advocated better working-class accommodation, among other civic improvements. The topics, however, grew increasingly eclectic, ranging from the desirability of a school journal to the pros and cons of cremation, military volunteering, 'social problems' and a critique of the government's old-age pensions legislation.[62] These discussions did not galvanise armies of active citizens, and by the end of 1900 the Citizens' Union was no longer active. One contributing factor might have been William's election to the Wellington City Council in September 1900, where he served as a councillor for the Mount Cook ward until April 1905.

By the early 1900s the Forward Movement seemed past its peak. This was partly because it had witnessed the realisation of some key goals, notably the creation of Victoria University College and Hogben's education policies. An increasingly confident national economy also helped to lessen the poverty and unemployment experienced in the capital during the economic depression, which had spurred the creation of the Forward Movement. Nevertheless, in the early years of the new century, William and Kate continued to work diligently for the cause. In 1902, for example, the *Observer* in its gossip column hailed William as 'one of the most strenuous men now in public life in the capital', and a hard worker 'wherever he sees a chance of promoting the good of his fellows'. It succinctly and admiringly described William and Charles Bradbury's aims in setting up the Forward Movement and referred to Kate as 'the power behind the throne'.[63]

In 1904 Kate ceased to be the sole family breadwinner, and the Forward Movement effectively ended, when William successfully applied for the position of minister to the Constable Street Congregational Church in the working-class suburb of Newtown. The Evanses moved to a house at 19 Hiropi Street, close to the church. Kate continued to run her girls' classes from this new home, while also throwing herself into the role of minister's wife. Her niece Dora Judson, writing to a friend in 1911, described 'Aunt Katie' as 'a terribly busy creature; I think a parson's wife is almost harder work than a farmer's wife, she has so many things to do for the Church, and now Aunt Katie has taken up the organ and plays for the services every Sunday.'[64]

For the common good

If the envisioned brotherhood of evangelical citizens working towards the benefit of those less fortunate had not exactly transformed Wellington life, the Forward Movement had achieved some key goals. It spearheaded improvements in the distribution of charitable aid, and Kate and her husband both worked hard to help the lives and prospects of those who had fallen on hard times. For many Forward Movement members, such as Ernest Beaglehole, the movement's intellectual and cultural activities enriched their lives. Some Wellington citizens were able to advance to further education because of its continuation classes. Significantly, a number of Forward Movement members became figures of real power and influence in the Liberal government and managed to effect far-reaching educational reforms. For a time, the movement filled an intellectual void in the city, offering the serious-minded intellectual engagement that those pushing for a university felt was necessary for a progressive and enlightened community. The Forward Movement helped to spur the creation of a university that is still thriving.

When the Labour Party was formed in 1916, a number of its more prominent members, including Walter Nash and Peter Fraser, adhered to a form of Christian socialism that advocated a moral economy and a society that offered opportunities for self-improvement through education, community health and environmental reform, and a political culture that encouraged interclass co-operation and unity. Socialism of this kind was underpinned by a Christian philosophy that 'asserted the superiority of moral principles over economic appetites.'[65]

The Forward Movement could not have continued for 11 years without Kate's financial support and involvement, achieved while keeping the family afloat and raising three sons. Her achievements are even more impressive because she was also actively supporting a range of other social reform movements, from temperance and prohibition to pioneering social work on behalf of women and children.

"Disguise our bondage as we will,
'Tis woman, woman rules us still."

Tom Moore.

6

Suffrage and the Demon Drink

[You] must lay aside the remembrance that you are a conservative or a liberal, and feel that you are just women – that a vote is A SACRED POSSESSION for the protection and welfare of your sex, your homes and the moral benefit of the community at large.

Prohibitionist, 21 October 1893

In working for the abolition of the liquor traffic we are doing the work of God – we are making happier homes and we are working for the uplifting of humanity.

Annual Report, WCTU Dunedin Branch, *Otago Daily Times*, 3 February 1897

In the early 1890s Kate Evans participated in New Zealand's energetic, high-profile and controversial women's franchise campaign. She signed the massive women's suffrage petition presented to Parliament on 28 July 1893 and spoke at public meetings supporting the cause.[1] When, on 19 September 1893, New Zealand led the world by granting all adult women the franchise, she hoped, like many others, that the female voting influence would help to usher in a more morally sound and compassionate society. She also hoped that New Zealand would soon lead the world again with another ground-breaking reform: banishing the demon drink.

Kate was a lifelong stalwart of the Women's Christian Temperance Union (WCTU). Her support for both the suffrage and prohibition campaigns was based on liberal enlightenment ideas about natural justice and equality. All adult women, regardless of religion or ethnicity or wealth, should have the right to vote. If the cause of prohibition triumphed, New Zealand women's rights would be augmented and they would no longer have to endure the dangers and degradations excessive drinking inflicted on their homes and families.

A cartoon from 1893 illustrating the popular perception that women voters – 'She that is to be obeyed' – would clean up a host of male vices. Auckland Libraries Heritage Collections, 7-A12543

As one historian has noted, '"Serpent" alcohol was male; "strong drink" was the very essence of male sex energy, of uncontrol, and destruction.'[2] Then, as now, excessive drinking tended to increase the prevalence and severity of domestic violence. It led to loss of income and employment, sexual licentiousness in both sexes and the deterioration of health and well-being, especially among the poorer working class. The crusade for prohibition drew on religious belief in attempting to preserve the sanctity of the home and women's revered role in it. It was also a feminist cause that aimed to protect women and children from the impacts of alcohol.

Like many other religious nonconformists, Kate perceived prohibition as a panacea for a wide range of social ills, something that would usher in a dry utopia, but wanted the sale of alcohol eradicated by the will of the people, not imposed from above by state decree. In October 1893, not long after women won the vote, prohibition advocates achieved a legislative aim they had pursued for some 30 years: the Alcoholic Liquor Sales Control Act established triennial referendums in which New Zealanders could decide whether the liquor trade should continue in their electorate. Kate and William celebrated this victory and crusaded against the demon drink with renewed vigour, undaunted by the fact that a 60 rather than a 50 percent majority was required to achieve the desired end. They were not alone: for some three decades, about half of the New Zealand electorate supported the cause.[3]

The moral absolutism of the temperance movement has earned Protestant evangelical nonconformists, who formed the backbone of the crusade in New Zealand as elsewhere, a reputation as a joyless, puritanical force. Yet the reality was much more complex than the stereotype suggests. Promoting temperance and prohibition was an attempt to solve a serious source of social and economic problems but also, for campaigners like Kate Evans, a feminist issue. The varied negative impacts of alcohol struck at the heart of the evangelical domestic ideal of womanhood, marriage and family, and ruined the lives of many women and children.

The New Zealand Women's Christian Temperance Union

Kate Evans joined the Nelson branch of the New Zealand WCTU in 1886, its founding year, and was busy addressing wrappers for the organisation's *White Ribbon* newspaper a few days before her death in 1935. She was dominion recording secretary from 1916 to 1920, president of the Miramar branch from 1922 to 1930 and associate editor of the *White Ribbon* for many years.[4] The WCTU originated in the United States in 1874 in response to a series of women's 'crusades' against alcohol that swept through the Mid-west. In 1879, under the presidency of Frances Willard, it added women's suffrage to its list of social reforms.

When the American WCTU missionary Mary Leavitt toured New Zealand in 1885 on behalf of the World's WCTU (also recently founded by Willard), her message fell on receptive ears, and a New Zealand organisation was soon up and thriving. This receptivity, as Barbara Brookes has observed, 'attests to the strength of feeling against the drink trade amongst middle class women'.[5] It also attests to their perception that in order to restrict or ban the liquor trade, women needed the vote. With the motto 'For God, Home and Humanity',[6] the union was never a single-issue organisation, but rather offered its members the chance to take concerted action on a wide range of social matters, such as women's suffrage, temperance and prohibition, social purity, health and dress reform, prison reform, aiding fallen women, equal pay for equal work and improving women's legal status and rights within marriage. WCTU members worked within efficiently organised departments in local branch unions, each under the charge of a local superintendent.

In the mid-1880s, when Kate first joined the WCTU, the causes of female suffrage and prohibition were linked in many people's minds and it was widely believed that women voters would support the latter. For the WCTU, then the only national organisation of New Zealand women, female suffrage was not only an end in itself but also a means to another greatly desired goal: vanquishing the demon drink. A large proportion of its members, like Kate, came from a religious culture that had involved women in such triumphant crusades as the anti-slavery movement and in Josephine Butler's recent opposition to Britain's Contagious Diseases Act.[7]

Although led by predominantly white middle-class evangelical nonconformists, both the suffrage and prohibition crusades involved and affected Māori women: all adult women, Māori and Pākehā, would receive the vote, and Māori women rallied to the temperance cause, 'concerned at the effect of alcohol on their communities, and its relationship to land sales – some men were getting drunk and signing sales papers, or selling land to pay debts to tavern owners or to buy alcohol'. The first Māori WCTU unions were formed in 1894. Their members often also belonged to Nga Komiti Wahine, tribally based committees associated with Te Paramata, the Māori Parliament. Seven unions were represented at the first Māori conference of the WCTU in 1911.[8]

The WCTU encouraged a strong sense of female solidarity. Members referred to each other as sisters; America was the mother union. They placed great value on women's higher moral purity and elevating role. All members wore a white ribbon as a symbol of purity. When they received it they made a pledge to 'uphold the pledge of purity as equally binding upon men and women'.[9]

The idea of social, that is sexual, purity and a monogamous sexually virtuous 'white life for two' has an emphatically Puritan ring when viewed from our present age. In the late Victorian period, however, this line of thought was associated with radical movements promoting women's equal rights and the reformation of men's sexual behaviour. Those who advocated social purity wanted the sexual double standard removed. Why were there 'fallen women' but no 'fallen men'? Men had to be held to account for their behaviour and marriage laws needed to equalise the rights and duties of spouses. For WCTU members, the family was the foundation stone of the nation, and laws and attitudes must ensure that both men and women abided by just and equitable rules. Alcohol abuse, by its nature, threatened the family; women and children were its most frequent victims.

The WCTU vehemently opposed New Zealand's Contagious Diseases Act, which came into force in 1869. In common with its English counterpart, the legislation subjected women prostitutes to forcible examination and detention, but applied no sanction to their male customers. The police had discretionary powers to decide who was a 'common prostitute', a term that was not defined in law.[10] Although only sporadically invoked for short periods of time in Auckland and Canterbury, the legislation angered feminists because it both enshrined the sexual double standard and violated women's rights as citizens. The WCTU and other women's organisations such as the National Council of Women energetically campaigned to have the act abolished, finally succeeding in 1910.

The WCTU was never a mass movement. It numbered some 600 women during the early 1890s; membership rose to a peak of 3474 in 1912. Although it embraced only 0.43 percent of New Zealand's adult women in 1893, and just 0.94 percent in 1915,[11] the union punched well above its weight. It was prominent, efficient, organised and extremely determined in pursuing its goals. One admiring columnist referred to it as 'not only one of the grandest philanthropic and religious movements, but the most perfect organisation the world has ever known'.[12]

Kate Sheppard, leader of the WCTU's women's suffrage
campaign and New Zealand's most celebrated first-wave
feminist, photographed in 1905.

Alexander Turnbull Library, Wellington, 1/2-C-09028F

Campaigning for women's suffrage

The women's suffrage campaign had some well-known nonconformist leaders. The
most outstanding and effective, Kate Sheppard, was a devout Congregationalist
and, from 1887, the WCTU's national franchise supervisor. Under her inspired
direction, the campaign for women's suffrage, which had attracted both male and
female supporters in New Zealand since the 1860s, rapidly gathered momentum.
An outstanding public speaker and writer, Sheppard organised petitions and
wrote letters and used her consummate diplomacy and charm to make strategic

connections with important parliamentary figures. The question of whether women should vote began to attract unprecedented levels of public interest. Enthusiastic supporters and indignant opponents squared off at public meetings and in newspaper correspondence columns.

Kate Evans, already busy, supported the suffrage movement through the WCTU. The size of the union suffrage meeting she attended in Nelson on 10 March 1891 so exceeded expectations that the initial venue, the Wesleyan schoolroom, proved too small for the audience of 280. Accommodatingly, the Reverend Frank Isitt moved the gathering to the nearby St John's Church. Isitt was both a supporter of female suffrage and a dedicated prohibitionist. His brother Leonard, also a Methodist minister, was a renowned orator and the country's leading advocate of prohibition for many years. The motion that 'the time has come for women to be admitted to equal privileges with men as regards the exercise of the Parliamentary franchise' attracted only two adverse votes. One woman opposed the motion on the grounds that women were not sufficiently educated; another felt that voting in public could subject women to potential abuse and insults. Maria Atkinson who, like all the women speakers, was identified in the press account of the meeting by her husband's name, quickly dispatched these arguments, noting 'there was no more publicity about voting by ballot, than there was about telegraphing'. Separate polling places, or even postal ballots, could easily be organised.

Kate then made a speech that, according to the *Nelson Evening Mail*, had 'the special charm' of being spoken rather than read. She considered some of the arguments for and against women's suffrage, beginning with a basic but salient point. The government's purpose was to provide for the welfare of society, and since society comprised men and women, both genders needed to be interested in government. 'Women contributed to taxation … they bought things; they paid rates; and if they contributed the money it was only just that they should have something to say about the spending of what they contributed … women played as important a part in social life as men.'

> In the strikes, for instance, last year, who suffered the most? Surely the wives and families. If women had had a voice in the matter, those strikes would never have taken place, as they would have looked further ahead, and seen that they could not effect the desired object. With regard to the liquor trade, who suffered most from the vice of drunkenness? Why the women again, and yet they had very little say as to the laws which regulated the drink traffic.

In contrast to those who argued that only women of property, single women and widows should have votes, Kate stressed that 'the real principle of women's franchise lay deeper down and included *all* adult women, and the question should be fought out once and for all on the broader basis'. Regarding the assertion that women should not stand for Parliament, Kate observed: 'Perhaps not in our day. Parliament would have to be a very different place to what it was now for women to *wish* to go. The presence of women in Parliament would purify it.' In response to arguments that women's home duties prevented them from entering public life, she did not deny that their sphere was the home, 'but what about the women who had no homes or special spheres? Were not these the women who would go into Parliament?' It would be 'preposterous' for a woman with young children to want to go, but 'very many women were not married, and lived independent lives, with neither husbands, brothers, nor fathers to represent them'. She also rejected the idea that if women had the vote there would be discord in the home. 'Was it impossible to think differently without quarrelling? The interest of discussing and arguing on public questions was surely an additional bond of union rather than a bone of contention.'

In closing, Kate drew attention to great advances women had made. 'Fifty years ago it would have been hardly possible for such a question to have been raised. Very much had been done for the emancipation of women since then; they had equal educational privileges with men, and must be able to exercise the vote as intelligently as men.'

Maria Atkinson, in her final words to the meeting, stated that women's suffrage would have a moral and protective impact: 'who would protect the women's interests, if women were not represented? Who would see that women were not ousted from legitimate channels of employment? Who would see that they were not paid less for doing the same work as men?' Equal education had undermined claims of female intellectual inferiority: 'The lawgivers had decided that ignorance did not debar men from voting; any man with certain residential qualifications provided he were neither under age, lunatic, or criminal, could vote, and why should the women be classed with the lunatic and criminal?'[13] These arguments mirrored those of New Zealand's pioneering feminist Mary Ann Muller, also from Nelson, who in 1869 had made the same arguments in a published pamphlet entitled *An Appeal to the Men of New Zealand*, but used a pen name, 'Femina', to disguise her identity from her disapproving husband. A June 1892 *New Zealand Herald* editorial took a similar line and as an example of injustice mentioned Lilian Edger, who was then

Gender balance, early 1890s style: Lilian Edger, the first female member of Auckland University College Council, with various local luminaries, including Auckland Mayor J.J. Holland (standing left), Bishop William Cowie (seated, second left) and farmer, investor and philanthropist James Dilworth (seated, second right).

Auckland Library Heritage Collections, 7-A11252

serving as a member of the Auckland University College Council. She was the first female in the country to sit on a university council.

> All adults in New Zealand have a vote except criminals, lunatics, and women. Adult Maoris, if they are only males, have a power and a position in the State which is withheld from our most educated and patriotic women. A lady like Miss Edger may sit upon the University Senate, but when election day comes round she is denied a right which is not withheld from a sailor, a sundowner [tramp] or a pauper.[14]

Patricia Grimshaw has suggested that, for anti-suffragists, women like Kate 'were the exceptions, the extremist wing of a dangerous, atheistical doctrine which was fraught with calamity for society'.[15] But most New Zealanders in the early 1890s, even conservative anti-suffragists, could hardly have failed to note the earnest, committed Christianity of WCTU members.

Early feminists like Kate found strength and empowerment in strongly gendered roles, but many others, male and female, who shared such a view, reached different conclusions. Fears about the impacts of women's increasing involvement outside the domestic sphere did not abate. In England, where women were still campaigning for the vote, some anti-suffragists placed a high value on women's moral and maternal roles. Women who had been early and prominent supporters of female education joined the anti-suffrage movement because they feared the potential overshadowing of women's role within the home.[16]

When New Zealand women won the vote on 19 September 1893 there was much proud national self-congratulation. Once again this remote young colony was leading the way in providing equal rights and opportunities for women while the 'old country' lagged behind. Achieving the suffrage did not signal an end to the activism of women's rights advocates, however. The suffrage campaign had give women opportunities to develop skills that enhanced their political effectiveness and confidence. Many now felt a strong desire to continue improving society, to make it purer and more moral, more just towards women, more supportive of those in need, and to rid it of the scourge of drink.

Maintaining the momentum: Active citizenship

After 1893 women formed groups to educate one other on social and political issues, to maintain the bonds of sisterhood experienced during the suffrage campaign and to exercise their new-found political influence for the common good. For example, several former franchise leagues (non-temperance groups that had sprung up during the suffrage campaign) transformed themselves into social and political leagues. In April 1896 a National Council of Women (NCW) was formed to federate women's organisations and provide a platform on which to meet and discuss topical issues. This council, linked to the International Council of Women, gave members the continued sense of belonging to a worldwide movement for women's progressive rights. Kate, who gave birth to her third son, Vryn, in 1895, was not on the NCW executive but in later years attended NCW conventions; in 1898, for example, she delivered a discussion paper on prison reform (see Chapter 7).

For a number of years there was a regular women's page in the temperance newspaper, *The Prohibitionist*, but in May 1895 the WCTU launched its own journal, the *White Ribbon*. The first issue proclaimed:

We are a body of Christian women called by His name and doing His work. The Evangelistic Department is the 'backbone' of our organisation, and we desire through all our work to have entwined, like a thread of gold, the evangelistic spirit; and the Gospel of our Lord Jesus Christ carried with its healing power far and wide. When we think of the meaning of an evangelist – 'The bearer of glad tidings or messenger of good' – how encouraging it is. But to fulfil this mission we need the anointing of the Spirit and to know that all our well-springs are in God.[17]

Although evangelical fervour remained a feature of the paper, there were long-standing tensions between WCTU members on religious matters. Between 1890 and 1892, Christians in the WCTU, including its then president Catherine Fulton, had wanted to impose a compulsory faith test on WCTU office-holders. Sheppard, writing in *The Prohibitionist* early in 1892, opposed this as sectarian and 'opposed to the spirit of Christ's teaching', adding that to achieve the primary goal of abolishing intoxicants, the WCTU should 'gladly enlist rich and poor, high and low, Priest, Levite or Samaritan'.[18] Her view prevailed and an abstinence vow and payment of annual fees remained the sole requirements to belong to the union.

Kate worked as an associate editor for the *White Ribbon* for decades. The paper provided a means of communicating between WCTU branches, with other women's groups and with temperance organisations throughout New Zealand and abroad. Often included were articles from American or English feminists, portraits of high-achieving women both within New Zealand and overseas, special reports from the regions and departments, and in-depth accounts of WCTU and NCW conventions. There was considerable continuity in substance and opinion in the paper over the years: prohibition and more active citizenship by women featured perennially, but many divergent and even conflicting views were aired within its pages.

A lack of unanimity was even more evident in the NCW where, from the outset, Lady Anna Stout made waves. Perhaps piqued that Sheppard was elected president rather than herself, she resented what she saw as a dominant, radical, politically oriented 'faction' from Christchurch: Kate Sheppard, Ada Wells, Wilhelmina Sheriff Bain and others. She objected, too, to the omission of less political women's groups, predicting, with some prescience, that this would be a source of future trouble. Unless more educational and philanthropic societies were included, the council was not, in her view, truly national. After 1897 she ceased to attend its annual conventions.[19]

Stout formed the Southern Cross Society in 1895 in Wellington with the aim of providing opportunities for women to gain 'sound and accurate knowledge'

LADY VOTERS GOING UP TO POLLING-BOOTH, ELECTION DAY, AUCKLAND.

'Lady voters' at a polling booth in the Drill Hall, Rutland Street, Auckland, 1899.

Auckland Libraries Heritage Collections, 7-A12353

of the political and economic questions they would need to use their new voting rights most effectively. The society wanted women to insist on the moral probity and purity of candidates, to consider adjusting laws to make them more fair for women, to ensure equal pay for equal work, to promote temperance and improve the administration of charitable aid and to meet to discuss the issues and positive work the society could effect.[20] Anna Stout, who would later adopt a much more radical feminist stance in England, did not at this stage believe that women were yet ready for Parliament, on the grounds that they must educate themselves more fully in the study of politics. She was elected president of the new society and Lily Kirk vice-president.[21]

Kate and William were by this time moving in the same progressive liberal circles as Lily Kirk, her future husband Arthur Atkinson, and Anna and Robert Stout, all of whom were involved with the Forward Movement, and all of whom shared strong prohibitionist views. William spoke at an early Southern Cross Society meeting about its objects and goals, and on another occasion on 'The Social Question'. Kate later presented a paper on charitable aid reforms.[22] Neither she nor William served on the executive of the Southern Cross Society, but they agreed with its aims, and endorsed Stout's opinion that women were not yet ready to stand for Parliament. Kate made this view clear when delivering a February 1896 paper entitled 'Women's Part in Politics' to the Women's Social and Political League, a group with direct links to the ruling Liberal government. Its president was the premier's wife, Louisa Seddon.

In her paper Kate 'urged that, now women had the franchise, they should endeavour to vote the men who had the best moral character into Parliament, and not depend so much on those men who were ready to promise everything they were asked, and whose promises turned out to be like piecrust. She also thought that the members of the League, as women, should vote for Prohibition, and she considered that women were not ready for Parliament.' Those who attended agreed with all her points except prohibition – they advocated moderation instead – and thanked her profusely for giving the talk.[23]

In the *White Ribbon* in April 1899 Kate Sheppard used arguments based on women's familial role to urge more active female citizenship.

> If we have good and happy families, we shall have a good and happy community. Whether she be mother or daughter, sister, wife or aunt, a woman who is a good citizen will find her first duty in her home, which she will strive to make all that

a home should be … The woman who is a good citizen cannot be content with things as they are. She will be anxious to see the principles which she strives to carry out in her home extended to the community … The welfare of the State, like the welfare of the family, of which it is an enlargement, needs the care and attention of both men and women.[24]

The first wave of feminism had receded by 1900. Various groups that had come together during the suffrage campaign lost a sense of common purpose once the major goal had been attained. Most women were satisfied, and those who pushed for further feminist reforms were often perceived as zealous radicals or cranks. By the early 1900s the National Council of Women was weakened by internal disagreements over whether to condemn or support the South African War, and by conflicts between its more radical and conservative members.[25] In 1906 it went into abeyance. Many of the educated, activist, largely nonconformist women who had played a key role in the suffrage campaign, however, continued to exercise active citizenship. In March 1913 Kate presented a paper at the Dominion Convention of the WCTU on women's responsibilities as citizens. Although women had possessed the franchise for almost 20 years, they 'had not realised the sacred right of that vote'. It should be 'used as a sacred duty, and it should be exercised on every opportunity'. To be prepared for the highest political offices, women should be represented on school committees, charitable aid boards, city and borough councils. Their influence in practical affairs, such as planning public buildings and spending public money, would be advantageous to society.[26]

Marion Judson, Kate's eldest sister and the WCTU's national superintendent of the Good Citizenship Department for many years, argued on the same lines a few months later in the *White Ribbon*. She stressed that 'in claiming rights, we are claiming duties' and that the burden in social matters should fall on 'the strong rather than the weak; that those who are the best off, not only in material possessions but in character, education, and general development' should take responsibility for 'making the world a better place for all to live in.' There should be no 'sex war'; rather women should 'find out what is our true position, our right work in the community, that which will best promote the welfare of the whole.'

Like Kate, she urged women to seek places on a wide range of bodies, to educate themselves about issues and legislation, to train their children to adopt sound views and to help in every way possible to make their communities better places. In America, 'energetic women' had achieved, among other things, the 'planting of trees, the formation of parks, the cleaning up of towns and getting rid of unsightly rubbish, securing inspection of dairies and bakeries, the sanitary inspection of schools, penny lunches for school children, drinking fountains, playgrounds, evening schools, public reading rooms and libraries'.[27]

The prohibition panacea

Advocating prohibition had been a significant component of the Forward Movement, but Kate and William also played a prominent role in the New Zealand Alliance for the Abolition of the Liquor Traffic. This national umbrella organisation, formed in 1886, incorporated numerous prohibition groups, including the WCTU, and spearheaded prohibition campaign tactics. Kate was made an Alliance vice-president in 1915, usually a lifelong position. She was one of a small number of women who played a leadership role in the organisation, sitting on committees and discussing tactics.[28]

The temperance movement originated in England in the early 1830s when religious middle-class men, most either nonconformist or evangelical Anglicans from the north of England, aimed to encourage the middle-class values of self-control and delayed gratification among the working class. Initially they encouraged not giving up drink altogether but moderating alcohol consumption and renouncing hard liquor. The message was well received. The phenomenon spread rapidly. In the late 1840s the Band of Hope, founded in Leeds, encouraged children as young as six to take 'the pledge' – to vow never to drink alcohol, unless it had been prescribed for medical reasons. Many British temperance groups were founded by working-class men and women concerned to improve their social conditions; some Chartist groups even saw drunkenness as a barrier to the achievement of full political rights for that class. In 1853 the United Kingdom Alliance was formed to fight for legislation to eliminate or limit alcohol. Baptists and Congregationalists were particularly prominent in the push to abolish alcohol altogether. The first Church of England temperance organisation, formed in 1862, accommodated moderate drinkers as well as teetotallers. Catholics generally did not support the cause, although it had some prominent advocates. In Ireland, from the late 1830s until his death in 1856, Father Theobald Mathew became a one-man temperance league, travelling across the country convincing hundreds of thousands to sign the pledge.[29] By the 1900s the British temperance movement had lost momentum, but this was not the case on the other side of the world.

It is difficult to overestimate the passion and commitment of those promoting prohibition in New Zealand in the late nineteenth and early twentieth centuries. Advocates like Kate fervently believed that this one reform would cure all of society's economic, social and spiritual ills. For both the WCTU and the New Zealand Alliance, the goal was nothing less than prohibition of everything to do with alcohol, from making to selling to importing. It was a black and white matter: to drink or not to drink. Individuals could choose good over evil by giving up drink or stand idly by and watch it exploit and degrade their fellow human beings. Every temperance publication, and there were many, included one or more accounts, in suitably purple prose, of the dire contribution of alcohol to child and wife abuse, and its role in suicide, murder, bankruptcy, theft and murder. Those involved in the infamous 'trade' were condemned for making profits out of exploiting their fellow men. Overturning this tyranny was presented as a great campaign of liberation which, like the anti-slavery campaigns of the past, would extend the boundaries of human freedom. It would do so, moreover, not by setting class against class, or requiring an overhaul of the economic and political status quo, but by all New Zealanders working together and making a morally sound choice. If everyone saw the light and opted to ban alcohol, poverty and crime would rapidly recede, if not fade away altogether.

The term 'crusade', often used to describe the prohibition cause, is pertinent on several levels. The millenarian aspect of the campaign resonated with many nonconformists, who firmly believed that after prohibition a new era of righteous morality and justice would dawn. New Zealand would become a sober utopia. In his 1876 'Annual Sermon on Intemperance', Samuel Edger referred to the drink question as 'one of moral right and wrong, close to every man's conscience; as a question of universal degradation, individual and national'.[30] If prohibition occurred the nation would be on the path of progress towards a more elevated, moral society.

As in Britain, the cause in New Zealand was dominated by nonconformist congregations. By 1891 nearly 37 percent of New Zealanders were Presbyterians, Methodists, Baptists, Congregationalists or members of the Church of Christ; these churches supported prohibition unequivocally and were disproportionately represented in its leading ranks.[31]

Many people assumed that, after achieving suffrage, women would vote en masse for prohibition. That never eventuated, and there is no evidence that women voted for the cause any more than men.[32] There was no doubt in the mind of Kate and other WCTU prohibition stalwarts, however, that women, as society's moral standard bearers, would eventually rally to the cause. Kate Sheppard, speaking at the 1893 NZWCTU national convention, confidently anticipated women voters' moral impact: 'Laws need altering for the protection of our sex and those dear to us. On women devolves the special duty of seeing that our legislators are men who honour purity and probity more than party, men to whose names the title of "Honourable" is a fitting prefix, and not a biting sarcasm.'[33]

Writing in the *White Ribbon* in 1897, Lily Kirk described anti-alcohol campaigning as a subject

> pre-eminently fitted for women to take up. In the home, the nursery, and the social circle her influence is still supreme, and whatever changes politics may bring, this supremacy is one which she is never likely to lose. If her power to mould the minds of the young and the social customs of the adult – a power mightier than any legislative power, because law is weaker than opinion and powerless without it – if this great power were exerted by her constantly and strenuously to promote the cause of temperance, women might … effect a glorious and bloodless revolution, the like of which the world has never seen.[34]

Groups like the WCTU and the Alliance focused their tactics on education and propaganda, carried out through journals, leaflets, pamphlets, lectures, processions, clubs and concerts. Their aim was to encourage greater support at the licensing polls, along with political measures such as petitions and lengthy written and oral submissions to parliamentary select committees. The Alliance urged members and the public to vote for political candidates who stood for prohibition. By 1908 only 12 out of 76 electorates had voted to go dry, but another 38 were close to doing so, with over 50 percent of their voters opting for no licence.[35]

In the early 1900s success in a related cause augured well. The WCTU and the NCW had long objected to women working in public bars. Attractive barmaids were perceived as lures, drawing vulnerable young men away from the path of virtue. There was also concern for the women doing this kind of work because it was perceived as detrimental to their moral well-being. The issue attracted controversy in the press. In 1906 the *Observer* commented, with some indignation, 'Where has it ever been shown that "public opinion is strongly against females being employed in the bars of the city hotels?" … The Christian Temperance Women have spoken … but public opinion – never.'[36]

In 1910 the Liberals introduced a ban on hiring new barmaids – a victory for the WCTU, the NCW and all those opposed to the perceived morally corrupting influence of bars and alcohol. In the same year the prohibitionists received another boost when Joseph Ward's government legislated for triennial polls on national prohibition, with the same 60 percent majority required. In 1910, too, the minimum drinking age, which had been raised from 16 to 18 in 1904, was raised further to 21. In 1911 a 'women's crusade', spearheaded by Annie J.P. Driver of Dunedin and adopting the popular temperance motto 'lips that touch wine shall not touch mine', urged women to withhold conjugal relations if their husbands drank alcohol. It is not possible to measure the success of this tactic because membership figures of those engaged in the crusade were not made available, but the 1911 prohibition poll was large, following a steadily upward trajectory from 38.83 percent in 1896 to reach 55.83 percent, and among prohibitionists it was thought to have had a considerable impact.[37] An article in the *White Ribbon* in December 1914 spoke of the prohibitionists' confident sense of inexorable advance: 'We know our cause is a real live cause to-day, and that it is bound to conquer. The forces of righteousness never suffer ultimate defeat; the fight for freedom, though baffled oft, is ever won … The fight may be long, but victory is certain.'[38]

The armoury of tactics and arguments employed to advance the cause received a new weapon during the war years: concern about maintaining and enhancing national strength.

National efficiency

After the declaration of war in August 1914, 'national efficiency' became a concern among many combatant countries. In Britain anxieties about falling behind owing to a lack of scientific planning, technical expertise and a tendency to 'muddle through' had begun to surface in the 1880s in response to Germany's rapid military, industrial and commercial rise. The worry had intensified in the wake of the military humiliations and recruiting problems of the South African War. The perception that Britain, and by extension its dominions, needed to improve national efficiency in order to staunch deterioration and maintain pre-eminence, was widespread throughout the Edwardian era. What one historian has called 'an incongruous amalgam of middle-class technocrats, reform-minded aristocrats and Fabian social engineers' dedicated themselves to the cause.[39]

When World War I broke out, the belief that national efficiency, and therefore military success, would be impeded by alcohol had a positive impact on the prohibition crusade internationally. In New Zealand, as elsewhere, the war brought an upsurge in anti-alcohol sentiment, though not among those on the front line.

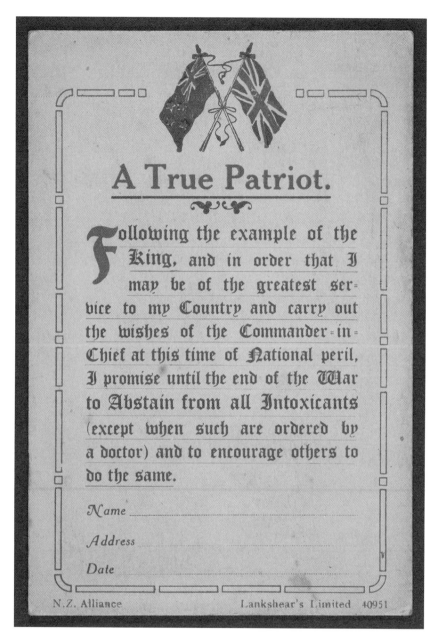

During the war, abolishing the liquor traffic was presented as a patriotic duty. This New Zealand Alliance card signifies the bearer's pledge to relinquish all intoxicants, unless strictly medicinal, during wartime.

Alexander Turnbull Library, Wellington, Eph-A-Alcohol-Temperance-1915-01

There was more willingness now to adopt austerity measures for the good of the nation, to keep it strong and fighting fit. Fears that young troopers might be led astray by drink, both at home and abroad, or have their physical fitness impeded by the strength-sapping impact of excessive drinking, accelerated. Wasting precious national resources on making and selling alcohol while young soldiers were dying for their country abroad seemed potentially weakening and morally wrong. When a National Efficiency Board was created in February 1917, 'to protect and advance the industries of the Dominion',[40] three of the five businessmen on it were staunch prohibitionists.

The WCTU had not been idle. In 1915 a petition with over 60,000 signatures was presented to Parliament, calling for public bars to close at 6pm. This measure was argued for primarily in terms of national efficiency. As Lily Atkinson emphasised, it had nothing to do with drunken soldiers: 'This is demanded solely as a war measure, on the ground of national economy and efficiency, the petitioners believing that the struggle in which the Empire is engaged is so serious that the waste on alcoholic liquors and similar luxuries constitutes a distinct menace at a time when every penny and every ounce of efficiency may be needed to ensure victory.'[41]

The WCTU presented two further petitions to this end in conjunction with the New Zealand Temperance Alliance in 1916 and 1917. Kate, as then WCTU president and an Alliance vice-president from 1915, was in the midst of this campaign. On 4 April 1916 she talked to members at a Wellington WCTU meeting about the organisation's 'monster petition' for early closing and asked for everyone's support.[42] By 1916 all but two Australian states had banned liquor sales after 6pm, which set an important precedent. New Zealand followed suit in December 1917, as a temporary wartime measure; the change was made permanent in 1918. Six o'clock closing remained in place for the next 50 years. Ironically, the notorious 'six o'clock swill' became a national institution.

In the short term, however, prohibition appeared to gain momentum. In 1917 the National Efficiency Board recommended holding an extra licensing poll, with compensation provisions for the liquor industry should prohibition prevail. The government acted on this recommendation in 1918 and, crucially, reduced the required majority to the long-desired 50 percent. As the first poll loomed on 10 April 1919, Kate, as recording secretary of the WCTU, wrote excitedly in the *White Ribbon* about this crucial chance to achieve the long-desired goal. In the 18 February 1919 edition she advised her 'Dear White Ribbon Sisters' that the national WCTU convention would be postponed until 23 April, 'seeing that all would be busy in their respective districts with enrolment work, the distribution of literature, or other preparation for the poll'. She urged all branches to attend the convention in Napier, because 'If the poll … is in our favour, as we all hope and pray it may be, and as many signs seem to show that it can be – it will be a historic occasion, in which all will wish to have some part. To that end, let us all devote our best energies, that to us, as to the woman of old, it may be said, "According to your faith, be it unto you."'[43]

A month later, in a letter to the editor of the *White Ribbon* headed 'Stop! Look out for the bogey!', Kate urged women not to be put off voting, among other things by 'the mistaken notion that if the present poll is in favour of the Trade, there will be a better chance before long of striking another blow, without the "compensation" clause, that is a stumbling block to so many staunch Temperance partisans'. To anyone considering not voting for this reason she would say: 'Do not fall into the error of supposing that you will be able in a few months to vote out the Trade without compensation. If this poll fails, it will be years before drink is banished, for it will be years before so favourable an opportunity offers itself for securing a majority against it.' Kate then pointed out that the 'hated compensation was given years ago when that clause was inserted in the Licensing Bill making Prohibition, if carried, inoperative for over four years'.

The National Efficiency Board was, to all intents and purposes, 'paying four and a half million [pounds], or less, for the purpose of seeing immediate Prohibition'.

> Will anyone seriously maintain that it is not worth paying that sum to save the country the misery and degradation resulting from four more years of the drink curse? Nay, rather, it is a good business proposition! Think of all the bright boys, the promising young men, who will fall victims to the temptations of the open bar during that time; think of the unhappy, poverty-stricken homes, the ruined manhood, the impaired efficiency of the nation, to say nothing of the millions that will have to be spent in dealing with the crime and poverty produced by the Liquor Traffic.

Even those opposed to compensation should 'take a broader view and let nothing prevent you from casting your vote for Liberty on the 10th of April!' She concluded: 'Do not risk the bitter regret that will assuredly be yours if you let the golden opportunity slip, and fail to record the vote that will help to make New Zealand free from this curse …'[44]

The 1919 poll and beyond

The April 1919 poll, when the home-based advantage of a 10,000-vote lead was overturned by some 40,000 overseas soldiers' votes, is often cited as the great turning point, after which 'wowsers' no longer posed a serious threat to the drinking classes. Prohibition, however, remained a force to be reckoned with throughout the 1920s. Writing in the *White Ribbon* in the immediate aftermath of the poll, an undaunted writer (possibly Kate) asked: 'Are we downhearted? No! If beaten this time, we will rally for the next fight. We make no compromise with this infamous traffic.'[45] A less well-known referendum, held in December 1919 alongside the general election, showed that this 'never say die' approach was warranted. Despite the addition of a potentially vote-splitting option of state purchase and control of alcohol, the prohibition vote increased to 49.7 percent. Only 1623 votes prevented a majority vote for the cause.[46]

This 1919 pro-prohibition cartoon shows a submarine armed with liquor, having sunk one ship, preparing to destroy three more, named Health, Happiness and Hope.

Alexander Turnbull Library, Wellington, Eph-A-Alcohol-Prohibition-1919-02

The following year the advent of American prohibition gave the cause a fillip. Overnight it seemed less like a minority or 'faddist' issue than a viable reality. Throughout the 1920s the nonconformist churches were united in support for the cause, while the Alliance became a more professional and effective lobby group, although its public support levels remained largely unchanged. The real blow to prohibition came with the advent of the Great Depression in 1929. Alcohol consumption dropped considerably, and the fact that the economic downturn had begun in the US belied arguments about the economic benefits of proscribing alcohol. Prohibition in the United States ended in 1933.[47] By the mid-1930s, when Kate died, the cause that she had so ceaselessly and energetically worked for had weakened dramatically.

The fact that, for decades, temperance dominated so much political discourse, generated such passionate responses and influenced the national culture through increasingly restrictive licensing laws, has led one historian to describe it as 'the most important mass social movement in New Zealand's history'.[48] This judgement certainly captured the perspective of Kate and her allies, who saw their work for prohibition in a religious light but also as part of a crusade based on humanitarian social concern.

7

Protection and Redemption

If the tone of morality is to be raised, there must be only one standard of morality by which it is measured.

KATE SHEPPARD, *White Ribbon*, October 1896[1]

I do not know the reason why all these sex Bills are brought in; I do not know whether it is in consequence of 'hysterical women,' or some so-called purity society, or whether it is simply a softening of the brain …

THOMAS KELLY, debating the proposed legislation to punish incest, 1900[2]

After Kate died in 1935, an obituary praised her as 'a social worker and educationist of eminence'.[3] For decades, on behalf of the Society for the Protection of Women and Children (SPWC), she helped vulnerable women and children and promoted legislation that enhanced their rights and interests. With other feminists, she worked hard to change a world in which men could sexually and physically abuse their wives and children almost with legal impunity and/or abandon them without any means of financial support, in which young single women could become social outcasts because of unwanted pregnancies, and women of all ages could be infected with life-threatening venereal diseases by husbands and lovers. Kate and her colleagues pushed for legislative sanctions against the negative impacts of men's all too frequent failure to uphold the evangelical ideal of social purity and faithful monogamy. For them, the way to achieve a more enlightened, fair and progressive society was to strengthen legal protection for women and children, enhance welfare provisions for them and offer struggling families moral assistance and practical support through philanthropic agencies. In undertaking this work, they often broached sexual subjects that had formerly been kept secret or denied altogether. Kate and the SPWC played a prominent role, for example, in the protracted but ultimately victorious battle to have incest recognised as a punishable offence. They also helped to bring about special children's courts and a more just and rehabilitative prison system.

Kate and other feminists who were keen to reform family law and the prison system did so through women's organisations, notably the SPWC, the WCTU and the NCW. Drawing on skills and experience they had gained during the suffrage campaign, they wrote articles, petitioned government, spoke at public meetings, gave evidence to royal commissions and participated in delegations to leading politicians. As Barbara Brookes has noted, getting the vote was but 'a first step in a wider feminist agenda'.[4]

In arguing the case for improved social welfare and prison reform, Kate used the language of religion, of natural justice and equal rights, and a new language of scientific evolutionism and evolutionary fitness. She and other Wellington SPWC members also worked closely with several like-minded men who moved in the same progressive liberal circles, had supported the Forward Movement and now occupied positions of power in the Liberal government. As welfare historian Margaret Tennant has observed, 'Voluntary agencies were not opposed to state interference that would further their own moral agenda or advance their own powers.'[5] Self-help and moral restraint were important, but so was legislation that would help to produce stronger, more prosperous families and rehabilitate those who had strayed from virtue's path.

Protecting women and children

Like the WCTU and the NCW, the SPWC, established in Auckland in April 1893, was concerned with maintaining the happiness, sanctity and purity of family life. The movement's founder Henry Wilding was a devout Methodist who emigrated to New Zealand from England in 1878. After trying his hand at various occupations, he eventually became a broker and general agent, with an office on Auckland's Queen Street. Despite having been born and raised in the poverty and degradation of London's East End, Wilding found the material privation and moral malaise of his adopted city saddening and appalling. He initiated the SPWC to help women and children who were abandoned, neglected, abused or made destitute and also assisted them to defend their legal rights in court.[6] Community-minded people from all the Christian denominations, members of the Auckland Jewish congregation and many women interested in helping those less fortunate than themselves, soon began working voluntarily for the cause.

These initiatives were necessary because New Zealand's hospital and charitable aid boards, set up in 1885, could not adequately address the varied practical and moral needs of the most vulnerable sections of society. Charged with providing both health care and charitable relief, these boards were locally controlled and financed by bequests, voluntary contributions, local rates and a pound for pound government subsidy. The poor, many of them elderly, and people who were unable to look after themselves, were cared for within institutions. Deserted wives, widows and the unemployed received 'outdoor relief', that is, relief beyond an institution, frequently in the form of food, coal or help with rent. The relief system was varied and gave much discretion to local board members and to the relieving officers who interviewed people to judge whether they should receive assistance. Many institutional homes for the elderly and helpless were spartan, dirty and reminiscent of workhouses in the old world.[7]

The modus operandi of the boards reflected the mid-Victorian aversion to subsidising a putatively lazy, dependent 'pauper class'. Women and children were the major recipients of outdoor relief, and many women seeking assistance found the process demeaning. Attitudes towards them were often harsh and judgemental. Grace Neill, appointed assistant inspector of hospitals and charitable institutions in 1895, famously decried 'brazen-faced beggars of the female sex'.[8] In his 1897 annual report to Parliament, Dr Duncan MacGregor, the forceful and volubly opinionated inspector of hospitals and charitable institutions, denounced the state subsidy for indiscriminate outdoor relief as an 'incalculable evil' and 'the most effective scheme that could be devised for the systematic cultivation of social parasites'.[9]

When the Wellington SPWC branch was formed, Kate and William Evans were deeply involved with the Forward Movement. Although William, working in the slums of Wellington, strove to ensure that those in need received adequate assistance, like MacGregor he had little sympathy for the morally feckless or undeserving poor. In 1896 he wrote a report criticising the Wellington Charitable Aid Board for not adequately vetting charity recipients, and on a number of other occasions he commended the work of England's Charity Organization Society, founded in 1869 and vehemently opposed to any poor law relief not rigorously scrutinised to weed out loafers and wastrels.[10] Unlike that entity, however, William believed that the state should play an active role in helping the urban poor, notably the respectable working class, whose need of charitable aid was frequently due to factors beyond their control. He wanted the system of aid in New Zealand improved and rationalised, with the goal of creating self-reliant citizens.

In late July 1896 Kate, who shared these views, gave a lecture about charitable aid. To attain its end, charity should 'not demoralise the recipient into pauperism but elevate him and make him as far as possible, an independent, self-supporting citizen of the state'. As for 'the section of the unemployed who would not work – the drunkard, loafer and the professional tramp – the State should take charge of such, and by means of confinement in reformatories do what could be done towards converting them again into useful citizens.'[11] Like other Forward Movement activists, Kate recognised that many people in need of charitable aid were not personally culpable and deserved compassionate support, not further shame or stigma. Although the services and resources required to assist New Zealanders in need simply did not exist, unpaid 'social workers' for the NZSPWC, mostly middle-class women, helped to fill this void.

The members of the SPWC, a voluntary association with vice-regal patronage, worked away quietly in the wings doing good deeds, helping the needy and often, in the process, keeping people from the necessity of receiving charitable aid. Praised in the press for their 'quiet, active kindness' and 'doing good by stealth', these SPWC Samaritans posed no threat to the established order.[12] Yet they initiated new areas of social welfare and promoted and encouraged the implementation of some unprecedented progressive legislation to protect the interests and rights of women and children.

The Wellington branch differed from its Auckland predecessor in being formed and run by women. On 29 September 1897 Wellington members of the WCTU, worried about 'juvenile depravity' – a phenomenon that included male larrikinism and young girls parading in the streets at night – met to discuss how best to stamp it out. At the end of the meeting, Lady Anna Stout 'gave an outline of the system' of the Auckland SPWC.[13] On 20 October church delegates and representatives of various societies met at the Wesley Church Sunday School. Lily Kirk, then WCTU president, was in the chair. The gathering resolved to found a Wellington branch of the SPWC. When the officers were elected on 11 November Kate became president, a position she retained for the first five years. She then stayed on the executive committee, serving as vice-president from 1919 to 1924, and was a vice-patroness (an honorary position) from 1928 until her death.

Each SPWC branch operated independently and possessed a distinct character: Wellington's was notably feminist, maintaining links with national and international women's organisations and advocating equal pay for equal work. Although its operations and executive were exclusively female, influential men figured among its subscribers and trustees. At the time of its first annual report in October 1898, the Wellington branch executive consisted of Kate as president, Annie Williams and Margaret Fell as vice-presidents, and Lady Anna Stout as temporary honorary secretary. William Evans, Edward Tregear, F.H.D. Bell, J.W. Aitken and J.R. Blair were trustees.[14] Tregear, one of the country's most prominent, colourful and controversial intellectuals, was briefly a theosophist and was a long-serving secretary of the Bureau of Industry (later the Department of Labour). John Aitken was a prosperous merchant, Wellington mayor from 1900 to 1905, a devoted Presbyterian and a prohibitionist. Subscribers and supporters included, among others, Chief Justice Sir Robert Stout, Arthur Atkinson and other members of the Richmond–Atkinson clan plus several clerics. Women supporters included the Catholic nun, nurse, teacher and pioneering social worker Mother Mary Joseph Aubert,[15] and progressive-minded female doctors such as Elizabeth Platts-Mills, as well as the wives of leading merchants and politicians, including Mary Anne Kirkcaldie, whose husband John co-founded the Wellington department store Kirkcaldie & Stains, and Josephine Findlay, who was married to John Findlay.

Each of the four SPWC branches, in the main centres, had an unpaid executive, but employed a visitor or secretary to investigate allegations of domestic violence, marital strife, financial struggles or the abuse and neglect of children. The Wellington branch had a room in the Alliance Chambers, in upper Willis Street, with the secretary in attendance from Tuesday to Friday from 10am to 12.30pm. It was usually the secretary who visited homes, but other members of the committee, which generally comprised some nine or 10 women, also did so.[16] They wrote up their findings in case form, after which the society decided how best to address the problem: organising subsequent visits, finding private or institutional accommodation, offering advice and moral guidance, liaising with the police or the local charitable aid board about possible solutions, helping women to find employment, and acquiring clothing and other materials for destitute children from charitable groups and the Salvation Army. The Wellington SPWC took cases to court to obtain maintenance and prohibition orders, and helped to chase up unpaid maintenance. In some cases involving child neglect or abuse they informed the police, and the offenders were subsequently fined or convicted.[17]

The branch's key aims, outlined in 1900, included agitating for more protective legislation for women and children:

1. to prosecute in cases of cruelty outrage or excessive violence to women and children

2. to give advice and aid to women and children who have been cruelly treated

3. to make provision in homes for children when it is found their parents or guardians are unfit to have charge of them

4. to agitate for the improvement of the Statute laws with a view to more effective protection of women and children.[18]

Kate, Lily Atkinson and Anna Stout used tactics employed during the suffrage campaign – letter writing, petitions and appearing before select committees – to push for legislative change. The SPWC's first legislative success, however, had come in 1894, before the birth of the Wellington branch, when, following letter-writing campaigns, the age of sexual consent was raised from 14 to 15, and then to 16 in 1896, under amendments to the Criminal Code Act.

Despite enthusiastic rhetoric about family responsibility and self-help, the SPWC was willing and effective in calling on the state to support its goals, but at times the Wellington branch was censured for calling on government to help protect women and children. At the 1899 annual meeting, when Kate mentioned the possibility of government-funded homes for unwed mothers, Governor Lord Ranfurly, as patron, magisterially dismissed her suggestion, observing that 'New Zealanders were … too much accustomed to look to the State for assistance'. At the same time, the SPWC was often lauded for being a voluntary endeavour, without government funding, one that helped keep many 'out of the category of people who were merely objects of charity'.[19]

In 1898, after its first full year of operation, the Wellington branch summed up its record of work. It had arranged for three illegitimate children to be adopted into comfortable homes and improved the welfare of 17 others. It had dealt with 26 cases of cruelty and neglect by husbands towards their wives, the same number of instances of cruelty and neglect of children, two cases of desertion of wife and family, and 38 other situations requiring advice and support. The secretary had written 151 letters and received 133. SPWC members had made some 148 home visits.[20] The *New Zealand Times*, reporting on the first annual meeting in 1899, quoted Kate's comment that 'There was plenty of work for sympathetic hearts and willing hands.' In addition to the executive, the paper named the nine women on the committee and mentioned several 'honorary solicitors'.[21] By 1900 the Wellington branch's caseload had increased to 188, from 109 in its founding year.[22]

The work of the Wellington SPWC bore witness to the legal vulnerability of women and children over many decades. Although by the early 1900s New Zealand was enjoying unprecedented prosperity, men who abused or neglected their wives and children were still often impossible to trace; many wives were too worn down or concerned about 'respectability' to leave abusive relationships.[23] Young women who had been raped usually felt ashamed and told no one. Deserted wives forced into the workplace often left their babies and small children with unlicensed, negligent or cruel minders. In one case recorded by the branch, a wife, made to do labouring on a farm in addition to raising her family, had sunk to such a nervous state through ill-treatment by her husband that she asked him to shoot her to put her out of her misery. Another case, reminiscent of a Victorian melodrama, involved a father who tried to incarcerate his daughter in a mental institution with the aim of acquiring her inheritance.[24] Drink often played a large role in familial problems, fuelling the push for prohibition.

But the accounts of the cases also make for uplifting reading, as solutions and assistance were found for women and children in need. In a precursor to modern social work, each SPWC branch kept systematic files, followed up on visits and became involved in constructive counselling, domestic support and legal assistance. Counselling and moral guidance often worked in a way that mere monetary or material aid could not. As Kate emphasised in 1903, 'The society recognised that moral suasion was better than legal compulsion, and as far as possible acted on that principle.'[25]

Punishing incest

Incest was one particularly sensitive area where Kate and the Wellington SPWC played a key role in raising public awareness. In 1897 Sir Robert Stout introduced a bill that would have made incest punishable under an amendment to the Criminal Code Act, but the Legislative Council rejected it. Undeterred, the Wellington SPWC resolved that Kate should interview Seddon about introducing legislation to criminalise incest. After she did so in late September 1899, Kate could report that he 'expressed sympathy and was greatly shocked by the state of affairs disclosed. [He] remarked that it [the proposed legislation] was publishing our own dishonour but certainly it ought to be done if such a step was likely to diminish the evil.'[26]

In 1900 when the bill was again introduced in the House, many MPs expressed disgusted disbelief that incest existed, apparently unable to accept that something so reprehensible could happen in New Zealand. The SPWC was able to counter this response with written evidence from doctors, ministers, police inspectors and officers of charitable institutions documenting 50 cases of proven incest. Other MPs took the line that this legislation would harm New Zealand's reputation overseas by making people think badly of the country. One MP, Thomas Kelly, stated: 'I do not know the reason why all these sex Bills are brought in; I do not know whether it is in consequence of "hysterical women", or some so-called purity society, or whether it is simply a softening of the brain.'[27]

Despite such resistance, the bill became law on 9 October 1900 in the form of the Criminal Code Amendment Act. From that time, every male or female over the age of 16 who committed incest would be punished by 10 years' imprisonment with hard labour. This legislation passed almost entirely because of the SPWC's intervention, particularly the solid evidence it had provided from a range of reputable sources.

Protecting young people

Less successfully, Kate was directly involved in promoting the Young Persons' Protection Bill of 1899. This was the result of strong moral concern about 'larrikins' roaming city streets at night, and young women falling prey to, or themselves becoming, sexual predators. The word then was more the equivalent of the modern lout: a larrikin could be responsible for anything from spirited high jinks to sexual and other crimes. Larrikins were regarded as symptomatic of society's decay and parents' failure to be responsible for their families. There was also the problem of unwed girls becoming 'fallen women' as a result of pregnancies. The word rape was never used but was implicit in many of the calls by groups like the SPWC for more control over unruly youths.

As president of the Wellington branch of the SPWC, Kate was invited to a select committee of the Legislative Council in September 1899 to answer questions about the bill. It called for the appointment of protection officers who would watch for youths – 16 and under, male and female – who were loitering unsupervised after 9pm. Initially, young offenders would be reported to their parents; repeat offenders could be taken to a shelter and eventually put before a magistrate. Negligent parents could be liable to penalties and even imprisonment. The aim of the proposed measures was preventive, an attempt to ensure that young people took a safe and morally sound road through life.

Kate spent most of her appearance before the committee explaining the nature of the SPWC's activities. She hoped that the legislation would 'have a very good effect in preventing the immorality which is so prevalent in our large towns. I do not think it would stop it altogether … I think there are other causes which lead to immorality; but still, the custom of young people of both sexes parading the streets at night very frequently leads to immorality.' She was 'not prepared to say', when asked, if the Contagious Diseases Act would do a better job of clearing the streets. This apparent missed opportunity seems hard to comprehend, given Kate's strong antipathy towards the iniquitous Contagious Diseases Act and the different aims of the legislation under consideration. When asked if the efforts of the Wellington SPWC in reclaiming these young people had been successful, she admitted that she could 'hardly point to a single case where the reformation has been lasting'.[28]

Although the Young Persons Protection Bill did not make it into law, it engendered a huge amount of often acrimonious discussion, and revisions, in both the upper and lower houses from 1899 to 1902. One MP, faced with yet another version of the bill in 1901, referred to it wryly as his 'old friend'.[29] The politicians' debates throw light on contemporary attitudes, especially regarding women and their perceived role. Those who supported the legislation greeted it as a welcome measure to protect vulnerable young people and accepted that both men and women would serve as protection officers. Opponents felt the measures painted New Zealand in an unflattering light, as a 'morally tainted' place, and objected to the involvement of women in a form of policing. As one MP observed, 'I do not believe in policemen in petticoats. I do not think the power the policeman has under this Bill should be given to women, nor should it be proposed in any measure to give such power to them. We admire and reverence women because they are women. When they put on the breeches we change our opinion.'[30]

Others shared this view, expressing distaste for 'mischievous meddlers … poking their nose into other people's business' and 'petticoated termagants who seem anxious to jostle with the midnight rabble … It is a man's duty which they want to take upon themselves.' The 'temperance people' and 'those who advocate moral purity and the elevation of the people to the higher grades of intelligence' also came in for derision.[31] Defenders of the bill argued that 'good motherly women would have greater influence dealing with young girls than would any man who might have to carry out the work'.[32]

Not long after Kate appeared before the select committee, the Wellington correspondent for the *Hawke's Bay Herald* railed against this 'utterly idiotic' proposed measure. The bill was a step too far by 'old women of both sexes'; it existed only because of 'the idiosyncrasies of antique virgins and vinegary mothers who are unable to rule their own households'. The writer concluded by hoping that the 'natural good sense of the people will prevent New Zealand ever again being delivered over to the faddists, busy-bodies, notoriety-hunters, and the vicious who pose as virtuous because they have never been found out'.[33] Seddon effectively kicked the bill into touch in 1903. After being asked if he had plans to reintroduce legislation along similar lines in the next session he observed that 'far more could be done by the establishment of truant schools under the School Attendance Act'.[34]

Prison reform: The new penology

The SPWC did achieve a significant legislative goal in 1906 with the Juvenile Offenders Act, which aimed to protect young people and prevent them from becoming hardened criminals. In the late 1890s, alongside her SPWC involvement, Kate began advocating for prison reform.

Protestant nonconformists in Britain had a long tradition in this area. Britain's John Howard and Elizabeth Fry, a Congregationalist and a Quaker respectively, had campaigned for a more humane and compassionate prison system and in the process earned fame and public respect. Throughout his life, Samuel Edger keenly kept up with the latest progressive ideas about the treatment of criminals. In the early 1870s, he supported his friend Mary Ann Colclough when she wrote to Auckland's *Daily Southern Cross* about the 'quite disgraceful' conditions faced by women prisoners in Mount Eden Gaol: 'Old and young, hardened past all shame and quite new to that hot-bed of vice, sent there to have every good impulse laughed out of them – all are herded together.' Colclough also initiated schemes to find employment for women recently released from prison.[35] In 1873 Samuel began crusading against capital punishment, spurred by a controversial case involving Joseph Eppright, who was charged with murder after stabbing another seaman during a drunken brawl in Russell. A petition with over 700 signatures pleading that the sentence be commuted fell on deaf ears, and Eppright was hanged on 29 July. In an ensuing pamphlet entitled *The Folly and Evil of Hanging Men*, Samuel argued that hanging was effectively another murder and provided no deterrent. There was always a chance for criminals' reformation and redemption. With 'wise and judicious treatment', they could become useful citizens.[36]

In the 1880s Inspector of Prisons Arthur Hume had introduced significant reforms making New Zealand gaols more uniform, efficient and economical. But his policies emphasised control and surveillance rather than reformation and rehabilitation, and even on the former front fell short. Escapes were common and each institution still followed its own sets of rules and procedures to a considerable degree. The mentally ill and drunks often ended up in prison, largely because the services needed to deal with them did not exist. Probation, introduced in 1886 for first offenders only, was rarely used. Moreover, crime rates rose disturbingly from the late 1890s. Wounding and homicide rates in the 'Better Britain' between 1909 and 1913 were worse than in England.[37]

Hume's penal policies increasingly came up against criticisms from individuals and groups advocating 'the new penology'. This trend in prison reform entailed a different focus – on the criminal, criminal psychology, criminal typology, the rehabilitation of the offender and the individualisation of punishment – and a more interventionist role for the state. Criminals were 'sick' and needed restoration to health and normality. Kate shared her father's commitment to rehabilitating prisoners but argued for this end using a new language of 'illness' and 'cure'.

In a paper entitled 'The Treatment of the Criminal', presented to the 1898 NCW Conference, Kate outlined some recent trends in prison reform and advocated a reappraisal of the issue. She commended John Howard and other early reformers, who had pushed for more humane treatment of prisoners. Their emphasis, however, was on the external conditions of prisons, whereas over the last 25 years a new approach towards 'criminal anthropology' and improved prison systems had emerged: 'The work of reform has been carried on along two distinct lines, which yet bear a close relation to each other – namely criminal anthropology, or the study of the criminal from a physiological and psychological standpoint, and the treatment of the criminal according to improved systems, such as that of Elmira.'[38] Along with the United States, Italy was now the standard-bearer of progressive penal reform. It was the home of criminal anthropology, promoted particularly in the work of criminologist and physician Cesare Lombroso.[39] The famous Elmira Reformatory in the state of New York, which Samuel had commended in the early 1880s, was the model for improved systems. These two components – criminal anthropology and progressive reformative systems of incarceration such as practised at Elmira – were key aspects of the new penology, which stressed the reform of individual prisoners through understanding their personal psychology. As in medical settings, the emphasis was on monitoring the condition of the patient/criminal. The new penology differentiated prisoners by their behaviour and character. Imprisonment would no longer aim to produce a regimented body of obedient inmates but would seek to address and resolve the particular non-chronic problems that had led each individual convict into crime.

This emphasis on the individual, and his or her moral redemption, had particular resonance with Protestant nonconformists. It mirrored their perception that conscience was paramount, and that each Christian had a direct, unmediated relationship with God. As Kate argued, 'The first necessity is that we cease to regard the crime as all important and instead think of the criminal; study the disposition of and character of each individual, and bring such influences to bear on him as are best calculated to eradicate the evil tendencies faster and develop the good.' The system needed to be elastic enough that 'we shall be able to apply to each case its appropriate treatment. The first reform necessary is the total abolition of the definite and predetermined sentence.'

In contrast to a definite sentence for a prescribed period of time, an indeterminate sentence meant that the length of incarceration depended upon a prisoner's conduct. This could result in a short stint or a lifelong stay. Indeterminate sentences allowed prisoners to be released when they were again found to be 'normal' and no longer criminally inclined; that is, when it was deemed their personality had changed. Prisoners would be treated for what was described as an illness, and only released upon cure. 'Should prisons be abolished?' Kate asked. 'No, say the best authorities; for they are an institution too deeply rooted in modern civilisation to be suddenly overturned. But with the light that has been thrown on the subject by criminal anthropology, it is possible to transform them from nurseries of crime to reformatories of the criminal.'

Morality and moral choice remained vital and Kate described the Elmira Reformatory in admiring detail: 'the school classes, the lectures and discussions conducted by the best professors attainable, the library, the weekly paper, and all the similar means whereby the prisoners are brought into contact with all that is likely to exert a refining and humanising influence. The whole educational department is based on moral tendency, its object being to unfold the moral faculties together with the mind.' Physical training also received attention and care was taken with the prisoners' diet. The statistics to September 1889 showed that 83 percent of the men who had passed through Elmira did not reoffend and were deemed permanently reformed.[40]

The paper was imbued with Kate's deep Christian faith. She spoke of 'the leavening influence of Christianity' through which 'we realize more than ever before the sacredness of human life' and 'recognise every human being as a child of the Divine Father, with practically unlimited capacity for development and culture'.[41] Other speakers also emphasised Christian redemption. Annie Hutchinson of the

Salvation Army, for example, after speaking feelingly of the degrading influence of the cell system and of flogging, observed that prison surroundings 'should be bright, beautiful and healthy, to help elevate them [criminals] to the position God intended they should occupy'. After further discussion, Ada Wells successfully moved that the object of incarceration be the reformation of criminals rather than their punishment.

There was a sense in this discussion, as Kate had noted, that the intense individualism of former times was giving way to more demands on the state to help ameliorate 'the conditions of life for all classes of society, and particularly the poorest and most degraded'.[42] This focus on individual needs, on collective Christian and social responsibility and on enhanced calls for state involvement in social welfare, was prominent among women's groups and others concerned with progressive social reform. Laissez-faire individualism now seemed inadequate; the state needed to step in to help achieve the desired 'common good'. The NCW passed the motion that the duration of all sentences be decided by the reform of the criminal and limited by the maximum penalty attached to the crime. It also voted, by 12 to four, to support the abolition of capital punishment.[43]

The NCW, the WCTU and the SPWC were all deeply committed to a more compassionate redemptive approach to criminal justice. The WCTU, for example, set up 'prison-gate missions' to help those newly released from prison, particularly women, rebuild their lives. There were, of course, male advocates of prison reform, many of them devout Christians, but women played a particularly prominent role in pushing the cause. Elizabeth Fry, who by the mid-nineteenth century was a celebrated figure in Britain and the colonies, had exhorted women not to 'forsake their province', but to use their 'gentleness, their natural sympathy with the afflicted' and 'their openness to religious impulses' to engage outside the 'domestic and social relations' with 'a far more extensive field of usefulness'.[44]

From the late 1890s, resolutions supporting the new penology were regularly passed at NCW conferences. Male and female members of various Christian denominations endorsed these views, as did secular progressive liberals like Robert Stout, who were drawn to progressive scientific explanations to solve society's various problems. Like Kate, other advocates of the new penology used the language of moral illness and social health. In 1897 Fabian socialist Eveline Cunnington argued: 'We must have cumulative or indeterminate sentences. A short period of detention for long-standing moral disease is simply worse than useless.'[45] She endorsed policies to educate and reform prisoners and also lamented that 'From the moment a woman commits a crime, she passes into the hands of men', advocating instead the appointment of female prison inspectors, police, doctors, jurors and government officials.[46] Women would bring to these jobs special skills and sensitivity, and also be more likely to be confided in regarding sexual matters.

In her SPWC work Kate strove ceaselessly to get more women into positions within the justice system, most notably the police force, but progress proved elusive. In 1913 and again in 1916 she was among SPWC delegations attempting to persuade politicians about the advantages of female police officers. At the end of October 1916 she expressed how 'greatly disappointed' and 'aggrieved' the SPWC was by government inaction, noting that female police officers were employed in the United States and in Europe with 'signal success' and that 'nothing should be left untried' that might help to protect boys and girls.[47] Despite repeated appeals for female police from the SPWC, the WCTU and the NCW, it was not until 1941 that between 24 and 30 unmarried women who could use a typewriter were allowed into the police force; women were not officially received into the force on an equal basis, and their appointments gazetted in the *Police Gazette*, until 1952.[48]

A small number of Liberals on the left wing of the party, who supported the new penology, gradually built up a platform of support for it in the House. In 1905 Thomas Kay Sidey, MP for the Dunedin seat of Caversham, introduced a bill that advocated indeterminate sentences for habitual criminals. These individuals would perform labour in reformatories, which could be separate or part of regular prisons. That bill, deemed insufficiently punitive, did not pass. In 1906, however, a revised version became law as the Habitual Criminals Act. Although it did not introduce indeterminate sentences, it went a certain distance in that direction, for deterrent rather than rehabilitative reasons. Designed to deal with those who had opted for a life of crime, indeterminate sentencing was argued for as a measure offering greater protection to society. In fact, it was very little used, perhaps because the number of offenders who fitted the habitual category was relatively small.[49]

Those campaigning for more rehabilitative and nuanced penal reform now shifted focus, directing initiatives at peripheral segments of the criminal population, notably prostitutes, juvenile offenders and drunks. Without addressing the reformative needs of each of these groups, they argued, the prison system would remain inefficient and ineffective.

Creating children's courts

The SPWC had long campaigned for juvenile offenders to be dealt with in a separate court, a cause in which Kate was centrally involved. In 1903 the SPWC urged that all offences involving children be heard in camera, with judges and magistrates able to clear the court at their discretion. The society believed that when neglected or criminal children were taken to trial or made to mix with hardened criminals the impact was always negative and dire. They aimed to make the system more humane and decrease the chance of young offenders opting for a life of crime. In August 1904 the *White Ribbon* reported a meeting of various women's groups and religious organisations, including the Canterbury Women's Institute, the Anglican Prison Gate Mission and the Salvation Army, and several MPs, which called for a separate children's court and affirmed that indeterminate sentences should be introduced into the colony's penal system.[50]

In 1906 Frederick Baume, MP for Auckland East and a vice-president of the Auckland SPWC, introduced the Juvenile Offenders Bill into Parliament. After speeches illustrating the impact of the success of children's courts in other countries, the legislation passed with relative ease. The act created separate courts for young offenders, a move very much in line with the new penology. In debating this legislation, Minister of Justice James McGowan described it as the result of 'requests that have been made by the societies for the protection of women and children' and went on to boast that 'we lead the Mother Country in this as in other matters'.[51]

The approach in the juvenile courts was to be more that of an investigative tribunal than an adversarial contest. Magistrates were not obliged to enter a conviction even if they considered the case proved, and in no case were offenders required to remain in a jail or a lock-up pending the hearing. In 1906 Arthur Atkinson congratulated the SPWC on the establishment of the children's courts, a measure it had 'long advocated'.[52]

Influential champions

The Habitual Drunkards Act of 1906 stipulated that a person had to be convicted of drunkenness three times within a nine-month period before being detained in a reformatory institution for treatment. Two years later the Inebriates Institution Act provided for state-funded homes, as opposed to relying on privately funded ones. Prisons were becoming less and less the dumping grounds for members of society with alcohol or mental health problems. George Fowlds, a leading Congregationalist and minister of education and of public health from 1906, advocated reforms that resulted in increasingly specialised functions in the field of health and social welfare; his friend John Findlay, the man who became justice minister in 1909, shared this view.

With Findlay's appointment, the new penology made real strides. A former legal partner of Robert Stout, Findlay moved in the same progressive liberal circles as Kate and William Evans, and like Fowlds, had contributed articles to *The Citizen*. By the early 1900s, Findlay, a cultured erudite man with strong humanitarian principles, had become a powerful figure in the Liberal government, and remained so after Seddon's death in June 1906. He served as both attorney general and leader of the Legislative Council from 1906 to 1911, a period when the upper house played an active role, not just amending and revising measures but initiating 17 important bills.[53] Findlay pushed for more individualised prison sentences to fit the character and previous history of the offender, more indeterminate sentences, more specialised reformative institutions and a generally more proactive state involvement in crime and reformation.[54]

He introduced various pieces of legislation that put these key objectives into practice. In 1909 the Reformatory Institutions Act moved towards tailoring punishment to suit offenders; prostitutes could be ordered to live in a reformatory for up to one year. Because these offenders were perceived as sick or defective, the state, in attempting to normalise them, would now provide more assistance and a different and more extensive mode of regulation. Under the 1909 Industrial Schools Amendment Act, inmates in reformatories could be detained beyond the age of 21 if they remained, in the minister's view, unreformed and a threat to the public interest. In parliamentary debates on this proposed legislation, Findlay argued against those who saw the proposed changes as restricting individual rights and liberty. Instead he used a familial analogy: 'the State has a higher duty to perform than merely play the part of policeman and seeing that liberty of the subject is protected. It has to become an intelligent parent, and especially the intelligent parent to which this Bill applies.'[55]

The new penology's ability to link the moral reformation, or cure, of individual criminals with the health of society was one of its major appeals. It extended the state's role but did so with the redemption of the individual criminal foremost in mind. In order to best achieve this goal, the penal system became more specialised. Findlay's Scheme for the Reorganisation of the New Zealand Prison System, introduced in 1910, set out various strategies for reform, which now extended to include the whole criminal community and the entire system of penal institutions.[56] It stipulated that criminals should be classified according to type and matched to an institution appropriate to their offending. There would now be prisons for 'hardened' criminals, for sexual predators and 'criminal lunatics', agricultural and industrial reformatories for men and for women, a women's prison, prison camps and homes for 'incorrigible drunks'.

This scheme found legislative form in the Crimes Act Amendment Act of 1910, which introduced reformative detention by extending the indeterminate sentence until the prisoner was deemed to have reformed. Judges' sentencing powers were no longer definitive; now a Prisons Board 'of not less than three nor more than seven persons', only one of whom was a judge, decided the extent of reformatory treatment required and when prisoners could be released.[57] The probation service expanded and prison officers became more professional and accountable. Findlay's language and arguments in promoting the bill mirrored Kate's 1898 paper. He, too, lauded Elmira and cast the new penology as an evolutionary step away from primitive 'eye for an eye' justice towards enlightened, curative reformation.[58]

The contemporary press widely endorsed Findlay's reforms. The *New Zealand Times* in March 1910 commented enthusiastically: 'Humanity will be studied as much as justice by deflecting the anti-social instinct away from crime to good citizenship.' In August the *Evening Post* observed that the changes would 'bring the reform of our prisons up to the highest point that the science of penology has yet reached, and … undertake for the first time the reformation of our prisoners in a thorough and scientific fashion'.[59]

One strong appeal of the new penology was the way it incorporated religious ideas about individual morality and redemption with the language of scientific analysis and progressive social evolutionism. Reforming Liberals like Findlay, and indeed the broader New Zealand public, took pride in this latest example of New Zealand's progressive legislation. As often happens with prison reform, the reality ultimately fell short of the aspirations, but the initial optimism about the potential to enhance the good of society was remarkable. There would now, Findlay proudly assured the House in 1910, be 'less likelihood of releasing a prisoner unreformed under the indeterminate method than any other system that can be devised by man'.[60]

Social work pioneers

Kate began her voluntary social work in the late 1890s when the Forward Movement was still in full swing. Her SPWC involvement was fundamentally concerned with safeguarding the family. The founding executive of the Wellington branch believed that women were most suited to effectively undertake this sort of social assistance. They became social-work pioneers, liaising with politicians, select committees, prison inspectors, police and the press, and helping to push through some enlightened welfare initiatives. Kate and other advocates also helped to implement a more rehabilitative and specialised prison system.

Both Kate Sheppard and Kate Evans cited humanitarian legislation that assisted women and children as one of the most important outcomes of achieving women's suffrage. They believed that women voters and women's influence had resulted in 'a perceptible rise in the moral and humanitarian tone of the community'.[61] The SPWC had played a significant role in making the lives of contemporary women and children happier and more hopeful. If at times the tone of moral righteousness it employed seems puritanical or intrusive to modern ears, this should be balanced by an appreciation of the compassion that motivated its members at a time when there was little social welfare support and when most sexual crimes against women and children were unacknowledged or ignored.

Voluntary associations such as the SPWC also helped to lay the groundwork for social work in New Zealand. By the 1920s this area had become much more professionalised and responsibility for it had shifted largely to the public sector, a trend underlined by the creation of the Child Welfare Branch of the Department of Education in 1926.[62] Child welfare, in the words of historian Bronwyn Dalley, 'incorporated particular types of welfare that had little to do with the various benefits and pensions which characterised other areas of the welfare state, and which have largely dominated welfare history in this country'. Instead it was predicated on 'casework and investigation, inquiry and observation, supervision and non-monetary assistance'.[63] This was exactly the kind of complex and challenging work that the SPWC engaged in for decades.

8

Compulsory Domesticity

[O]ur social evolution is progressing on incorrect lines and diverging further and further from the home life which tends to the rearing of a healthy population.

DR FERDINAND CAMPION BATCHELOR, 1909[1]

What can be better for the life of the nation than to direct into channels of usefulness the strong forces of mind, the stronger forces of will and devotion that rise in a woman's soul?

KATE EVANS, 1914[2]

From 1917 all New Zealand girls holding junior free places at post-primary schools were to be instructed in home science for not less than three hours a week.[3] This compulsory curriculum change generated heated debate. Some women saw it as a beneficial move that would improve family life; others rejected it as an unfair imposition that might disadvantage females when competing academically with males. The normally united triumvirate of Kate Evans, Lily Atkinson and Anna Stout parted ways over the issue.

Kate supported the curriculum change. Rather than posing a threat to women's established right to an equal education, she saw it as a progressive measure that could improve family well-being and, in the process, help to alleviate the problems she witnessed through her social work for the SPWC. Her ideal education always involved not just academic rigour and success in examinations, but also the cultivation of a balanced character. Her support for an element of compulsory domestic education for girls reflected her Christian belief that men and women had particular different but complementary familial roles to play. But unlike many leading figures of the time, she did not endorse the view that women's higher education posed a threat either to their individual physical and emotional well-being, or to national efficiency.

To help the mothers and save the babies

In the early years of the twentieth century, scientific household management and parenting gained enthusiastic followers throughout New Zealand. Fostering and improving mothering skills and child health would benefit not just individual families but also nation and empire. The origins of this heightened emphasis on happy homes and efficient mothers lay in a range of contemporary concerns and anxieties. In 1900, 60 percent of British volunteers for the South African War proved unfit for military service, a statistic that seemingly confirmed contemporary theories about racial degeneration due to urban industrialism. Concern mounted that Britain and her empire were losing the neo-Darwinian race between nations. Falling birth rates in both the mother country and her colonies made a worrying contrast to burgeoning populations in the east.[4] Fears of a 'yellow peril', which could see populous Eastern nations overtaking and even potentially subjugating Western nations, gained momentum. In the United States, Canada, Australia and New Zealand such fears were exacerbated in the late nineteenth century by the advent of Chinese workers.

In New Zealand, the child-bearing rate among women aged 15–45 more than halved between 1881 and 1926 and remained low until the late 1940s, for a variety of reasons that remain difficult to ascertain accurately. There was a perception that middle-class people were restricting their family size and that this practice would adversely affect the strength of nation and empire.[5] Rapid urbanisation and new technologies were transforming New Zealand's predominantly rural society into something more complex, multi-layered and disturbingly unfamiliar. In the early 1900s young women flocked to work in towns and cities as typists, secretaries, factory workers, waitresses, cooks, housemaids, clerks, shop assistants and telephone operators, and women also entered the professions, most notably as teachers and nurses. Although most women gave up salaried work when they married, their status as independent wage-earners, however short-lived, combined with the competition they presented to male breadwinners, caused unease among some sectors of the populace. In 1910, for example, an editorial in *New Zealand Truth* entitled 'Women, Work, and Wages' complained that women's 'intrusion into the industrial world' tended to:

> keep wages low, crowd men out of employment, shrivel what chivalry is left in men, cheapen themselves, and diminish the operations of the marriage market. As a set-off they can claim a certain degree of artificial independence, and capacity

Dr Frederic Truby King,
founder of the Plunket
Society, c. 1913.

Alexander Turnbull Library,
Wellington,
PAColl-3861-31-01

to boast equality with man. They forget that meanwhile, they are exhausting their
youth and their charms, and that, when they fail, even the despised haven of
matrimony will be difficult of access.[6]

In 1904, to help counter the country's disturbing downward trend in births and
to reduce infant mortality, the government introduced state responsibility for the
training and registering of midwives and agreed to the establishment of St Helen's
Maternity Hospitals. The first opened in the Wellington suburb of Newtown in
May 1905, and eventually there were seven throughout New Zealand. But it was a
voluntary association, the Society for the Promotion of the Health of Women and
Children, founded in Dunedin in 1907 by Dr Frederic Truby King, that quickly
became the most influential force in helping to decrease infant mortality while
simultaneously elevating mothers' status. The call to 'help the mothers and save the
babies' was strengthened by a desire to augment national and imperial strength.
Combining modern scientific principles of childcare and reverential respect for
motherhood as women's highest and 'natural' calling, King's organisation immediately attracted enthusiastic support. By 1912, 70 branches had been established

Lady Victoria Alexandrina Plunket, vice-regal patron of the Plunket Society and devoted mother of eight, 1905.

Alexander Turnbull Library, Wellington, 1/1-014571-G

throughout the country.[7] It was eventually renamed the Plunket Society in honour of its early patron, Lady Victoria Plunket, wife of New Zealand's fourteenth governor, who was both its great advocate and a mother of eight.

During 1907 the Wellington SPWC, after listening to a 'lucid speech' by King, passed a motion that 'the Wellington Society for the Protection of Women and Children … take up work along the lines he has indicated for the promotion of the health of women and children'.[8] Following a meeting with Lady Plunket in March 1908, the members decided to set up a Plunket branch in the capital. It would be under the auspices of the SPWC but have a separate executive and name. The move was necessary because, as Lady Plunket explained, Plunket nurses did specialised and unique work: 'The district nurses mitigated the sufferings of the sick, the Society for the Protection fought the battle of wrongs done, the Government inspectors visited licensed homes and institutions, but it was not the business of any of these societies to educate mothers, or prospective mothers on their own health or that of their babies.' Anna Stout and Lily Atkinson were on the executive of Wellington's new Plunket branch, along with several other Wellington SPWC members such as Dr Elizabeth Platts-Mills and Mother Mary Aubert.[9]

Kate and her fellow members of the Wellington SPWC endorsed King's methods and goals, indicating that prominent feminists clearly had no qualms about an organisation that so revered the traditional maternal role. Indeed, when Anna Stout visited England in 1909, she gave talks in which she cited the existence and popularity of the Plunket Society as proof of the beneficial impact of women's suffrage in New Zealand. Voting rights had not, she hastened to assure her audiences, caused women to behave in a more masculine manner or to neglect their homes.[10]

Home science and the curriculum

The heightened prominence of improving family life and valuing motherhood influenced ideas about the school curriculum for girls. Increasingly, there was a call, not just from King but also from the government, to place more emphasis on teaching girls to be better mothers and homemakers. Kate, Anna Stout and Lily Atkinson agreed that improving and extending the teaching of domestic science was beneficial. In their SPWC work they encountered many families adversely affected by lack of knowledge about health and welfare and an inability to budget effectively. Domestic science, a new weapon in the armoury of progressive reform, would aid the cause of those battling for happy families. In countries such as the

Young women in a domestic science class, c. 1880s–1920s,

Alexander Turnbull Library, Wellington, 1/1-017752-G

United States and Britain it was a popular subject, endorsed by those on both the left and right of the political spectrum. Kate hoped to see domestic science flourish in New Zealand but did not see its promotion as an either/or proposition, replacing or restricting women's rights to attain academic education qualifications on equal terms with men.

By contrast, several prominent male Plunket supporters, a number of them doctors, viewed the physical and mental legacy of higher education for girls and women in a negative light. In 1909 at the annual meeting of the Society for the Promotion of the Health of Women and Children, Dr Ferdinand Batchelor lamented that education was pushing the 'first and main object of life' for girls – that is, being wives and mothers – into the background and making it 'a secondary consideration'. New Zealand's current education system encouraged a young woman to enter 'a course of study for which Nature had never intended her' and which weakened her physically and emotionally. In the course of a 20-year medical practice, Batchelor claimed he had daily evidence of higher education's debilitating impact: 'When we see them [women] entering professions, eager to obtain clerkships, office work

Kate Evans, c. 1910.

Jill Smith Collection

and typing, and when the work in our factories is largely conducted by female labour, one cannot but realise that our social evolution is progressing on incorrect lines and diverging further and further from the home life which tends to the rearing of a healthy population.' King agreed that educating women for the learned professions was an 'absolutely indefensible thing'. Giving girls and boys identical education was 'a preposterous farce'.[11]

Such opinions evoked some spirited critical responses from, among others, Emily Siedeberg, the first woman to qualify from Otago Medical School in 1896 and the first New Zealand female medical practitioner, and Dr Agnes Bennett, who became the first medical officer of St Helen's Hospital in the capital. The latter wrote an indignant 'rejoinder' in the *Dominion*:

> Who will arrogate to themselves the right to say what Nature did intend women, or men, for? … Is woman to stifle the inborn yearnings of her intellect that she may be no more than a healthy animal to minister to and apparently compensate for the impaired vitality of the man? Can true progress possibly consist of a man of highly-cultured intellect pacing side by side with a woman who is no more than an intelligent vegetable?[12]

Yet neither Siedeberg nor Bennett questioned that women's natural environment was the home and family, and both supported more training for women in the domestic arts.[13]

The WCTU, with its motto 'For God, Home and Humanity', had always valued traditional domestic roles. At its 1911 convention, members 'heartily endorsed' proposals by the Christchurch branch for 'more thorough training in Domestic Economy' for all the girls in the dominion.[14] Some of the support arose because the WCTU's predominantly middle-class membership wanted to augment the supply of domestic servants. In 1912 Miss M.B. Lovell-Smith, superintendent of the WCTU's Legal and Parliamentary Department, sent a report to the Cohen Commission, which was assessing the rights and powers of New Zealand's various education authorities, noting that decreasing the amount of time girls spent studying mathematics and increasing their domestic instruction could help to solve 'the domestic help difficulty'.[15] Kate did not adopt this argument, emphasising instead the benefits improved domestic science instruction might have for family life.

Progressive panacea

As with prohibition, the reform-minded middle-class women of the Wellington SPWC seemed to view improved instruction in the domestic arts as an almost magical cure-all, conjuring up visions of well-cooked meals in happy, comfortable homes. Many familial problems were linked to the inability of struggling working-class wives and mothers to satisfy their husband's expectations. In 1910 Dr Elizabeth Platts-Mills, addressing the Wellington SPWC annual meeting, congratulated the members on their work, yet deplored 'the necessity for the existence of such a society in a country so young and vigorous'. Lack of basic domestic skills could potentially lead to serious marital problems:

> Now, I believe that the trouble at home usually begins when the husband finds that his wife can neither cook nor make a home. It is a humiliating fact that our emotions depend to a great extent upon our digestions. To a very much greater extent is this the case when the emotions are untrained, uncontrolled, so that a badly cooked dinner means a fit of ill-temper on the part of the husband. It does not require a vivid imagination to picture the constantly recurring annoyances on both sides originating in this cause alone, and when at last matters become so complex that nothing remains but separation, what happens? The wife, in the ordinary course of events, expects to be kept by her husband. Failing this, she must either go out into the world as an unskilled labourer to work for herself, or the law must interfere and force from the man a reluctant maintenance.

Platts-Mills urged parents to first teach their daughters to work and make a home, and second to give them a means of earning a livelihood if necessary: 'By so doing you at once protect her from the most of the humiliations that women are called upon to suffer. You give her an independent, an unassailable, position in the world.'[16]

The creation in 1909 of a chair in home science and domestic arts at Otago University, endowed by Colonel John Studholme and supported by King and Batchelor among others, helped to raise the subject's academic status. Winifred Boys-Smith, the woman chosen to be inaugural professor, New Zealand's first, was a crusader in the cause of female higher education. Perceiving domestic science as a potential 'great force', she aimed to lift the status of domestic arts through a strong education grounded in science and augmented by technical instruction. In 1906–07, while working as a science lecturer in the training department at Cheltenham Ladies' College in England, she had spent four months studying the teaching of 'Home Science' in America, where it was a well-regarded and well-established subject in schools and colleges. She emphasised science, most notably chemistry, as part of the

Otago programme, and from 1911 had the able assistance of Helen Rawson, who lectured in chemistry, applied chemistry and social and household economics.[17]

The new department, which offered a three-year Bachelor of Science degree and a diploma course, was an unprecedented development: a tertiary course of study with female lecturers and students, most of whom would go on to teach domestic science at secondary school. That a university programme recognised and taught elements of traditional 'women's work' was notable in itself. The Education Department played its part by providing bursaries for future home science teachers and, from the early 1900s, offering subsidies to secondary schools to encourage the teaching of such subjects as cooking and dressmaking.[18]

Home science also featured prominently in technical education, a cause Kate and William Evans both supported. Their friend George Hogben, who became the country's first director of education in 1915, aimed to lessen the academic and privileged bias of secondary school education and provide more practical instruction, relevant to most pupils' environment and employment expectations. He actively promoted the establishment of manual training schools and colleges, under the Manual and Technical Education Acts of 1895, 1900 and 1902. There was, of course, gender differentiation in the curriculum: training courses in domestic skills for girls and subjects such as woodworking for boys. Girls, however, proved more interested in commercial than domestic courses: in 1915 only 16.7 percent took the domestic course.[19] To some, this was cause for concern. When giving evidence to an Inquiry into the Cost of Living in New Zealand, which reported in 1912, the respective directors of the Auckland and Christchurch Technical Schools argued for compulsory domestic training for girls on the grounds that it would benefit family life. The commission's final report agreed and urged the implementation of 'a proper system of training in domestic economy'.[20] As well as making home life more comfortable and efficient, this would reduce the cost of living.

In 1913 Kate Evans and other members of the Wellington SPWC asked the Wellington Education Board to hold a conference in the capital to discuss the possibility of establishing a chair in domestic science at Victoria College and how best to establish a 'thorough system of domestic science instruction'. Numerous prominent education officials, principals, college governors, teachers and Education Board members attended the 25 June gathering.[21] Hogben spoke first, assuring listeners that domestic science instruction was being given whenever possible in primary and secondary schools, and noting that all teacher trainees had to take a course in the subject. Kate moved that the trustees of the Macarthy Fund, set up in

Female students in a Wellington Technical School typing class, c. 1900.

Alexander Turnbull Library, Wellington, PAColl 3271-3

1912 under the bequest of brewer Thomas Macarthy for educational and charitable purposes in the Wellington district, be asked to consider supporting either the establishment of a chair or the setting up of hostels associated with training colleges to provide further home science training. After some discussion, and a speech by William LaTrobe, Director of Wellington's Technical School, the conference passed a resolution to approach the Macarthy Fund regarding money for hostels.[22]

In 1914 home science was introduced as a subject for the Public Service and Intermediate examinations, the first step towards making the subject compulsory

177

for all girls during the first two years of secondary school.[23] In the same year, an article entitled 'Sketch of the Movement for Higher Education of Girls' appeared in the *White Ribbon*, commending the recent moves toward educational differentiation in the curriculum. Although unsigned, this piece was in all likelihood written by Kate. Both the views and manner of expression certainly match her writing elsewhere. Moreover, in surveying the history of higher education for girls in New Zealand, the author does not refer to Kate Edger by name, but pays tribute to the Reverend Samuel Edger and Farquhar Macrae.

The author sees two major motives behind the push for women in tertiary education: the desire for personal development and the necessity for gaining the power to earn a livelihood. As time went on, however, a third motive emerged, 'the value to the community of the work of a great mass of educated women, the social utilisation of their intellectual and moral capacities. What can be better for the life of the nation than to direct into channels of usefulness the strong forces of mind, the stronger forces of will and devotion that rise in a woman's soul.'

After telling how the first women's degree in higher education came about, the writer asks 'to what extent should there be differences between girls' and boys' education?' and concludes that 'If girls and women have special duties, if their place in the world, their work in the social order, differs from that of boys, then their education must be to some extent different.' One contemporary view, which the writer describes as 'extreme', but which Lily Atkinson espoused with her trademark rhetorical flair and confidence, was that home science 'ought to occupy somewhat the same place in a girl's education that military training does in a boy's'. Whether or not one agreed with this, 'the movement towards including at least some instruction in Home Science in the ordinary routine of school work for girls [was] gaining ground'. The Otago domestic science chair had helped this advance by supplying trained teachers, and by giving the subject more rigour and academic credence. Rapid progress in domestic training was being made in the United States and Europe, where the subject was being taught in primary and secondary schools and 'many technical institutions that are entirely concerned with the preparation of girls for home life'.

In New Zealand the perfect system of education for girls was still evolving and much remained experimental. 'On the one hand, we have the multiplication of subjects and the difficulty of making a wise choice among them; on the other is the tyranny of examinations and the danger of filling the school days so full as to crowd out home life altogether.' The overarching aim was to ready each girl 'to live her own life fully as possible' and to be able to contribute to the community to the best of her ability. By keeping this end in view, 'we shall, though it may be slowly, advance along the path of true progress, and future generations will have cause to look back with gratitude upon the work achieved by pioneers in this great movement of woman's education.'[24]

War, eugenics and the 1916 General Council of Education recommendations

The *White Ribbon* article recommending home science in the curriculum was published just days after World War I broke out. In the course of that protracted conflict, public support for teaching domestic science increased; motherhood, domesticity and happy families enjoyed an emotive and increasingly hallowed status as concerns about national efficiency and the need to increase the birth rate mounted.[25] Minister of Education Josiah Hanan, writing in 1915, observed that while girls might for a time occupy paid work positions, in 'the great majority of cases' this was only temporary, and that 'nearly all of the girls soon become wives and mothers'. This was necessary if New Zealand was to 'stand in its present high position, which is due in the greatest measure to the influence of devoted mothers in our British homes'.

> Let us give our girls a good education, even a temporary occupation in the business or industrial world, but let us act so that we and they may realise that not even the lawyer, doctor, statesman, or merchant has a calling so richly fruitful of all that is highest and noblest in national life as the mother of a good home. To this end we must see that every girl, both in her secondary and primary education, shall have such training in domestic affairs as will render her great future work a source of interest and pleasure, and will enable her to meet its demands with the confidence and success that a good training can give.

It had never been 'more imperative, or more urgent' for the state to 'secure the health and physical efficiency of our girls' and ensure that they received 'an all-round practical education … To save child life is an axiom of State preservation; to remedy defect is an axiom of State economy.'[26] Healthy mothers producing healthy children who would go on to serve their country and the empire was seen as a form of patriotic duty. This was the way to improve racial strength and fitness. The failure of many World War I recruits to pass physical fitness standards was often attributed to poor mothering.[27]

In Auckland, Kate's sister Eva Hemus fed this trend towards the elevation of motherhood when she helped to found the Mothers' Thought Guild in mid-1916. Members of this group, who numbered more than 500 after the first 12 months, were asked to read daily the affirmation on their member's card: 'I am a mother, therefore I must be loving, patient and gentle that I may make my home happy and train my children wisely.' As the Auckland guild observed in July 1918, 'Anything that can be done to help the health of the race is helping the Empire, and the welfare of the future lies so much in the hands of women of to-day, who must wake up and use their brains if we, as a people, are not to lag behind in the race.'[28]

While Eva played her part in publicly promoting maternal domestic paragons, the school curriculum was being changed to ensure that instruction in the domestic arts played a stronger role. The General Council of Education (GCE), an advisory body created in 1915, appointed a committee of four men and four women in that year to consider the curriculum for New Zealand girls. In 1916 it recommended differentiation between the sexes and advocated compulsory 'vocational training bearing on home life' for girls at secondary school. Because boys' and girls' 'work in life is different', differentiation in the curriculum should start earlier and be more marked. Differing mental capacity and physical strength was another factor cited: boys were 'more original' and girls 'more imitative', and there was 'more danger' of girls suffering from overwork.[29] Kate's old mentor, John Macmillan Brown, at this stage in his life an enthusiastic eugenicist, was one of the committee members.

Brown was not alone in holding such views, which lay behind many contemporary policies designed to augment the teaching of domestic science, improve family life and raise healthy children, both in New Zealand and throughout the developed world. Francis Galton, a cousin of Charles Darwin, had coined the term eugenics in 1883, defining it as 'the study of agencies under social control that may improve the racial qualities of future generations, either physically or mentally'.[30] In the early 1900s, eugenics attracted some prominent supporters in Britain, including Fabian socialists such as George Bernard Shaw, H.G. Wells, and Beatrice and Sidney Webb; prominent economists such as William Beveridge and John Maynard Keynes; and Conservative politicians such as Winston Churchill and Arthur Balfour. In the United States it had a particularly high profile, attracting finance from such deep-pocketed bodies as the Rockefeller Foundation and the Carnegie Institute, and influential exponents like the distinguished biologist Charles Davenport and the wealthy cereal magnate J.H. Kellogg.[31]

In New Zealand the subject attracted little interest among the general population but was enthusiastically endorsed by advanced liberals and social reformers.[32] The list of members of the Eugenics Education Society, founded in Dunedin in 1910, was a veritable roll-call of Kate and William Evans' friends and colleagues in various moral and social reform movements. They included H.B. Kirk (Lily Atkinson's father and professor of biology at Victoria College); Phoebe Myers, a demonstrator in biology at the same college; J.C. Johnson, professor of biology at Auckland College; several prominent medical doctors including King, Batchelor, Siedeberg and Lindo Fergusson; and a number of former contributors to the Forward Movement, who were now leading political and legal figures, such as Stout, Findlay, Fowlds and Hogben.[33] The WCTU and the NCW also supported eugenics and the work of the Eugenics Education Society; the WCTU even had a 'Heredity Department'.[34] The values and aims of many feminists and the eugenicists overlapped since both were concerned with the conditions of social well-being.

Supporters of eugenics in New Zealand, with one or two notable exceptions, endorsed 'positive' prescriptions; that is, rather than emphasising heredity and employing negative policies such as sterilisation of the 'unfit', they advocated improving environmental factors and education to ameliorate the mental and physical state of those whose living conditions posed a threat to national and imperial health. King, for example, feared that putting too much emphasis on heredity would lead to fatalism and neglect of childcare; 'environment was ten times as important' as inherited deficiencies.[35] Stout, though an office-holder in the Eugenics Education Society and a firm believer in the idea of a 'criminal class' and the dangers of racial degeneration, always maintained faith in self-improvement and education as a way to lessen their threat.

Kate and William Evans did not belong to the Eugenics Education Society, and as evangelical Christians with firm beliefs in moral choice and redemption, would have rejected any focus on heredity. They had a keen interest, however, in progressive reform that would benefit the disadvantaged, and a strong belief in education's ability to bring about a better society. They also, like most progressive social reformers of the time, used language that now has a disturbing eugenicist ring, and they advocated policies and institutions that eugenicists supported. In 1911 Kate addressed the Wellington SPWC about the need to keep pressing government on the creation of a school for 'defective' girls.[36] An institution for defective boys, the Otekaike Special School, had already been created on a rural estate in South Canterbury in 1907 and was thriving. Its headmaster, George Benstead, was a member of the inaugural council of the Eugenics Society.[37]

The facility was regarded as a success not only because it removed the boys from the rest of society and prevented any unwanted procreation that might 'increase the helpless and hopeless section of the Empire', but also because the mental and physical benefits of being educated in such a healthy rural environment would help the boys to become useful members of society rather than 'absolutely useless units, with physical and mental deterioration slowly but surely awaiting them'.[38] Kate and the SPWC wanted a similar institution for girls on the same estate and had requested it often; she noted in 1911 that the government 'had the matter in hand'. Everyone would agree 'as to the necessity of making provision for children of weak intellect' who, though not 'insane', were not suited to 'the ordinary school course'. It was 'the duty of a Government with the welfare of the people at heart', as New Zealand's was, to care for these children. All kinds of girls would be taken into the facility but they would have to be carefully classified first. She was pleased that 'the Government was determined that these children should receive what advantages could be given towards making them useful citizens'.[39] A special school for girls eventually opened in 1916, not on the Otekaike estate but in Richmond, near Nelson.

In arguing her case, Kate focused only on providing a useful and beneficial education for girls who could not benefit from mainstream schooling. She made no mention of how such a facility would impede racial degeneration or restrict procreation of the unfit in the interests of national and imperial health, but others did. In 1905, for example, King gave a speech that tapped into contemporary anxieties about physical and moral degeneration:

> If women in general were rendered more fit for maternity, if instrumental deliveries were obviated as far as possible, if infants were nourished by their mothers, and boys and girls were given a rational education, the main supplies of population for our asylums, hospitals, benevolent institutions, gaols and slums would be cut off at the sources: further a great improvement would take place in the physical, mental, and moral condition of the whole community ...[40]

And when a deputation from the Eugenics Education Society and the Charitable Aid Board of Dunedin visited George Fowlds in March 1911 they emphasised that 'feeble minded' girls were especially dangerous to the race because they were 'unable to withstand temptations that arise from their own defective natures', defectiveness that led to indulgence in alcohol and 'frequent matings'.[41]

A subject of dispute

Within the Wellington branch of the SPWC there was unified support for King and Plunket, and agreement that more and better domestic science teaching was a good thing. But there was disagreement about the GCE recommendation to make domestic science compulsory at secondary school. In October 1916 Kate attended a meeting at Victoria College called by the Women's Social Investigation League – founded in 1916 to examine questions of public interest – to discuss the GCE report.[42] Some speakers emphasised that the report was vague and made no provision for girls who had to become independent wage-earners. It was also pointed out that 'when girls had been taught to use their brains and think, as a rule they are successes in the domestic arena, whether they have had any academic training in domestic arts or not'. At the end of the meeting a motion was passed stating that the training recommendations tended to restrict girls' 'all-round development, being based on narrow, rather than on broad, general lines'.[43]

The press originally attributed this motion to Mrs W.A. Evans, but a few days later acknowledged the mistake. In the course of the meeting Kate had in fact said that she considered the GCE report to be on the 'right lines, though possibly in some points it went rather too far'. She had voted against the motion and noted that 'so little enthusiasm had been evoked by it that out of the large audience present only about a dozen thought it worth while to vote either for or against, upon which a second show of hands was called for'.[44]

Lily Atkinson, like Kate, endorsed the GCE recommendations, but the Stouts were in the opposing camp. In July 1917, at a meeting called by the Wellington SPWC to discuss the GCE's proposals, Anna Stout spoke emphatically against them. While not denying the importance of domestic science – she referred to it jokingly, much to the amusement of the audience, as 'so essential for husbands' – she suggested 'a certificate of responsibility for fatherhood should be demanded equally with a knowledge of domestic science in women'. Some women who were 'totally unfitted for motherhood … were splendidly equipped for a commercial or professional life'. Professor Thomas Hunter from Victoria College also objected strongly, arguing that the existing equality between the sexes in the education system worked well, and describing the University Senate's requirement for a girl to study domestic science before she could matriculate as 'pernicious and unfair'. If compulsory courses were introduced, they must be of the highest quality: there was 'nothing worse than that which was cheap, nasty and compulsory'. The meeting ended with the motion that, 'while in full sympathy with domestic training for women', it 'strongly protests against any alterations of our educational system that will place disadvantages on women and deprive them of educational rights equal to those of men'. The GCE proposals, if adopted, would have 'disastrous consequences'; the Education Department must not give effect to them.[45]

In June 1917 Nellie Peryman, a teacher and the editor of the *White Ribbon*, wrote an editorial objecting to the GCE proposals. Her article, entitled 'Differentiation in the Education of Girls', noted that:

> The men of the past have said that women's place was the home, and so they shut all the doors leading to a liberal education and the learned professions against her. We should be false to the noble women who endured obloquy and shame in their fight for equality of opportunity for our girls if we allowed that opportunity to be taken from them. Once admit that there should be a difference on the ground of sex, and then it is only a question of degree to go back to the early Victorian period of education. We believe that all difference should be on the ground of *ability*, not of *sex*.

She did not adhere to the Kaiser's view that women were only good for 'the church, the cradle, and the kitchen', but quoted WCTU leader Frances Willard: the ideal woman's mission was to 'make the whole world home-like'. Peryman concluded by observing that younger teachers were less keen about making domestic science compulsory at secondary school than older 'and presumably more conservative' ones.[46]

In the next issue Kate, then the associate editor of the *White Ribbon*, wrote a letter in response to Peryman's editorial and a letter that had followed it. Although 'no sensible woman' could regret the struggle to obtain for girls an intellectual education equal to that of boys, in the process 'other sides of the ideal education' had been 'more or less neglected':

> It is ever thus that human progress is made – not by the steady unswerving unbroken advance of the lava stream down the mountain slope, but by the ceaseless alteration of the forward and backward movement of the incoming tide. I do not therefore believe that we shall go back to the educational methods of the early Victorian period, as some seem to fear, but that before long the ideals that are seeking realisation through the increased prominence of such subjects as Home Science, will be acknowledged as of equal importance with those aimed at the training of the purely intellectual subjects, and both groups will find thus their true balance.

Home science was becoming wider in scope and when 'better understood and fully developed' might well train the intellect and reasoning powers as effectively as studying language or mathematics, 'besides doing much for the social and home-loving side of a girl's nature'. Kate found it 'strange, and one might almost say pathetic, that a Society that has for its object the protection and welfare of women and children, should set itself in opposition to a movement that is really seeking so to improve the condition and the spirit of the home as to reduce the necessity for such a society'. Much of the criticism of the GCE proposals failed to take a sufficiently broad view of the matter.[47]

Kate's hope that 'the subject will be still further ventilated in these columns' was fulfilled by Nellie Peryman's response, which followed immediately. She was pleased to have a letter from Mrs Evans, 'a recognised expert on this subject'. Although she agreed entirely that education's purpose was to train and develop a child's latent powers, 'and where a girl shows a talent or bent for Home Science, then train her and send her out as an expert', but not every girl had that interest 'and we object to her being compelled to take it as a subject'.[48]

The compulsory domestic science curriculum changes provoked polarised responses in the daily press. Nellie Coad, a Wellington College teacher, energetic promoter of educational opportunities for women and secretary of the Wellington branch of the New Zealand Women Teachers' Association, was elected onto the GCE after the 1916 report.[49] She argued that the compulsory domestic science component disadvantaged girls, while Emily Chaplin, president of the New Zealand Women Teachers' Association, did not believe that the result would be an inferior education: 'Equality of opportunity … does not mean identity of studies.'[50] There had been considerable gender differentiation in New Zealand education for some time, with domestic courses for girls and compulsory military drill for boys from 1904. But many considered that the *compulsory* element of the regulations might disadvantage girls and force on them a subject for which they lacked interest and aptitude. Some also feared that the course of study, as Hunter had pointed out, might be second rate. There were also concerns that this development threatened the curriculum equality gained decades earlier.

The amendment to Clause 6 of the Free Place Regulations ensuring that home science would be taken by every girl attending secondary or district high school remained in place until 1943. A controversial issue in 1917, its impact and import have continued to provoke debate. Some historians present it within the context of a state-supported 'cult of domesticity' that both disadvantaged women, by adding domestic science to an already crowded syllabus, and hindered their study of science and medicine at university, which they entered with an insufficient grounding in the pure sciences. Others point out that there was strong resistance to domestic education by both girls and their parents, that the state's commitment to it was only 'half-hearted', and that the number of girls actually exposed to the domestic curriculum remained small, because the number going on to secondary school was still low.[51] In 1917 only 37 percent of pupils went on to secondary school; the figure in 1932 was 55 percent. When girls were supposedly being imbued with the 'cult of domesticity', more were entering paid employment with vocational qualifications than ever before. Also, the Education Department's commitment to a broad liberal education for both sexes remained fundamentally intact, despite a degree of gender differentiation in the curriculum.[52]

In her exchange with Kate, Nellie Peryman suggested that women who supported the GCE recommendations belonged to an older and more conservative generation. Although a generational divide between female social reformers became more notable both during and after World War I, Anna Stout's views illustrate that not all older women agreed with the compulsory element of the new regulation, however positively they might view the domestic training of young women.

Between 1910 and 1920 ideas about the importance of women's role as wives and mothers were endorsed by both liberal progressive reformers and the more conservatively minded. Kate's views on the subject remained constant and unwavering. In a speech entitled 'The Ideals of the Modern Woman', delivered in December 1917 at Christchurch Girls' High as part of the school's fortieth anniversary celebrations, Kate paid tribute to modern women 'who had thrown themselves wholeheartedly into work which no one had ever thought them capable of. The girls of to-day were the moulders of the future. On them rested the responsibility of building up the civilisation that had been so nearly ruined. They were the mothers of the future generation, and she urged upon them that, no matter what career of usefulness they chose to follow, not to lose sight of the sacred duty of motherhood.' Her last words were, 'Keep in mind the necessity for truthfulness and unselfishness, and your service will be the best you can render to the world.'[53]

9

War, Social Purity and Moral Fibre

I desire to assure the women of this country that I recognize the responsibility which has been placed upon me, and to assure them that it will be my great desire to uphold the sacredness of the pure and virtuous womanhood of New Zealand.

GEORGE RUSSELL, Minister of Public Health, on the
War Regulations Amendment Act 1916[1]

We contend that we send our sons to fight for purity and righteousness and we utterly discountenance everything that slackens moral fibre …

Resolution passed at the New Zealand Women's Christian Temperance Union
National Convention, March 1918[2]

In the early years of the twentieth century the New Zealand women's rights movement, formerly so energetic, visible and effective, appeared to be languishing. A number of prominent first-wave feminists were growing old, dispirited or ill – in 1905 Amey Daldy suffered a paralysing stroke and Margaret Sievright died – and some lamented the lack of continued involvement with women's rights issues.[3] In 1906 the NCW had gone into recess, beset by factional strains. Its leaders seemed increasingly unrepresentative of women as a whole, most of whom did not feel the need to press for further equal rights reform.[4]

There was, at the same time, a gradual loosening of manners and sexual mores, which had began before the war and accelerated rapidly during it. The high-minded crusading feminism of the early 1890s was increasingly being superseded by a different version of the 'New Woman' who 'was as likely to express her rebellion by smoking, drinking alcohol, or having sex before marriage – sometimes almost simultaneously – as by petitioning Parliament or getting a university education'.[5]

The war years, however, also witnessed an upsurge of crusading social purity feminism and Kate was among its most committed exponents. Along with Anna Stout and Lily Atkinson, she vigorously opposed legislation designed to combat the increasing ravages of venereal disease. Social purity feminists perceived the proposed 1916 War Regulations Amendment legislation as a new incarnation of the hated Contagious Diseases Act, threatening women's equal rights as citizens under the law and challenging the evangelical ideal of purity and chastity for both men and women. When, in 1917, Ettie Rout proposed prophylactic kits for Kiwi soldiers overseas, she outraged not just social purity feminists but the vast majority of New Zealand women.

In 1918 Kate, Anna Stout and Lily Atkinson again joined forces to protest against the police and judiciary's handling of the 'Kelburn Case', a much-publicised scandal concerning the arrest and trial of several women purported to be prostitutes. The males involved escaped censure. Matters of social purity and sexually transmitted disease presented an opportunity to channel concerns about the moral direction of society, changing standards of behaviour and the hated sexual double standard. To many younger women, however, this moral righteousness seemed out of step with the increasingly complex realities of contemporary wartime society. A minority of women on the political left also resented what they perceived to be the entitled 'bourgeois' authority assumed by the older generation of women's rights activists.

1914: War, service and a suffrage twenty-first

A strong element of pacifism had long prevailed among women's rights organisations in New Zealand. The WCTU had a peace department and the NCW a peace and arbitration department. In 1897 the NCW had passed a resolution stating that war was 'a savage, costly and futile method of solving disputes hostile to the realisation of brotherhood which is essential to the progress of humanity'.[6] A 1904 article in the *White Ribbon* discussed the menace to the 'further development of civilisation' posed by the growth of militarism. Two years later the WCTU passed a resolution decrying war and advocating the progressive feminine, Christian qualities of conciliation and arbitration.[7] Nevertheless, in 1914 the WCTU threw its support behind the war effort.

Kate was 57 in 1914. She had closed her classes two years before, possibly in order to devote more time to social reform work in the SPWC and WCTU. She remained involved in education, however. At a Wellington SPWC meeting in October 1914, she indignantly protested against the injustice of placing experienced and highly ranked female teachers on a lower pay scale than junior male teachers. Her resolution against the measure was carried unanimously and was then passed on to the minister of education.[8] In 1916 she ran unsuccessfully for a place on the Wellington Education Board. She still worked as an examiner as well: for the Public Service Examination in 1914, and for the Department of Education Junior and Senior National Scholarship and Senior free places in district high schools and technical schools in 1914, 1916 and 1917.[9]

Her three sons had all benefited from their education at Wellington Technical School. By 1911 James was farming in Pakaraka, Northland, on land Kate had purchased in the 1880s. Elwyn passed the Civil Service Junior Examination in 1910 and worked all his adult life as a civil engineer for the Public Works Department in different parts of the country.[10] Vryn studied history and economics at school, then went on to acquire an MA in economics at Victoria College. Like his mother, he became a popular, well-respected secondary teacher and eventually headmaster at Northcote College in Auckland.

By this time all Kate's sisters had embraced theosophy. Lilian had moved to India in 1900, where she lectured and taught for the Theosophical Society, eventually becoming headmistress of the Theosophical Girls' School at Benares. Marion also worked for the society in India from 1904 to 1909. Eva and Charles lived in Auckland, in the old Ponsonby College building, which their daughter Geraldine described as 'a centre of theosophical activity for about thirty-five years'.[11] They eventually moved to Epsom, where they helped to set up the theosophical Vasanta Garden School. Frank Edger had died in 1909 after a short illness and operation, aged only 56. Several Māori chiefs, who appreciated his work as a liberal Native Land Court judge and Māori Councils advocate, attended his funeral. Apirana Ngata and Native Minister James Carroll telegraphed messages of condolence and regret. Lilian and Marion sent floral tributes from India.[12] Because he and his wife Augusta were childless, Frank's death marked the end of the Edger family name in New Zealand.

With the outbreak of the war, Kate's long-standing advocacy of active female citizenship and family support found a new focus. In 1914, through the SPWC, she urged the government to create a Guild of Service to help families suffering because of the war, and also organised sales and bazaars to raise funds. In 1916, for example, she participated in a Red Cross sale of work in the Newtown Congregational School in Constable Street to help 'crippled soldiers', was involved in the Mayoress's Patriotic Fund, and also raised money for the war effort through the WCTU. When presiding over a meeting in 1916, during which women were informed about the government's plan to train women to fill jobs left vacant by men, she noted that 'in

This photo of Kate's brother Frank appeared in the *New
Zealand Graphic* on 5 May 1909, a week after his death in
Auckland, aged 56.

Auckland Libraries, Heritage Collections, NZG-19090505-30-10

war women, to a great extent, had to play the waiting game, and it was incumbent
upon them to undertake whatever work was offered'.[13]

Women's rights activism was also playing a waiting game. In Britain, when war
was declared, suffragette leader Emmeline Pankhurst instantly called a halt to all
militant activity. When her daughter Adela, a pacifist, visited New Zealand in 1916,
Anna Stout, who had supported the Pankhursts' cause while living in England
between 1909 and 1912 and now had sons serving overseas, made no effort to
contact her.[14] On 28 September 1914, Kate and Anna Stout, under the auspices of

the WCTU, held a celebration of New Zealand women's suffrage's 'coming of age' on its twenty-first birthday, albeit a few days late. Kate spoke first, emphasising New Zealand's important influence as a role model in helping 'women in other parts of the world … in the brave fight for the vote'. There were great benefits at home too: 'We have had the vote here for a long time and I don't think any country has done more for the position of women and children.' Although Anna Stout agreed on this point, generally she was less positive, believing that New Zealand women 'had secured the vote far too easily, and that the majority had taken it too indifferently'. (She would reiterate this view in future years.) She spoke about the 'big fight' of the British suffragists and the encouragement of New Zealand's example. 'We have done a great deal … but we can do more and must do more. But the majority of women in the Dominion who are comfortable themselves don't trouble at all.'[15]

Social purity and the red plague

The departure of thousands of men for foreign military service once again raised the spectre of the sexual double standard. Proposed 1916 amendments to the War Regulations Act appeared to reintroduce, with no attempt to involve or consult women, another version of the reviled Contagious Diseases Act, which had finally been repealed in 1910.

Even before the war, 'the red plague', as it was often known, posed a serious health threat to both men and women. In 1909 Ferdinand Batchelor, at the Otago Medical School, reported that 'fully 50 per cent of the decent married women who enter the gynaecological ward of the Dunedin Hospital do so as a result of these [venereal] diseases'.[16] In 1910 Attorney General John Findlay suggested that an estimated 35 per cent of all hospital outpatients suffered from venereal disease. Until the invention of Salvarsan in 1911, there was no effective treatment for syphilis – and even Salvarsan frequently had toxic, even occasionally lethal, side effects.[17] Both syphilis and gonorrhoea, if untreated, could have numerous damaging impacts such as sterility in women, and insanity, blindness, deafness, deformity, rheumatism, heart disease and paralysis for both sexes.[18] Sexually transmitted diseases also carried a great social stigma. Findlay saw the 1910 repeal of the Contagious Diseases Act as an ideal opportunity to urge for more effective legislation against venereal disease, making sure to emphasise that this time it would target promiscuous males as much as promiscuous females. He spoke up and down the country on the subject and called for new legislation and a commission of inquiry. He did not succeed in those aims, but with the outbreak of World War I venereal disease became a pressing public issue. New Zealand soldiers needed to be safeguarded from infection, and civilians protected from infected members of the armed forces.[19] The threat that VD posed to the family, its potential harm to mothers and babies, and its ability to swell the ranks of the 'degenerate' and impede national efficiency, made it an emotive, controversial issue.

Feminists feared that part of the War Regulations Amendment Bill of 1916 would lead to a reincarnation of the Contagious Diseases Act and its infamous double standard. Kate and Anna Stout were involved in public meetings protesting against this negation of women's civil rights and the fact that 'vice' (i.e. the use of prostitutes) was punishment-free only for men. Rather than such legislation being imposed by men, they wanted it to be first discussed in Parliament by representatives from the country's various women's organisations. The WCTU argued that the inspection provisions of the bill should be clearly and strictly defined in a separate piece of legislation. Despite such objections from women's groups around the country, the bill became law in August 1916.

At the WCTU National Convention in March 1917, the same month her eldest son James was conscripted to serve overseas, Kate commended an article in the *Auckland Star* that drew attention to the problem of venereal disease and urged 'that all publicity should be given to the facts' of the kind the article disclosed 'as a means for stirring up the public opinion to demand effective action'.[20] The motion was carried unanimously. In August Kate was part of a women's deputation to Prime Minister William Massey, urging, again, that female police be appointed to ensure better protection of young people. They also requested that the age of consent be raised to 18, and that a campaign of education on venereal disease and free clinics for VD sufferers be introduced. The deputation wanted all treatment for venereal disease to be volitional rather than compulsory.[21]

On 3 October 1917 a Social Hygiene Bill, described as 'a measure to prevent the spread of venereal disease', was introduced into Parliament. It provided, among other things, for the establishment of prison hospitals where prostitutes and their clients could be confined for no more than six months. Despite the fact that both sexes could be punished, feminist activists suspected that in practice women would be the primary detainees. On 6 October Anna Stout called a public meeting to discuss the bill. This time Kate did not, as was often the case, act as chair, but she sat on the platform. The attendance was so great that many had to stand. Anna Stout called the Social Hygiene Bill 'panic legislation' and stressed that a measure of such importance to women should have involved women in its framing. The meeting endorsed resolutions that treatment for VD should be voluntary, that education about the disease be increased and that voluntary clinics be promoted.[22]

Kate attended a further meeting, held on 10 October, during which Anna Stout spoke again at length on the proposed legislation and moved that 'this meeting of citizens of Wellington calls upon the Government to withdraw the bill at present before Parliament … holding that such legislation would have the effect of driving the evil underground. It further invites the Government to place the matter of social hygiene before the women's societies which have for the last twenty years been suggesting solutions of this problem.' This was unanimously passed, as was a further motion, that when appointing female health officers or police, 'Parliament should invite the co-operation of such women's societies with a view to securing suitable women for such positions'. The government should 'follow the example of the Canadian and South Australian Governments in appointing women justices and magistrates to deal with cases where women and children are concerned.'[23]

Their representations had some effect. When the Social Hygiene Act was passed at the end of October 1917, it introduced female health officers to assist in the four main cities of New Zealand. Aged over 40, and paid a small stipend, they would help to guard the health and morality of young people. The first such positions were not appointed, however, until 1919.[24]

Although feminists like Kate, Anna Stout and Lily Atkinson strongly upheld prostitutes' rights as women, they rigorously opposed prostitution, advocating instead loyal monogamy within marriage by both men and women. They soon found themselves at odds with an outspoken woman who held very different views about moral purity and sexual relations during wartime.

Social purity feminists vs Ettie Rout

In 1917 Ettie Rout began pushing the benefits of prophylactic kits for New Zealand soldiers overseas. An energetic, strong-minded, unconventional woman who had run her own public typist business in Christchurch, she had gleaned considerable knowledge about VD in her capacity as an official reporter for court cases and on commissions of inquiry before the war. Rout held very liberal views on sexual relations between men and women. She was a former student and friend of Kate Evans' old teacher at Canterbury College, the free-thinking Alexander Bickerton. Rout was also a socialist and from 1910 to early 1911 edited the *Maoriland Worker*, a successful radical Labour newspaper, which she had helped to found. She organised a group of women aged between 30 and 50 as a Volunteer Sisterhood to provide nursing care for the New Zealand troops overseas. She led the first group to Egypt in late 1915 and as soon as she arrived, immediately recognised the severity of the VD problem.[25]

On 24 October 1917 the *New Zealand Times* published a frank article written by Rout in London in August, in which she noted that New Zealanders 'topped the poll' in terms of incidence of VD among soldiers serving overseas, and that attempts by the military to curb the problem by patriotic pleas, moral suasion, counter-attractions and so on had patently failed. Her prophylactic kits had gained approval at the highest military and diplomatic levels and she would soon be opening a Soldiers' Medical and Health Club at Hornchurch in Essex, the site of the New Zealand Convalescent Hospital.[26]

This piece created an instant nationwide furore, arousing repulsion and indignation among New Zealand women. An emotional letter to the *New Zealand Times*, signed 'A Soldier's Sister', typified the response:

> The letter in your paper last week from Miss Ettie Rout has filled many
> women with deep sorrow and shame, shame that it is possible for a woman to
> unwarrantably besmirch the character of their sons and husbands and brothers,
> and to cast a blot on the dead heroes of the war ... Is it possible that Miss Rout has
> been empowered by the Government to ask for funds to foster and encourage vice?
> To make a trade of it?[27]

The correspondent also pointed out that Salvarsan was hardly a reliable cure and often resulted in serious side effects. Although the NZEF had adopted Rout's kits for free and compulsory distribution to the troops, her name was promptly censored in the press and she received little or no contemporary recognition for her input. For her part, Ettie Rout had no time for social purity feminists' point of view. She mocked their fear of the 'white slave trade' – a reference to claims about the forced prostitution of young British women dating from the 1880s[28] – deriding it as both mythical and unnecessary: 'There is no necessity for it [i.e. abduction], there are plenty of volunteers available – women who may be described as neither moral nor immoral but simply non-moral.'[29] Rout's mockery reflected her view that young single women could choose to be sexually active.

As early as 1914 the WCTU had resolved at its annual convention that chastity was the only solution to VD, and that 'present palliatives' could never ensure the safety of a man's wife and future children. Such remedies only did harm 'by

Ettie Rout and the first members of her Volunteer Sisterhood, who worked in Egypt during World War I, photographed in 1915. Ettie is in the middle, without a hat.

creating a false sense of security'.[30] In March 1918 the WCTU unanimously carried a resolution rejecting Rout's position and her baneful influence: 'We contend that we send our sons to fight for purity and righteousness, and we utterly discountenance everything that slackens moral fibre and self-control, and place on record our emphatic repudiation of prophylactics and the woman who advocates them.'[31] In April, Kate, Lily Atkinson and Anna Stout were part of a women's deputation to Massey complaining about Rout's club and her prophylactic kits. Stout described Rout's club as 'an insult to the women of New Zealand', and Atkinson lamented the 'corruption of the innocence of many a young man' that would result from visiting it and using the kits. There was 'not a mother in New Zealand who would tolerate any communication of Miss Rout with her son'.[32] Massey promised to investigate the scheme when he got to London.

On 1–2 April 1918 a conference of the newly reconstituted NCW convened in Wellington, its aim to 'unite all organised societies of women, to arouse them to a keener sense of their responsibilities as citizens, and to support all social movements which make for the welfare of the community'.[33] It was hoped that the emergence of a powerful and united women's organisation would help to offset some of the impact of the war and the way men had assumed control over legislation that apparently condoned a double standard of morality; and that the revived council would help to reverse slipping moral standards and protect the family.[34]

The Kelburn case: Gender, class and sexual equality

Just days after the the revival of the NCW, a case hit the headlines that confirmed social purity feminists' worst fears about the War Regulations Act. It also brought into focus social anxieties about a perceived decline in wartime morals among women, and pointed up political, class and generational divides among women's rights advocates. The case involved a police raid on a 'house', in other words a suspected brothel, in the Wellington suburb of Kelburn. This house, on Upland Road, was rented by Molly Gibson, her two children and another woman, Winifred Olsen. Both women appeared to be respectable and middle class. Since January 1918, however, police had been keeping a watch on the address after neighbours complained about suspicious behaviour there: male guests, drinking, hilarity, music and alcohol. On the night of the raid, 27 April 1918, Gibson, Olsen and five other women were enjoying 'a musical evening' in the company of 10 men, many of whom were military officers. Five women were arrested and imprisoned and their names published in newspapers. Two were let off, having proved they were visitors. None of the men at the house were arrested or initially named in the press. The arrested women had compulsory medical exams; two were dismissed but the other three went to trial.[35]

By the time the case was heard before the Magistrate's Court on 6 May, public interest had intensified. The fact that the women lived in an upmarket suburb increased the sensational element: as Katherine Sanders has observed, 'much public interest was undoubtedly spurred by titillation'.[36] On 4 May *New Zealand Truth* had published the names of the 'gentlemen visitors' involved.[37] Women's organisations, most notably the WCTU, registered unqualified disapproval of how the case had been handled.

The large crowd that assembled to witness the trial included representatives from eight different women's organisations, including the Women Teachers' Association, since one of the accused was a teacher at Brooklyn School. *Truth* described the 14 women from these organisations as 'a solid phalanx … commanded by Lady Stout' and facetiously dubbed them the 'Up-Lifts', a label that played on the idea of social reformers keen to morally uplift society.[38] The magistrate stipulated that members of the public could not watch the proceedings, but allowed Anna Stout and her associates to remain, 'seeing that they were representatives of women's protection and welfare societies, etc.', though he warned that they 'must be prepared to listen to some very unsavory evidence'.[39] Given her ongoing role in the affair, it is highly probable that Kate was among their number.

It was revealed during the trial that one of the accused, a 19-year-old, was a virgin. Only Gibson and Olsen were sentenced, under the War Regulations Amendment Act, to 12 months' reformative treatment. They had spent one month in prison when their appeal was upheld in the Supreme Court in July on the grounds of lack of evidence that sex had been for hire or gain. In the process, however, their personal lives were examined by the court and the public, and they were irreparably disgraced.

Anna Stout called a meeting in early June, before the Supreme Court decision, to protest the outcome of the trial, and the fact that while the men went scot free, adequate protections for the women involved had not been enforced. Those attending were in a disaffected, feisty mood, and Kate was commended in the press for the 'clear and unimpeachable' manner with which she chaired the proceedings.[40]

In a brief opening speech, she began by saying that 'this agitation for reform in regard to women's disabilities was not a sudden thing'; it had been going on for years, through groups such as the WCTU and the SPWC. The Kelburn case, however, had brought matters to a head. She stressed that the intention of the meeting was not to promote the overturn of the sentences imposed on the two women, but to 'affirm the necessity for three great reforms':

> (a) the equality of punishment for the same crime, regardless of sex; (b) more protection for women and girls, whether they have fallen or not; to obtain greater decency in court proceedings and avoid undue indignity, and for those who are yet innocent but in danger of falling to adopt better preventive measures; (c) to secure that punishment meted out to the guilty shall be better adapted to secure the real object … the reform and restoration to the status of respectable law-abiding citizens.

She then read several messages of support from around the country, including one from Kate Sheppard.[41] Kate's list of principles included issues fundamental to first-wave feminists: the need for women to have equal rights as citizens, the removal of the sexual double standard, a reformative rather than punitive system of criminal punishment, more protection for women in the court system to protect their dignity and reputation, and legislative measures and policies to help young people make the right moral/sexual choices.

Anna Stout spoke at length, stressing the unequal treatment of men and women involved in the Kelburn case, and the fact that the reputations of innocent women had been sullied because their names were published in the press. Although New Zealand women had the vote, they had fallen behind other countries in not having female police, magistrates or justices of the peace. The meeting decried the double standard of morality permitted under the law, and passed resolutions asking for separate courts for women and the introduction of female justices of the peace, jurors and police.[42]

There was some unexpected drama during the meeting. As the *New Zealand Times* reported, 'a certain section of the meeting had been showing signs of unruliness all the afternoon' and several speakers raised the Alice Parkinson case. One individual reportedly even caused 'some obstruction', until Kate ruled her out of order.[43] In 1915 Parkinson, a 21-year-old domestic servant, had become pregnant to a younger man, Bert West, aged 18. He agreed to marry her, but then reneged on his promise when the child died. During an impassioned argument the couple struggled with a gun and only Parkinson survived. A jury later found her guilty of manslaughter and recommended mercy on account of the provocation she had endured. Chief Justice Robert Stout had delivered what many people believed to be a harsh sentence of life imprisonment.[44]

From the outset the case attracted enormous publicity and generated a wave of public support that rippled on for several years. *Truth* painted the circumstances in emotive prose, and letters soon filled the correspondence columns from people angry at the harshness of Stout's decision. A nationwide petition against the sentence attracted some 20,000 signatures, public meetings were held and a Release Alice Parkinson Committee was formed. People on the left of the political spectrum were notably angered by what they saw as an injustice towards a working woman, with Harry Holland in the socialist *Maoriland Worker* lending his voice to the public outcry: 'We of the Social Democratic and Labour Movement … will direct our efforts to swing outward her prison doors and thus do something to redress the black wrong Society has committed against her and also to remove the stigma her sentence has cast upon the whole people of our country.'[45] However, when the petition was eventually presented to Parliament, it received a 'No recommendation' verdict.[46]

The 'unruliness' during the 6 June meeting caused some further discussion in the press. Anna Stout wrote to the *New Zealand Times* on 12 June in response to a letter to the editor, signed 'Fairplay', that had appeared in the *Evening Post* two days earlier. The writer had asked 'why those concerned in the Kelburn case should be whitewashed at the expense of the other unfortunate women?', that is, poor working-class prostitutes. It also queried the criticisms of the police and magistrate expressed at the meeting.[47] Stout described the whitewashing charge as 'class discrimination' and 'not founded on justice or Christian charity':

> I think I can honestly claim, that no woman has ever appealed to me in vain, but I know that the guilty woman, who had no excuse (I am always ready to sympathise with weaknesses in both women and men) will not come near me. In the Kelburn case the women were never warned of their danger – known evil women are always warned and given a chance to mend their ways. Girls whom the police stated they knew to be innocent were dragged to the police cells.

She went on to explain, in response to criticism during the meeting about the Parkinson case, that she had no sympathy for Alice because she had 'seduced a boy many years younger than herself, who had honourably met all liabilities in connection with the consequences but refused to marry the woman when the child died'. She took exception to claims that the meeting had broken up in conflict, or that questions from the floor had not been allowed. She also commended the earnestness of the women who attended the meeting, which, 'though in several instances neither courteous nor well-directed, augurs well for the future'. All resolutions at the meeting had been carried by a majority with the only 'dissentients' being some dozen women whom she described as 'the twelve apostles of disorder'.[48]

The patronising tone of this letter doubtless did not help endear Stout to the 'apostles'. Their criticism during the meeting had stemmed from a perception that the middle-class women running the meeting and organising the opposition to the Kelburn raid had become involved with the case because it involved middle-class women in Kelburn, not working girls. There is some irony here. Kate, Anna Stout and other middle-class feminists had for decades been arguing the case for prostitutes' civil rights; they wanted equality before the law, not one standard of morality for men and another for women. At the same time, the spectre of middle-class women who looked respectable but appeared to transgress social and sexual boundaries had both sparked the Kelburn women's arrest and arguably fuelled social purity feminists' indignation at their treatment.

In the pages of *Truth* on 22 June, columnist 'Lady Dot' quoted some of the criticisms directed from the floor at the stormy meeting:

> These are some of the interjections. Lady Stout smilingly confessed that she had been accused of shielding and sympathising with prostitutes. An interjector: 'So you are.' 'If they were Tory-street girls, instead of Kelburn, we'd never have heard a word from the likes o' you! You ought to be ashamed of yourself' … 'If they had been our husbands, you wouldn't have troubled yourself whether they were arrested or left!' said another dame, who became excited almost to tears. When reference was made to the women being in gaol whilst the men were free, a chorus of 'Serve 'em right', 'Good enough for them, too,' came from left and right.[49]

Elsewhere in the same edition of *Truth*, Isabel Hulbert, one of the 'apostles', gave an indignant account of the meeting. Upon being invited up onto the stage she had brought up the Alice Parkinson case, as an example of middle-class injustice towards a working woman. While agreeing wholeheartedly with the meeting organisers on the injustice of the sexual double standard, she was at odds with them on other matters, and annoyed that her views were seemingly being shut down. She complained about the 'irritatingly hostile attitude displayed toward a large part of the audience', adding: 'In the name of common sense, what is the use of calling a public meeting to protest and discuss anything if no discussion is allowed?'[50]

During the New Zealand suffrage campaign, women advocating for the vote had been primarily middle class, educated, liberal in politics and evangelical/nonconformist in religion. But those now involved in women's rights issues included a more prominent and vocal socialist element who, although they agreed about inequitable treatment and injustice towards women, resented the bourgeois feminists. This trend had become increasingly evident, from the 1890s, in the international women's movement, under the influence of the German socialist and feminist leader Clara Zetkin. This class-based opposition did not, however, involve any rejection of women's traditional domestic and maternal roles.[51]

A turning point

During the war years the moral certainty of women like Kate, Anna Stout and Lily Atkinson appeared both increasingly under threat from and out of step with contemporary society. The complexities of a wartime life in which young women lived and worked independently in cities, and where servicemen sought company and recreation, imperilled fixed moral codes. The class resentments and openly confrontational attitude of the 'twelve apostles' reflected a changed social and political reality. The New Zealand Labour Party represented a more class-based approach to politics, contrasting with the Liberals' notions of interclass harmony, conciliation, arbitration and progressive educated middle-class reformers legislating with their own view of the working class's best interests in mind. The vast majority of New Zealand women did not support Rout's ideas about free love but, at the same time, the moral rigour and righteousness expressed by first-wave suffrage campaigners seemed increasingly at odds with the changing times. The WCTU, for example, appeared to be attempting to hold back a turning moral tide. Its annual national conventions began to have a slightly besieged air as their views lost relevance for many younger women. In 1917 the annual WCTU convention noted that younger women were no longer joining the organisation, and a resolution was passed to make efforts to attract more.[52]

Most WCTU stalwarts were now in their late fifties or older. Although they held the same aims and ideas that had made them a progressive force in the 1890s, in some respects they looked conservative, attempting to preserve the vision of happy monogamous families living in a progressive, socially pure, alcohol-free utopia. But notions of respectability do not stand still. The older generation of feminists was still, as always, fighting for equal rights and to redress inequalities and injustices towards women under the law. But they still emphasised that women possessed distinctive and superior moral qualities and sensitivities. They argued for equality and inclusion on the basis of natural difference between the sexes and a clear emphasis on the moral impact and example of pure-living mothers. These same arguments were used by conservatives who resented women's higher education and widening sphere of involvement outside of the home.

During the war years, New Zealand women, like those in Britain and throughout the world, had stepped into a range of formerly undreamt-of occupations and roles, gaining independence and confidence in the process. Immediately after 1918, however, they relinquished most of those positions to returning soldiers, and there was a widespread belief that healthy homes, good mothering and domesticity would help to restore normality and rebuild shattered lives. Yet strains between an older ideal based on women's elevating influence within a morally pure family, and the complex realities of contemporary society, would continue.

10

A Just Community in a Happy Family of Nations

Each race has its own peculiar gifts and qualities, and underlying all, there should be a desire to understand each other.

KATE EVANS, 1930[1]

Whether Britain, or Russia or France do or do not agree with us, the moral righteousness of New Zealand's attitude is not affected in the least.

PETER FRASER on collective security and the League of Nations, 1936[2]

By 11 November 1918, the day Germany signed the armistice, some 18,000 New Zealanders had lost their lives in the 'the war to end all wars'. Kate and William were fortunate that their son James, who served in England from July 1917, did not see action due to a knee problem and returned home in 1919.[3] Commenting on the peace, one local newspaper succinctly observed: 'Thank God, it's all over.'[4] Throughout the country and around the world, people greeted the end of the war with jubilation and a heartfelt desire to resume normality. But then came a lethal influenza pandemic, which struck New Zealand between October and December 1918. By the time it eased, New Zealand's influenza death toll had reached almost 9000. Kate's nephew, Eva's son Claude Edger Hemus, an importer and talented portrait painter, died of the flu, aged 40.[5]

For Kate, the early 1920s were darkened by bereavement, and by concerns about the negative impacts of changing social and sexual mores on family life. More positively, she was involved, through the Wellington SPWC, in the successful push to grant New Zealand women the right to stand for Parliament, and from the later years of the decade worked enthusiastically for an idealistic new internationalist cause. The League of Nations, which held out the enticing prospect of a world without war, was an organisation that made all positions open equally to men and women. Its way of approaching international problems accorded with Kate's evangelical views in offering a model for a caring and supportive family of nations. In many respects, its aims corresponded with the evangelical feminine domestic ideal: understanding, compassionate, supportive, conciliatory, peace-loving, morally sound and dedicated to the welfare of all.

Women in the House

Although, as Kate noted when giving her speech at Christchurch Girls' High in 1917, the war that had 'so nearly ruined' civilisation, it had also shaken up society in innumerable ways, both tangible and intangible. Women's opportunities and expectations were altered, and new rights gained. In England in 1918, women over 30 who met a property qualification received the long-desired right to vote in elections, and also to stand for Parliament. Despite New Zealand feminists pushing for this latter right several times since 1893, the Women's Parliamentary Rights Act was not passed until October 1919. As a result of this legislation, women could stand for election to the lower house without meeting a property qualification. The Legislative Council remained closed to them, however, until 1941.

After New Zealand women gained the franchise, Kate and others believed that giving women the right to stand for Parliament was premature. They needed more time to educate themselves in political culture and political knowledge, and to gain confidence and knowledge as active citizens by serving in local government, and on charitable aid, hospital and liquor licensing boards. By 1919, New Zealand women had made a significant contribution in such areas; that year, for instance, a third of Wellington Hospital Board members were women.[6] In December 1918 the Wellington SPWC had passed a resolution that 'as a matter of Justice to Women', government needed to 'amend the law and make women eligible for election to Parliament'.[7] They had then sent a copy of their resolution to Liberal leader Joseph Ward, minister of finance, postmaster general and deputy prime minister in William Massey's wartime coalition government, formed in 1915. Both the recently reformed NCW and the WCTU had also supported the Women's Parliamentary Rights Act.

Fulfilling the promise of the new legislation, however, proved more challenging than anticipated. In the 1919 general election, Rosetta Baume in Parnell, Aileen

Cooke in Thames and Ellen Melville in Grey Lynn stood for election as MPs but failed. Melville, the second New Zealand woman to qualify as a lawyer and also a long-standing Auckland city councillor, ran a further six times, to no avail. It was not until 1933 that Elizabeth McCombs became New Zealand's first female MP through winning a by-election for the Christchurch Labour seat of Lyttelton, left vacant following the death of her husband.

The roaring twenties: Changing mores

However valued women's domestic role remained, their opportunities as single salary earners in the workforce were rapidly expanding, pushed along by techno-logical developments. By 1921, over 50 percent of young women between the ages of 15 and 24 were in paid employment, with an increasing number in white-blouse service occupations,[8] and their freedom as consumers and unchaperoned young 'flappers' around town caused consternation and moral concern in some quarters. In 1918 Englishwoman Marie Stopes who, like New Zealand's Ettie Rout, was a high-profile early advocate of birth control, wrote a bestseller called *Married Love,* which extolled the pleasures of sex between husband and wife, as distinct from sex for procreation. New Zealand banned Rout's 1923 book, *Safe Marriage*, which advo-cated various kinds of birth control, though middle-class women had clearly been quietly practising some form of birth control for decades.[9] As the 1920s began to roar, flappers, jazz, movies and dance crazes such as the Charleston all signalled a world far removed from the chaperoned 'courting' followed by earnest domesticity and a sexually virtuous 'white life for two' of earlier times.

Kate's personal life continued to be a notable example of many first-wave feminist goals, combining an advanced education, financial independence and a profession with motherhood, a happy family life, old-fashioned moral probity, teetotalism and selfless service to society. Her boys were proceeding on their own paths in life. In 1916 William had conducted the service when their son Elwyn married Marion Bold at the Evans family home in Newtown. In 1918, while serving overseas, James married his first cousin Morfydd in Wales. In January 1921, when Vryn announced his engagement to Myrtle Bell, Kate wrote a warmly affectionate welcome to her prospective daughter-in-law, which reflected her appreciation of the central importance of a rewarding family life:

Kate and William Evans with their grown sons, left to right: Vryn, Elwyn and James. Kate's companion Blythe Lindegaard is seated left. Jill Smith Collection

I cannot let my letter to Vryn go without a few words from myself to say how glad I shall be to welcome you as a daughter when the time comes. One of the deepest wishes I have always had for my boys is that they might find each <u>the one</u> in the world whom they could love and make a helpmeet, and I think from what I know of you that Vryn has that happiness to come to him in knowing you and winning your love.[10]

Before long William and Kate were enjoying being grandparents. Elwyn and Marion had two children, Beryl and William; James and Morfydd had one daughter called Olwyn; and Vryn and Myrtle three offspring: Laureen, Donald and Jill, the last born after Kate's death.[11] William, always full of fun and a great favourite with children, kept a supply of blackball sweets handy in his pockets as treats for his grandchildren. Kate, with characteristic kindness, would knit baby clothes for grandchildren, and also for former students who were starting a family, sending the garments along with a note of congratulations.

Kate Evans and fellow WCTU members wearing their white ribbons for purity, c. 1920s.

Jill Smith Collection

Lily Atkinson, c. 1912–16.
Alexander Turnbull Library,
Wellington, 1/2-233764-G

A year of loss

On 19 July 1921 Kate's friend and fellow social reformer Lily Atkinson died suddenly, aged just 55. Her obituary in the *Evening Post* included a commendation that could also have been applied to Kate: 'Her life should be an inspiration for women, for it showed how a woman could take a big part in the world's social work and yet be a home-maker of the best and highest description.'[12] In contrast to Kate's calm, judicious manner, Lily was an extrovert, never happier than when rousing audiences to support her various causes.[13] She and Kate had worked together amicably year after year, firm in their conviction that society would benefit from women's contributions both within and beyond the home.

While coping with Lily's sudden death, Kate was also nursing her beloved William, who was suffering from terminal bowel cancer. Vryn, by this time teaching in Wellington, regularly visited and helped his mother. He later recalled how his father, who normally never swore, cursed loudly during this protracted and painful illness.[14] William died, aged 63, on 6 November 1921.

Fulsome tributes appeared in the local press following his death. The *Evening Post* chose the word 'benevolence' to best describe his character. After recounting his humble origins, education, move to New Zealand and marriage to Kate, it praised his high idealism in founding the Forward Movement, which had 'as its object the brotherhood of mankind'. The paper extolled his contribution to education, and to the founding of Victoria University College, his service on the college council, the University Senate and the Wellington Technical School Board, as well as his role as a benevolent trustee and later as a member of the Wellington Hospital and Charitable Aid Board, and as a city councillor from 1900 to 1905. William was also hailed as 'a man who never sought the limelight and who eschewed publicity'.[15]

A later obituary, contributed to the same paper by an anonymous author on 14 November, described William as 'a local Ben Adhem', and lamented that Wellington had lost one of its most public-spirited citizens.[16] Even the populist *Truth*, frequently so unsparing about clerical do-gooders, praised Evans as 'a zealous social reformer', a 'Christian Socialist of the best type' and 'a lovable man without any of the vulgarity or push essential to "success" in these days'. Instead he 'pursued the path of duty in his quiet way, doing what good lay in his power'.[17]

In a notice thanking friends and well-wishers for their sympathy, Kate and the family acknowledged that many people would have expected a public funeral, 'in order to show respect … to one who had always tried to serve his adopted country'. The family was sure, though, that they would understand that this had not been William's wish. Kate also thanked the doctors who had looked after William during 'his long and painful illness'.[18] The funeral included a horse-drawn cortège, and the body was cremated rather than buried.[19] All the Edgers were advocates of cremation, a cause dear to many religious nonconformists.

Kate soon moved out of the large Hiropi Street house and into a smaller property at 62 Nevay Street, Miramar, accompanied by her long-time live-in companion Blythe Dungey Lindegaard. An attractive younger woman who shared many of Kate's interests, Blythe was the daughter of a member of the Newtown Congregational Church. Her eldest sister Alberta had married the Labour politician David McLaren in 1902. Blythe was a member of the Miramar branch of the WCTU of which Kate was president for several years, and both women belonged to the Lyceum Club, where they enjoyed social evenings, a play-reading circle and lectures.

After William's death Kate continued to contribute to the Newtown church, remaining in its congregation, helping to organise its various social activities and often playing the organ for services and weddings. She also kept busy with work on behalf of the New Zealand Alliance and the SPWC. In 1922, however, she found a renewed purpose and sense of mission.

An inspiring new cause

The League of Nations, launched in January 1920 at the end of the Paris Peace Conference, aimed to encourage disarmament, use collective security to prevent war, and encourage negotiation and diplomacy as a means of solving problems between nations, rather than violence and conflict. At the same time, it strove to promote the general well-being of nations, protect the rights of minorities and ensure that the 'products essential to the welfare and prosperity of mankind … be made available to all'.[20] If people benefited from living peaceful and comfortable lives on this basis, then, league advocates reasoned, they would never knowingly opt for war. Public opinion would ensure that the league became an enduring force for good in the world.

In October 1918 two groups already working for the cause of collective security and peace between nations, the League of Nations Society and the League of Free Nations Association, amalgamated to form the British League of Nations Union (LNU). Their key goal was to promote the League of Nations so as to 'bring about such a world organization as will guarantee the freedom of nations, act as trustee and guardian of backward races and undeveloped territories, maintain international order, and finally liberate mankind from the curse of war'.[21] The British LNU, which has been described as 'a key Liberal pressure group on foreign policy', aimed to ensure government adherence to the league's aim of peaceful conflict resolution in international affairs.[22] Members also worked to promote the league and its aims and to influence schools and universities to emphasise its nature and importance.[23] The LNU headquarters was in London, but branches sprang up around the globe, each with their own management structures. John Condliffe and Willis Airey, both young academics with high ideals and internationalist inclinations, founded New Zealand's first branch in Christchurch. In April 1922 a group of Wellington citizens held a meeting to discuss setting up a branch in the capital.[24]

The founding members of the Wellington group included the Reverend Doctor James Gibb, who had experienced a fervent conversion to pacifism during the course of World War I; Labour MP Peter Fraser; several members of the clergy; a number of schoolteachers and married women; and a bishop. Kate was not present at this first meeting but joined soon after. As in England, the make-up of the LNU in New Zealand was 'eminently respectable', 'high-minded' and comprising largely educated middle-class people. Most were liberal in their politics, and the nonconformist denominations figured prominently. Some LNU advocates, though, were more to the right of the political spectrum: men like Reform Party politician William Downie Stewart; Sir James Allen, who had been the wartime minister of defence; and two ministers in Massey's government, Francis Rolleston and the future prime minister Gordon Coates.[25]

When the Dominion LNU was formed during a conference in July 1922, Gibb was elected president, Presbyterian minister Robert Inglis treasurer and Thomas Sprott, the Anglican bishop of Wellington, a vice-president. The movement clearly attracted many committed Christians, but even for secular members its appeal incorporated elements of a crusade or a moral mission that attracted zeal and dedicated fervour.

The LNU's key aims and values dovetailed with Kate's own beliefs and those of her father before her. Showing tolerance and acceptance of different cultures and religions had always been a priority for Samuel Edger, who had opposed imperialism and endorsed alternatives to war. The theosophical beliefs embraced by Kate's three sisters also endorsed those concepts. There was a long tradition of Christian pacifism and internationalism among nonconformist denominations, especially the Quakers. Women's groups, both during and after World War I, were among those most determined to prevent future conflict. The NCW firmly supported the League of Nations, as did the WCTU. Within the LNU, women like Kate played a significant role in raising public awareness and support, educating students and adults alike.

The idea of a partnership between nations, working to ensure the welfare and prosperity of humanity, mirrored Kate's new liberal ideas about enhancing the common good and the state's role in effecting that aim. It also extended the evangelical Christian view of the primacy of family. The international order envisioned by the league was essentially an extension of the ideal family. Kate's belief in women's roles as moral arbiters of society also found an outlet in her LNU work.

A labour of love

In June 1924 Kate was appointed secretary of the Wellington branch and executive secretary of the Dominion LNU at a salary of £50 per annum. When her salary was raised to £60 four years later, she refused to accept the increase.[26] The work, varied and stimulating, brought her into contact with a range of interesting, like-minded people, both from within New Zealand and abroad. The salary was negligible compared with what she had earned as a headmistress in the 1880s, but this was a labour of love. Although less demanding and all-consuming than teaching, the position involved a considerable amount of time and energy.

Most of Kate's many tasks, great and small, related to spreading the message of the league and expanding membership. Between 1922 and 1931, when she was employed by the LNU, it grew steadily. For the first few years there were never more than about 2000 members nationwide and finances were often strained and precarious. By 1928, however, there were 24 branches throughout New Zealand and a total membership of 18,500: 2500 corporate members and 16,000 individuals. In Britain, membership sky-rocketed from 3217 in 1918 to more than 372,000 in 1924, 934,421 in 1931, and over a million supporters in 1933.[27] The LNU never achieved a comparable increase in public support in New Zealand, possibly because many people believed the organisation to be pacifist. Some members were pacifists, but the LNU did not reject war as such but rather endorsed disarmament and collective security policies as a means of maintaining peace.[28]

Kate's duties involved liaising with newspapers on how best to educate the public, enquiring into teaching about the League of Nations in history classes in schools, sending deputations to the Labour Party about increasing support among working people, organising the speakers and topics at the Dominion LNU's annual conference, communicating with branches about anything of importance received from the London office, and arranging for guest speakers. She also spoke herself. In 1925 she 'gave a good address' to the Women's Study Circle in Wellington, which included short sketches of the women delegates to the League of Nations, and distributed some literature.[29] When Englishman Sir Henry Lunn, a great advocate of the league, devout Methodist and founder of one of the world's most successful travel agencies, visited New Zealand in 1926, Kate booked the hall where he would speak, organised the lecture and civic reception and even obtained Lunn's distinguished visitor's railway ticket.[30]

Sometimes her efforts were more defensive than promotional. In June 1926, along with Peter Fraser and LNU President Gibb, she prepared a statement controverting a statement made by Commander J.R. Middleton in a speech at St Patrick's School in Wellington. Middleton had spoken of those 'who talk about various leagues and treaties and all sorts of ways of keeping peace in the world, but it is deeds and not words that are going to do that. It is wiser to rely on a good Navy, Army, and Air Force than on a strip of paper.'[31]

Kate became a vice-president of the Dominion LNU in 1926. At the annual conference in April, she seconded various remits and introduced one herself, which was adopted: to publish a series of leaflets in bold colours 'setting forth salient facts about the League of Nations and international peace and war'.[32] In September she was among a small deputation from the Wellington LNU that visited the Headmasters' Association to convey the principles of the league and advise about educating young people in its aims and functions.[33]

Later that month she chaired a meeting held for Wellington 'ladies' at a large private home in Thorndon, during which Sir James Allen spoke about the League of Nations. 'Women,' he said, 'were specially interested in the League, as the constitution admitted women to the Assembly, and the one lady who was on the Mandates Commission was, in his opinion, one of the best members.' He firmly believed that 'the personal meeting of men of different nations, closely associated round a table, and exchanging ideas, and learning from one another, was a mighty factor towards the peace of the world'. After Allen's speech, Kate expressed regret that the LNU had so few members in New Zealand. '[W]omen and people generally were intensely interested in war, and … they should surely be even more interested in peace, which meant the preservation of the civilisation of the world, and everything that was dear to women.' She asked everyone present to join the union, and also urged 'the education of all children in the tenets of peace'.[34]

In 1931, during a meeting of the Wellington branch of the LNU, Kate urged more Boy Scouts and Girl Guides to work for their World Friendship Badge, which required some knowledge of the League of Nations and its component parts.[35]

Peace in the Pacific

Like the LNU, the Institute of Pacific Relations (IPR) was devoted to internationalism and peaceful co-operation between nations, but with a focus on the Pacific region. It originated, and was made a permanent organisation, at a two-week conference in

Honolulu in July 1925, which included delegates, many of them intellectuals, from Pacific rim countries. Professor Condliffe of Canterbury College attended, and on his return described the new institute to the *Press* as:

> in no sense of the word a pacifist organisation. It aims to build up in each of the Pacific countries an organisation for the study of the real facts of international problems, and to organise periodical conferences in which men of influence and standing from these countries can meet to discuss ways and means of building up such an international organisation, on the basis of the Washington Treaties, as may prevent the possibility of war. The Institute is assured of ample funds from the United States and Hawaii, and I have been given the task of organising a branch in New Zealand.[36]

The New Zealand branch was formed in 1926, with Allen as chairman, and by 1927 there were groups in Auckland, Wellington, Christchurch and Dunedin.[37] Members of the LNU often belonged to the IPR: General Assembly Librarian Dr Guy Scholefield, for example, was the IPR secretary and an LNU member, and both Allen and Downie Stewart, among others, belonged to both organisations. Walter Nash, secretary of the New Zealand Labour Party and an enthusiastic LNU supporter, sold LNU promotional material through his Clarté Book Room in the capitals' Dixon Street, was also a national vice-president of the IPR, and served for a time as chair of the Wellington branch.

When a second IPR conference was held in Honolulu in July 1927, Nash led the New Zealand delegates. As his biographer notes, 'Meeting educated Asians, and people like [Sir Peter] Buck, made a permanent impression on Nash.' Upon returning to New Zealand, he opposed discriminatory immigration policy and began urging people to 'look behind the mask of race and colour and nation'.[38] Attending the conference also made him more conscious of New Zealand as a Pacific nation, a fact that its close ties with Britain tended to obscure.[39]

Condliffe, writing in 1928, described the IPR as 'an international shock absorber, fact-finder and interpreter', one which 'holds bi-annual conferences, stimulates research and disseminates information'.[40] Liberally funded both by big business and 'philanthropic giants', it was also an organisation in which America, which had opted not to join the League of Nations, could play a leading role.[41]

At an evening session during the September 1927 WCTU annual conference in Wellington, Kate gave a talk entitled 'Pacific Peace Relations', in which she praised the IPR and described the recent Honolulu conference. Over 40 varied research papers had been presented, and the ensuing mingling of all races had 'enabled a beneficial inter-change of opinions, ideas and knowledge between Pacific nations'. The IPR was 'not a League of Governments like the League of Nations, but a League of Peoples'. Its guiding aim was to overcome racial friction in the Pacific and increase understanding between East and West. This, in her view, represented 'the only way to preserve peace in the Pacific'. After quoting several well-known delegates who had expressed great confidence and enthusiasm in the institute's future, she concluded on a highly idealistic note: 'We can help this great aim of international peace in two ways. First we can do our best to help others, and secondly we can send out thoughts of peace to all the world.'[42]

In 1930 Kate employed a familial metaphor for the IPR during a talk entitled simply 'Gentleness', delivered at her sister Eva's house in Epsom at a meeting of the Mothers' Thought Guild. As the *Auckland Star* reported:

> Members of the same family should be bound together by feelings of love. Then comes the village – the clan or tribe, and gentleness is the attitude of mind which should characterise all the members … Both in families and in races, consideration should be shown for each others' likes and dislikes, and efforts should be made to understand one another. Each race has its own peculiar gifts and qualities, and underlying all, there should be a desire to understand each other. Such is the purpose of the Institute of Pacific Relations …[43]

From the outset the IPR enjoyed laudatory and extensive press coverage. In 1925, even before the first conference in Honolulu had taken place, the *New Zealand Herald* stated: 'Already there are signs that out of the conference, which is to be officially known as "An Institute of Pacific Relations", there will come an influence so strong and formative that it will foster political understanding and co-operation, and turn friction into cordial sympathy.'[44] Kate shared this positive hope. Her father, who had waged a protracted battle against anti-Chinese racism in late nineteenth-century New Zealand, would surely have approved of furthering cultural understanding with countries such as China, Japan, Korea and the Philippines.[45]

Dedication to the cause

In early June 1931 Kate resigned as executive secretary of the Wellington LNU branch, in response to some criticism regarding her failure to chase up subscriptions and obtain new members. In July she also resigned as dominion secretary.[46] In September, along with the presentation of a cheque, Gibb paid tribute to her

'broadmindedness, and her unfailing sense of duty', and concluded by reading out
a resolution passed at a recent meeting of the Dominion Council of the League of
Nations Union:

> She has discharged with rare fidelity and efficiency the always laborious and often
> difficult duties of her office. Her keen and disciplined mentality and whole-hearted
> devotion have been an asset of great worth to the union and the objects for which
> it stands … In accepting her resignation the executive most heartily thank her for
> what has been to her as a labour of love and to them a service of enduring value.[47]

At an earlier meeting Kate had been made, by unanimous decision, a life member
of the LNU.

Educating the young in the precepts of peace had always been a high priority
for Kate, and it was in this sphere that the New Zealand LNU arguably did its
most successful work. From the early 1920s, some school textbooks and the *School
Journal* contained praise for the League of Nations and for internationalism. The
journal began moving away from its former imperialist propaganda towards a pro-
league, anti-war message.[48] Condliffe's *A Short History of New Zealand*, published in
1925, conveyed an almost incredulous national pride in New Zealand having been
granted, in 1919, the mandate for the administration of Western Samoa and shared
responsibility for that of Nauru: 'No one in 1825 … foresaw the time when New
Zealand should be a prosperous, settled country, a member of the Commonwealth
of British nations, a member also of the League of Nations, with responsibilities
to undertake on behalf of the civilised world for the welfare of the natives of some
important Pacific Islands.'[49] Literature about the league was placed in the libraries
of schools throughout the country in the 1920s and 1930s. The 1931 New Zealand
secondary syllabus advised teachers to encourage study of the league and to
discourage a narrow nationalism.[50]

Kate's period of active involvement with the LNU covered a very positive time
in the history of the League of Nations. During these years it did valuable social,
economic and humanitarian work around the globe, and promoted the message
of international diplomacy and co-operation. In September 1931, however, Japan
invaded Manchuria and for the remainder of that troubled decade the league
consistently failed to respond adequately to a succession of aggressive acts by
member nations.

The leaders of New Zealand's first Labour government, elected in 1935,
were committed to the League of Nations and internationalism, and repeatedly

protested when the major powers, including Britain, failed to uphold collective security principles and take a stronger stand against aggression. As Peter Fraser said, 'Whether Britain, or Russia or France do or do not agree with us, the moral righteousness of New Zealand's attitude is not affected in the least.'[51]

Kate had begun supporting the LNU and the IPR during the 1920s, when in her mid-sixties, and did not live to see the league's failure to preserve world peace. Through these causes she came into contact with a younger generation who shared her values and ideals. She worked closely with Fraser and Nash, both of whom went on, after her death, to serve as prime ministers.

Nash's Christian socialist humanitarianism had much in common with Kate and William's views. He believed that 'happiness lies in self-sacrifice'. The election manifesto he wrote for Labour in 1935 set out that 'the first charge on the community' should be caring for the worker, the old, the young and the sick. Speaking in the House in 1937 he described co-operation, as practised by Robert Owen, as 'the most beautiful word in the English language'. In 1943 he wrote: 'I am a socialist in that I believe that a major responsibility of Government is to provide collectively for the economic welfare and security of the individual. But I am conservative in the sense that I look upon the family as the foundation of the nation.'[52]

The happy family of nations that Kate hoped the League of Nations would foster did not eventuate, but its legacy should not be underestimated. As Marie Curie once observed, 'the League has a grandeur that commands our support'.[53] Its ideas and aims did not end with the outbreak of World War II; the notion of social and economic co-operation between nations endured, and bodies such as the World Health Organisation and the United Nations are successors to the league ideals. As Leonard Woolf wrote in 1940, the league's failure did not make it a utopian cause, nor did that failure prove it was utopian.[54]

11

Last Years

*There are two kinds of thought, the negative and the positive – think of the positive
and you will help the world rid itself of its evils.*
KATE EVANS, speaking at the Nelson College for Girls Jubilee celebrations,
April 1933[1]

[A] New Zealand woman of unique distinction has passed away.
'Atalanta', tribute to Kate Evans, *Press*, 1 June 1935[2]

In 1930 Kate Evans turned 73. During the early years of that troubled decade, as
the Great Depression tightened its grip, some of her most cherished hopes for
women's rights and international peace were disappointed. She also experienced
losses and challenges in her personal life, though there were brighter times and
compensations during her final years.

Two feminist causes that Kate had long supported, women's right to work and
equal pay in the workplace, came under attack during the economic depression. In
the winter of 1931 New Zealand's registered unemployed reached 50,000, compared
with a little over 5000 a year earlier.[3] Many families suffered hunger and deprivation,
and social services and unemployment relief proved woefully inadequate. In 1932
angry citizens rioted in Auckland, Wellington and Dunedin. The 'Better Britain'
Samuel and Kate had worked so hard to foster seemed like a distant dream.

Female workers had no right to government unemployment relief and many
perceived their presence in the workforce as a threat to the now often uncertain
role of male breadwinner. An irate 1932 editorial in *White Ribbon* entitled 'No Sex
in Citizenship' worried that 'present expediency' was endangering hard-won rights:

This has been specially marked lately in the outcry by many, that a woman's
economic independence should be taken away from her. She should be made
economically dependent upon her husband or her father. If it is necessary that the

girl, whose father can afford to keep her, should be deprived of a job, to give it to one who has no one to provide for her, then why stop there?

We protest most emphatically upon sex being the ground for this distinction. If girls are compelled to be idle, then why not boys, whose fathers can afford to keep them? Why should they enter the labour market and deprive others, who need the money, of the few jobs to be had?[4]

Married women who wanted or, in a great many cases, needed to work were particularly disadvantaged.[5] In 1931, for example, education boards received legal authority to terminate the employment of any married women they employed as teachers, with three months' notice. From the 1880s onwards Kate had protested, and tried through the NZEI to draw attention to the injustice of pay disparities between male and female teachers. Those inequalities continued unabated. Male teachers earned more and were invariably promoted over more experienced female colleagues.

The international horizon steadily darkened. The League of Nations, for which Kate had set such high hopes, failed to respond effectively to Japan's invasion of Manchuria in 1931. In 1932 its Disarmament Conference made it clear that member nations were not prepared to give up their right to arm for war.

Kate was also facing a stressful, financially draining situation in her personal life: in 1930, her son James, who was farming in Pukekohe, was declared bankrupt.[6] Before the war he had been on Kate's 58 hectares in Pakaraka, but in 1918 she sold this, for £3,783, to the government for use in its discharged soldiers' settlement scheme.[7] A 1921 press report described the Pakaraka land as poor quality and full of gorse, whereas the land in Pukekohe that James farmed upon returning from serving abroad would in all likelihood have been better quality.[8] Although a favourite of his mother, the good-humoured and outgoing James developed a gambling problem which, together with commodity price collapses, proved a recipe for financial disaster.

On 27 March 1931 the long list of discharged bankrupts reported in the *Auckland Star* included a paragraph headed 'Mother's Heavy Loss': 'A mother who had provided capital for her son was stated to be a heavy loser in the bankruptcy of Edger James Evans.' Although James had been 'hopelessly insolvent' when he started out, his lawyer 'contended that any son would look at his mother as a tolerant and indulgent creditor, and, in carrying on with her capital, could not be considered to be acting dishonestly'. The amount involved in the bankruptcy was over £5,000,

The Edger sisters together late in life, in Auckland. Left to right, Kate, Lilian, Eva and Marion.

Jill Smith Collection

£4,000 of which – about $500,000 in today's currency – was owed to Kate, 'who had lost almost everything'. James was granted a discharge from the bankruptcy, the judge noting that 'it seemed to be a case of a man who came back from the war with nothing and was put on a farm by his mother'.[9] Kate's will, made in 1931, left nothing to James but £100 for his wife Morfydd; the interest of Kate's remaining money went to Blythe Dungey Lindegaard, until she married or died, and the rest was divided equally between Vryn and Elwyn.[10]

Lilian's visit

On the day the bankruptcy was reported Kate farewelled her sister Lilian, who had arrived in Auckland from India for an extended visit in mid-January 1930. Kate and Blythe drove up from Wellington to meet the traveller, who was staying with Eva in her home in Belvedere Street, Epsom. A family photo of all the Edger sisters taken at this time shows them looking relaxed and clearly happy to be together. There is something both benign and curiously Victorian about their appearance: despite the 1930s-style clothes, it is not difficult to imagine them in high-necked floor-length attire.

221

They did not have much time together in Auckland as Lilian soon began the first of many jaunts around the country. When not sightseeing she was delivering public lectures advocating her new hero Mahatma Gandhi, or the causes of world peace and anti-racism and the necessity to give the League of Nations more clout.[11] Although they lived far apart, her views were clearly closely aligned with those of Kate. Towards the end of January, Lilian and Marion visited Albertland to see old friends, then Lilian proceeded south on her own to Wellington, where she stayed with Kate and Blythe in Miramar. She gave several talks and lectures in the capital, which received considerable press coverage. In Auckland, where she concluded her stay, she spent time speaking to the WCTU annual peace meeting. She returned to India on the *Marama* on 27 March 1931. Kate never saw her younger sister again.

Losses and a departure

On 10 May 1931 Kate's old friend, fellow feminist and social reformer Lady Anna Stout died, less than a year after her husband's death in July 1930. She had long suffered from poor hearing and often wielded a formidable looking ear-trumpet as the problem worsened with age. Throughout the 1920s she gradually withdrew from active engagement in public affairs and social events. Despite their very different temperaments and social positions, Anna and Kate – and their husbands – had worked amicably and fruitfully together for decades on behalf of the same causes, and in their advancing years the two women continued to share interests. Anna was a member of the Wellington branch of the League of Nations Union, and she and Kate both enjoyed the Lyceum Club.

That year brought two more bereavements. Kate's former student Edith Searle Grossmann, the novelist and biographer, died in February 1831. Jessie Mackay, in a fulsome obituary tribute to Grossmann, described her as 'one of that bright girl-galaxy of Canterbury College following in the pioneer footsteps of the Edger sisters and Helen Connon'.[12] Then Kate's brother-in-law and cousin Frederick Judson died in September, aged 86. He and Marion had lived briefly in Auckland following their marriage, after which Frederick had settled on a large property at Nihotupu in the Waitākere Ranges where he became a familiar local identity, continuing to direct the local telephone station until well beyond his eightieth year.[13]

In 1932 Kate decided to move to Dunedin to live with her son Elwyn and his family in Roslyn. After 41 busy years in Wellington, this departure must have occasioned some sadness and regret. She was, after all, leaving her live-in

Sir Robert and Lady Anna Stout in 1929, aged 85 and 71 respectively.

Alexander Turnbull Library, Wellington, PAColl-7171-92

companion, her friends and fellow members of different clubs and social reform movements, as well as the Newtown congregation. Although the last three years of her life in Dunedin were quiet and circumscribed, Kate still assisted the WCTU and kept up with the League of Nations Union, of which she was a vice-president.

Jubilee celebrations

One notable highlight during Kate's final years was attending the fiftieth anniversary jubilee celebrations at Nelson College for Girls over Easter weekend in April 1933. Attended by over 700 old girls from all over New Zealand, the varied programme of events and entertainments included a morning tea, a motor picnic, an evening reception and cake, a pageant highlighting half a century of school fashions and a jubilee ball. The old girls had been busily organising and fundraising for these celebrations since 1930.[14] Four of the college's previous five principals attended the jubilee. Initially Kate had not felt robust enough to travel from Dunedin to Nelson and declined the invitation, but as the time drew near she began to feel that 'it was not right to be absent'.[15] With characteristic determination, she made the effort to go.

At the Saturday evening reception, as the founding headmistress of Nelson Girls' College was assisted onto the platform to deliver her speech, she was warmly received. When she began speaking, 'an intense silence came over the room'. Addressing the audience simply as 'Dear Girls', she noted, 'No doubt it would be possible to mention many things in the life of the school that had their origin half a century ago', but these she had not time to detail. Her message to past and present pupils was that 'they should cultivate the power of positive thought, by which they might help the world to rid itself of its evils'. After quoting Emerson, that 'thought was the most wonderful power in the universe', she advised:

> Be careful how and what you think for what you think makes your life what it is going to be. In the same way it is what a nation thinks that makes it what it is – a country owes what it is to the collective thought of its people. And so, if we want peace, we must think peace. If everybody thought peace and love it would do more than the League of Nations and would be more likely to bring peace on the earth than anything else. If you think rightly, and have your thoughts directed upwards, and not downwards, you will be helping to rid the world of its pain and misery.

As she resumed her seat, the 'revered' first principal received 'a rousing ovation with hearty cheers'.[16]

Pioneers

On 20 April 1935 Marion died aged 86. In addition to praising her 'long life of varied experience and useful work', her obituary paid tribute to her 'gentleness and sweetness and unselfish consideration for others', qualities that had 'endeared her to all who came in touch with her'. Marion's obituary was titled 'Pioneer's Death'.[17] By the mid-1930s, all the Edger sisters enjoyed that venerable status. They had arrived as children in a fledgling colony in the mid-Victorian era and lived to see it become a complex society linked to the rest of the world by telegraph, telephone, radio, luxury liners, aeroplanes and, last but not least, the universal allure of Hollywood movies. Roads, once so scarce and inadequate, were now extensive, and traversed not by horses but by cars, buses and trucks. Instead of candles or gas lamps, electricity lit houses and streets, and new electric household appliances made cooking and cleaning less time consuming and labour intensive. Society had altered in innumerable intangible ways, not least in women's opportunities, rights and expectations.

Kate died only weeks after her elder sister, on 6 May 1935 aged 78. The exact cause is not known, but her health had been failing for several years. Her niece Dora Judson, writing to a friend in June 1935, referred to Kate's recent death as 'a very happy release after a year of helplessness'.[18] On the day Kate died, her name was included in the press among the list of New Zealand recipients of the King's Silver Jubilee Medal, awarded to persons for 'faithful and distinguished public service during His Majesty's reign'. Women accounted for 300 (or 20 percent) of the 1500 medal recipients.[19]

Obituaries hailed Kate Evans as one of the trailblazers of women's higher education. They also extolled her pioneering social work through the Forward Movement and the Wellington SPWC, and her more recent role in promoting the League of Nations. The *Evening Post* tribute on 11 May stands out for its insight into a key element of Kate's character: 'Mrs. Evans had a gentle and charming personality which, in a way, masked her power and determination to work for what was right and just. She was not one to make any noise about her works, but they were carried through with ability and energy.'[20] Determination, or 'indomitable perseverance', had also been the quality that Kate's former headmaster, Farquhar Macrae, had emphasised in his testimonial when she embarked on her teaching career in the late 1870s.

On 1 June in the *Press*, 'Atalanta' described Kate as a 'woman of unique distinction': 'Advance of years and widowhood did not halt her straight and strenuous course. She was ever pressing toward the highest, obliterating self-advantage, scorning the need of rest, seeking only to serve the changing, emerging conditions of a world grown out of recognition since her early name was made in New Zealand's heroic moulding days.' The author lamented, too, the death four months earlier of John Macmillan Brown, who had 'carried the day for the entry of women into the young college on the Avon.'[21]

Unlike Lilian, who returned to New Zealand in the late 1930s and died in 1941, Kate did not live to see the outbreak of World War II as a blow to her League of Nations ideal. But neither did she live to see the election of the first Labour government at the end of November 1935, which implemented family-supportive welfare assistance and attached front-rank importance to education. In December Peter Fraser, her old friend and fellow League of Nations advocate and now minister of education, gave a statement to the press about the government's educational goals. These included one aim that had always been close to Kate's heart: 'every New Zealand child will have an opportunity of attaining the highest level physically, intellectually, morally and spiritually.'[22]

Epilogue

Writing in the *Listener* in 1976, W.J. Gardner suggested that Kate Edger's capping day, 11 July 1877, 'ought to be celebrated by tens of thousands of New Zealand women graduates'.[1] This has not happened, but Kate's pioneering role in women's higher education has been commemorated. Opposite the Old Choral Hall where she graduated is the sleek steel and glass façade of the University of Auckland's Kate Edger Information Commons, completed in 2003. The Kate Edger Educational Charitable Trust, based in Auckland, promotes and advances the cause of women's education, provides a range of scholarships, and runs the annual academic dress hire for University of Auckland graduation ceremonies. One of its trustees, Jill Smith, is both an Auckland graduate and Kate's granddaughter.[2]

At Nelson College for Girls Kate's memory and legacy remain central to the school's ethos and identity. According to the principal Cathy Ewing, the words of the school song, which encourages girls to go out into the world as 'bold young women, quite undaunted, building pathways for us to tread', 'epitomises Kate Edger's vision for what education for girls might accomplish'.[3] Kate is also remembered in Kate Edger Place in Stoke, outside Nelson. In the course of New Zealand's celebrations for the 125th anniversary of women's suffrage, she was honoured in ceremonies in Auckland and Nelson and her achievements featured alongside those of other first-wave feminists in various newspaper articles and exhibitions.

The profound importance and continuing beneficial impact of Kate's pioneering work in women's secondary and tertiary education cannot be overestimated. The fact that a young woman had calmly earned a university degree, and done so with distinction, did not put paid to arguments that women were intellectually inferior to men and unable to engage in academic study without doing themselves mental and physical harm. It did, however, provide ample ammunition against those making such claims. New Zealand women rapidly followed in Kate's footsteps and graduated in impressive numbers, proving that women both wanted to undertake tertiary studies and could do so successfully. In recognising women's equal rights as citizens and proving their intellectual ability, the opening up of tertiary education to women was an important precursor to female suffrage.

In another important break with the past, the secondary schools she helped to found took girls' education seriously. They built confidence, fostered a sense of female solidarity and opened up both future professional possibilities and economic independence. Kate and Lilian Edger, Helen Connon and other early teachers and headmistresses were inspiring role models. Moreover, by combining teaching and social reform activism with being a wife and mother, Kate gave the lie to the charge that women's higher education guaranteed 'spinsterdom'.

Kate's experiences as a university student and as a pioneering teaching professional provide a rare insight into the formative years of female secondary and tertiary education, a relatively unexamined but significant and influential aspect of New Zealand women's history. Her opposition to differential rates of pay for male and female teachers, and her work within the NZEI to improve professional working conditions and standards, are early examples of a teaching professional concerned with equity and justice for female teachers.

For Kate, the ideal education involved more than just acquiring knowledge and skills. It entailed fostering students' moral well-being and motivating them to go into the world and strive to make it a better place. She wanted women to be active citizens, selflessly helping others and pursuing the common good. In her own life she practised what she preached. She actively supported the campaign for women's suffrage, worked tirelessly to remove the scourge of alcohol with its many negative impacts on family life, and strove to protect the rights of vulnerable women and children.

During the Liberals' period in power, women's rights activists, in groups such as the WCTU, SPWC and NCW, had the ear of some highly influential politicians, and they helped to advance a raft of legislation specifically directed at increasing women and children's legal rights. Kate made two important contributions in this sphere: helping to raise awareness about incest and to initiate legislative sanctions against it, in the form of the Criminal Code Amendment Act 1900, and pushing for the creation of children's courts through the Juvenile Offenders Act 1906. For decades she also undertook unpaid pioneering social work, both in the Forward

Movement and under the auspices of the Wellington SPWC. In doing so, she helped many during years when welfare benefits and legislative safeguards for women and children were minimal or, more often, non-existent.

As Margaret Tennant has noted, 'Christianity was probably the single most motivating force within the voluntary social services within New Zealand, at least until the Second World War.'[4] This was certainly the case with Kate. Religion coloured every aspect of her life and shaped all her social welfare work. A strong belief in moral reform and individual redemption, for example, informed her efforts to introduce a more humane and reformative prison system. Similarly, her notions of fostering a mutually supportive, unified society – in which the more privileged and educated middle classes worked to assist those less fortunate than themselves – was an expression of the co-operative anti-materialist views inherited from her father.

In her later years Kate worked tirelessly to uphold the League of Nations. Like the evangelical domestic ideal, the family of nations needed to build selfless and mutually supportive policies for the good of mankind. There was an upsurge of pacifism and international arbitration among women's organisations in the aftermath of World War I. Preventing another conflict was a subject that women, as mothers, and in their role as moral arbiters, felt a renewed interest in endorsing.

The puritan element of nonconformism and its legacy on New Zealand culture is often portrayed in an unflattering light by historians and social commentators. There were, of course, zealous, fun-hating, religiously intolerant nonconformists, but there was another important and influential strain of nonconformist reformers who, like Kate, were liberal, religiously tolerant, supportive of women's rights, and concerned to improve the lives of those less fortunate.

In contemporary New Zealand, despite innumerable transformations and a second wave of crusading feminism, women and children still face many of the physical and sexual dangers that Kate and her fellow reformers worked so hard to alleviate. Violence against women remains a pressing issue. According to one recent study, 35 percent of New Zealand women will experience physical and/or sexual violence from an intimate partner in their lifetime, and the country has one of the highest rates of child abuse in the developed world. Speaking at a National Council of Women conference in Auckland in 2018, former Prime Minister Helen Clark described violence against women as a 'national crisis'. In its annual report for 2017–18, Oranga Tamariki, the Ministry for Children, recorded 92,250 reports of concern involving 64,950 individual children or young people.[5]

Kate Evans was a modest, unassuming person, but a determined and persistent battler for social reform, an aspect of her life's work that has not received the attention it warrants. In addition to pioneering higher education for women, she tirelessly campaigned to protect and augment the rights of women and children. She never ceased to believe that, with enough hard work and activism, womanly values of nurturing support and compassion could prevail.

Notes

ABBREVIATIONS

AJHR – Appendices to the Journals of the House of Representatives
AWMM – Auckland War Memorial Museum
ATL – Alexander Turnbull Library
NCC – Nelson College Collection
NPM – Nelson Provincial Museum
NZJH – New Zealand Journal of History
NZPD – New Zealand Parliamentary Debates

INTRODUCTION

1. 'All Sorts of People', *Free Lance,* 12 January 1901, p. 3.
2. Max O'Rell, an American journalist, originally made these comments in the *North American Review*. They were picked up and quoted in several New Zealand newspapers, e.g. *New Zealand Herald*, 3 October 1896 p. 2, cited in Deborah Montgomerie, 'New Women and Not So New Men: Discussions about marriage in New Zealand 1890–1914', *NZJH*, 51, 1, 2017, p. 50, fn 94.
3. 'Presentation of the degree of Bachelor of Arts to Miss Edger', *Auckland Star*, 12 July 1877, p. 3.
4. Barbara Brookes, *A History of New Zealand Women* (Wellington: Bridget Williams Books, 2016), p. 121.
5. Patricia Grimshaw, entry for Kate Milligan Evans in A.H. McClintock (ed.), *Encyclopedia of New Zealand*, vol. 1 (Wellington: Government Printer, 1966), p. 573.
6. Beryl Hughes. 'Edger, Kate Milligan', *Dictionary of New Zealand Biography*, first published in 1993. Te Ara – the Encyclopedia of New Zealand: https://teara.govt.nz/en/biographies/2e3/edger-kate-milligan; Megan Hutching, *Leading the Way: How New Zealand women won the vote* (Auckland: HarperCollins, 2010), p. 222. Kate wrote the 1923 article, entitled 'The First Girl Graduates', for the Canterbury College fiftieth jubilee celebrations. It appeared in a special supplement to the *Lyttelton Times* on 12 May 1923, p. 16.
7. Jock Phillips and Terry Hearn, *Settlers: New Zealand immigrants from England, Ireland and Scotland 1800–1945* (Auckland: Auckland University Press, 2008), p. 186.
8. Book-length biographies of New Zealand first-wave feminists are rare and often pay little

attention to religious belief. Judith Devaliant's biography *Kate Sheppard* (Auckland: Penguin, 1992), for example, does not examine Sheppard's Congregationalism in any depth. Raewyn Dalziel, in a celebrated article entitled 'The Colonial Helpmeet: Women's role and the vote in nineteenth-century New Zealand', *NZJH*, 11, 2, 1977, pp. 112–23, highlighted the fact that women who campaigned for the vote did not query their roles as wives, mothers and helpmeets, and perceived political (voting) rights as recognition of the worth of that vocation. The link between this strong attachment to women's traditional domestic role and religion was not explored, however. This article also appeared in Barbara Brookes, Charlotte Macdonald and Margaret Tennant (eds), *Women in History: Essays on European women in New Zealand* (Wellington: Allen & Unwin/Port Nicholson Press, 1986), pp. 55–68. Grace Millar, in 'Women's Lives, Feminism and the *New Zealand Journal of History*', *NZJH*, 52, 2, 2018, p. 134, makes the point that between 1993 and 2017, only 10 percent of articles in the *NZJH* focused on women's lives, and another 20 percent included women as historical actors. Discussions focusing on the relationship between religion and the social reform activism of first-wave feminists, either in the *NZJH* or elsewhere, are rare.

9. John Stenhouse, 'God's Own Silence: Secular nationalism, Christianity and the writing of New Zealand History', *NZJH*, 38, 1, 2004, pp. 53, 55, 57. This argument features in an expanded form in Stenhouse's 'Religion and Society', Chapter 14 in Giselle Byrnes (ed.), *The Oxford History of New Zealand* (Melbourne and Auckland: Oxford University Press, 2009), pp. 323–56.

10. Julie Spraggon, *Puritan Iconoclasm During the English Civil War* (Woodbridge, Suffolk and Rochester New York: Boydell Press, 2003), p. 98.

11. Julie Melnyk, *Victorian Religion: Faith and life in Britain* (London: Praeger, 2008), pp. 36–37.

12. Brian Harrison, in *Drink and the Victorians: The temperance question in England, 1815–1872* (Staffordshire: Keele University Press, 1994, 2nd edn), notes that the prominent role allotted to women by Quakers helped to get the temperance movement used to the idea of employing women in reforming work of all kinds. Harrison includes, on p. 163, a table listing the many and varied causes, 62 in all, pursued by prominent British teetotallers, a group dominated by nonconformist denominations, between 1833 and 1872.

13. Richard J. Helmstadter, 'The Nonconformist Conscience', in Gerald Parsons (ed.), *Religion in Victorian Britain, Volume IV: Interpretations* (New York: Manchester University Press/Open University, New York, c. 1988), pp. 70–73.

14. See James Belich's *Paradise Reforged: A history of the New Zealanders from the 1880s to the year 2000* (Auckland: Penguin, 2001), pp. 17–24, on longstanding 'myths of settlement' in New Zealand.

15. Census figures from 'Census 1871–1916, Religious Affiliation of the Population, 1871 and 1891': http://archive.stats.govt.nz/. Though Methodists had risen to 10.12 percent and Baptists to 2.37, Congregationalists dropped to a mere 1.07 by 1891.

16. Helmstadter, 'The Nonconformist Conscience', p. 62.

17. John Stuart Mill, *On Liberty, Utilitarianism and other Essays* (Oxford: Oxford University Press, 2015), pp. 409, 421.

18. The Unitarians were formed in Britain in 1774. Between 1800 and 1850 they moved from questioning the doctrine of the Trinity to questioning the miraculous inspiration of the scripture. They were not involved in the evangelical revival.

19. Melnyk, *Victorian Religion*, pp. 19–21. William Wilberforce, an influential MP and Anglican Evangelical, took the lead in the anti-slavery campaigns. The slave trade ended in 1803 and slavery in all British territories in 1833.

20. Ian Bradley, *The Call to Seriousness: The evangelical impact on the Victorians* (London: Jonathan Cape, 1976), p. 179.

21. John Tosh, *A Man's Place: Masculinity and the middle-class home in Victorian England* (New Haven and London: Yale University Press, 1999), p. 47.

22. Julia Bush, *Women Against the Vote: Female anti-suffragism in Britain* (Oxford, New York: Oxford University Press, 2007), p. 24.

23. John Ruskin, *Sesame and Lilies* (London: George Allen, 1905), p. 137.

24. Lucy Bland, *Banishing the Beast: Sexuality and the early feminists* (New York: The New Press, 1995), p. 52; Eileen Janes Yeo (ed.), *Introduction to Radical Femininity: Women's self-representation in the public sphere* (Manchester and New York: Manchester University Press, 1998), p. 7.

25. Jennifer Somerville, *Feminism and the Family: Politics and society in the UK and USA* (New York: St Martin's Press, 2000), p. 30.

26. Judith R. Walkowitz, *City of Dreadful Delight: Narratives of sexual danger in late Victorian London* (London: Virago, 1992), p. 92.

27. Barbara Brookes, 'A Weakness for Strong Subjects: The women's movement and sexuality', *NZJH*, 27, 2, 1993, p. 143.

28. Kate Sheppard, editorial, *White Ribbon*, 1 October 1896, p. 6 and *Woman Suffrage in New Zealand* (London: International Women Suffrage Alliance, 1907), p. 13.

29. Bland, *Banishing the Beast*, p. 84.

30. Katrina Ford, *Unpretending Excellence: A life of Kate Edger* (Auckland: The Kate Edger Educational Charitable Trust, 2017).

31. June Hannan, in *Feminism* (Harlow: Pearson Longman, 2012), p. 5, makes the point that 'women's attempts at reform in "quieter" periods need to be rescued from obscurity and seen as a key part of the history of feminism'.

32. Jenny Daggers uses the term 'spiritual womanhood' to describe this sense of a female civilising mission, which served as a vehicle for women's mobilisation in the nineteenth century as feminists, evangelicals and philanthropists. See Jenny Daggers, 'Josephine Butler and Christian Women's Identity', in Jenny Daggers and Diana Neal (eds), *Sex, Gender and Religion: Josephine Butler revisited* (New York: Peter Lang, 2006), pp. 99–100.

CHAPTER 1 **TO THE PROMISED LAND**

1. Miles Fairburn, *The Ideal Society and its Enemies: The foundations of modern New Zealand society, 1850–1900* (Auckland: Auckland University Press, 1989), p. 24.

2. Samuel Edger, *Autobiographical Notes and Lectures* (London: William Isbister, 1886), p. 83.

3. Sir Henry Brett and Henry Hook, *The Albertlanders: Brave pioneers of the 'sixties* (Christchurch: Capper Press, 1979, original edn 1927), p. 35 contains the 'Programme of the Farewell Gatherings'.

4. Lucy Sargisson and Lymon Tower Sargent, *Living in Utopia: New Zealand's intentional communities* (Aldershot: Ashgate, 2004), p. 21; Jock Phillips and Terry Hearn, *Settlers: New Zealand immigrants from England, Ireland and Scotland 1800–1945* (Auckland: Auckland University Press, 2008), p. 38.

5. Sargisson and Sargent, *Living in Utopia*, p. xv.

6. Edger, *Autobiographical Notes*, p. 79.

7. Ibid., p. 82.

8. Ibid., pp. 64, 71.

9. In an 1862 shipboard diary entry, Samuel referred to a dream in which he found himself still in his first parish of Kimbolton, while his family was en route to New Zealand. In an understandable panic, he 'jumped into a carriage to post off for Milligan to preach for me'. Samuel Edger Letters, 1862–63, MS-0711, B1507, ATL, p. 19.

10. Particular Baptists, strong followers of John Calvin's teaching, believed in a particular atonement: that is, that Christ died not for all but for an elect.

11. The Census, 1841, East Grinstead, Sussex, England; www.theweald.org/N10 ASP? Nld=4480273 lists these various siblings and their ages; Samuel was not in the house at the time of the census. See www.thekeep.info, file WHL 134, re the acquisition of Pixton or Pickstone Hill House by John Edger who, having leased it for many years, purchased it in 1852.

12. Edger, *Autobiographical Notes*, pp. 40–41.

13. See Edward R. Norman, *The Victorian Christian Socialists, Cambridge* (New York: Cambridge University Press), 1987.

14. F.D. Maurice's first tract on Christian Socialism, written in February 1850, cited in Bernard Murchland, *The Dream of Christian Socialism: An essay on its European origins* (Washington and London: American Enterprise Institute for Public Policy Research, 1982), p. 6.

15. Peter J. Lineham, 'Edger, Samuel', *Dictionary of New Zealand Biography*, first published 1993, Te Ara – the Encyclopedia of New Zealand: https://teara.govt.nz/en/biographies/2e4/edger-samuel

16. Edger, *Autobiographical Notes*, p. 328.

17. https://nzhistory.govt.nz/files/documents/peopling3.pdf

18. Brett and Hook, *The Albertlanders*, pp. 16–17, 22–23.

19. Ibid., p. 10; www3.stats.govt.nz, Statistics of New Zealand 1862, Table 1.1. Despite its apparent precision, this figure is estimated.

20. *Albertland Gazette*, Advertisements, Issue 2, 3 July 1862.

21. Samuel Edger Letters, pp. 15–16.

22. J.L. Borrows, *Albertland: The last organised British settlement in New Zealand* (Wellington, Auckland: Reed Publishing, 1969), pp. 36–37, 19–20.

23. Brett and Hook, *The Albertlanders*, pp. 36–37.

24. Statistics of New Zealand for 1862: www3.stats.govt.nz

25. Edger, *Autobiographical Notes*, p. 99.

26. This movement, under the leadership of the great Waikato rangatira and first Māori king Pōtatau Te Wherowhero, and his son and successor Tāwhiao, opposed land sales and aimed to protect Māori independence. War between the followers of the King Movement and the colonial forces began in 1860 and 'raged almost continuously for thirteen years'. James Belich, 'The Governors and the Maori', in Keith Sinclair (ed.), *The Oxford Illustrated History of New Zealand* (Auckland: Oxford University Press, 1999, 2nd edn), p. 88.

27. Brett and Hook, *The Albertlanders*, p. 78.

28. Samuel Edger Letters, p. 81.

29. Borrows, *Albertland*, p. 63.

30. Brett and Hook, *The Albertlanders*, pp. 78–82.

31. Marion Judson, quoted in Brett and Hook, *The Albertlanders*, p. 83.

32. Samuel Edger Letters, p. 64.

33. Brett and Hook, *The Albertlanders*, p. 85.

34. Michael Watts, *The Dissenters, Volume II: The Expansion of evangelical nonconformity*, Oxford: Clarendon Press, 1995, p. 563.

35. Edger Letters, pp. 186, 139, 187.

36. Edger, *Autobiographical Notes*, p. 83.

37. Ibid., p. 85.

38. 'Extracts from Diary, The Dark Features of the Future'; this entry, dated 13 August 1866, from Port Albert, is part of *Biographical Sketch of the Reverend Samuel Edger, B.A., late of Auckland, New Zealand, with extracts from diary and Auckland Herald* (East Grinstead: Hawthorne Printing, 1883), University of Auckland Special Collections New Zealand Glass Case 204 E 23b, pp. 11–13.

39. 'Extracts from Diary', p. 16.

40. 'Extracts from Diary', 27 August 1866, p. 14.

41. 'Extracts from Diary', p. 16.

42. Brett and Hook, *The Albertlanders*, p. 111.

43. Jenny Coleman, *Polly Plum: A firm and earnest woman's advocate, Mary Ann Colclough 1836–1885* (Dunedin: Otago University Press, 2017), p. 120.

44. Coleman, *Polly Plum*, p. 118.

45. Ibid., p. 12.

46. 'Pioneer's Death, Mrs. E.M. Judson', *Auckland Star*, 20 April 1935, p. 15; 'The Temperance Concert', *Auckland Star*, 31 August 1876, p. 3.

47. Edger, *Autobiographical Notes*, p. 88.

48. Information courtesy of Peter Marsh, Manager/Curator, Albertland Heritage Centre, Wellsford, February 2018.

49. 'Pioneer's Death'.

50. *Daily Southern Cross*, 21 May 1872, p. 1.

51. 'Lorne Street Hall Entertainment', *New Zealand Herald*, 9 October 1875, p. 3.

52. As Katrina Ford points out in *Unpretending Excellence: A life of Kate Edger* (Auckland: The Kate Edger Educational Charitable Trust, 2017), p. 16, Kate's involvement in the spelling bee indicated she was in a 'social milieu that took female intellectual achievement seriously'.

53. 'Lorne Street Hall Social Gathering', *Daily Southern Cross*, 29 August 1876, p. 2.

54. P.J. O'Connor, 'Keeping New Zealand White, 1908–1920', *NZJH*, 2, 1, 1968, p. 42.

55. See Samuel Edger, 'Anti-Chinese Agitation: A better way', *New Zealand Herald*, 13 September 1879, p. 5; 'Chinese and Saxons', *New Zealand Herald*, 22 September 1879, p. 6; 'Sir George Grey and the Chinese', *Auckland Star*, 24 May 1881, p. 3; 'The Chinese Question, *Auckland Star*, 1 June 1881, p. 3.

56. Auckland Institute and Museum, Minute Book IV, 1878–1883, MUS-1995-4, Auckland War Memorial Museum [AWMM].

57. Edger, *Autobiographical Notes*, p. 106.

58. Alfred J. Gabay, *Messages from Beyond: Spiritualism and spiritualists in Melbourne's golden age* (Carlton, Victoria: Melbourne University Press, 2001), p. 57.

59. See F.B. Smith, 'Walker, Thomas (1858–1932)', *Australian Dictionary of Biography*, National Centre of Biography, Australian National University: http://adb.anu.edu.au/biography/walker-thomas-4789/text7975, published first in hardcopy 1976. Walker embraced secularism in 1882 and later became minister of justice and attorney general in Western Australia.

60. Edger, *Autobiographical Notes*, pp. 107–08.

61. Robert S. Ellwood, *Islands of the Dawn: The story of alternative spirituality in New Zealand* (Hawai`i: University of Hawai`i Press, 1993), p. 35.

CHAPTER 2 'A LADY ADMITTED'

1. Charles Darwin, *The Descent of Man and Selection in Relation to Sex* (London: John Murray, 2nd edn 1888), p. 361.
2. 'A Lady Admitted', *New Zealand Herald*, 12 July 1877, p. 2.
3. Patricia Grimshaw, *Women's Suffrage in New Zealand* (Auckland: Auckland University Press; Oxford: Oxford University Press, 1987), p. 3; Linda L. Clark, *Women and Achievement in Nineteenth-Century Europe* (Cambridge: Cambridge University Press, 2008), p. 189.
4. Susie Steinbach, *Women in England 1760–1914: A social history* (New York: Palgrave Macmillan, 2004), p. 181.
5. For example, when Glasgow's Queen Mary College, set up in 1883 by a woman's organisation, merged with the University of Glasgow in 1892, there were separate reading rooms for women in the library and male and female students sat apart during official ceremonies; Clark, *Women and Achievement*, p. 183.
6. 'A Brief Biography of William Steadman Aldiss', n.p., n.d., unpublished ms, Auckland Public Library, cited in Grimshaw, *Women's Suffrage*, p. 5.
7. Dr. Harry Campbell, *Differences in the Nervous Organisms of Man and Woman* (London: H. Lewis, 1891), p. 612, quoted in Lucy Bland, *Banishing the Beast: Sexuality and the early feminists* (New York: The New Press, 1995), p. 74. Earlier in the century the noted sociologist Herbert Spencer made the comparison between Victorian women's intellectual stage of development and that of the 'savage races'; see 'The Comparative Psychology of Man', *Popular Science Monthly*, 8, 1875–76, pp. 257–89.
8. Samuel Edger, 'Mr. Mill and Women', *Daily Southern Cross*, 13 May 1871, p. 3.
9. John Stuart Mill, *On Liberty, Utilitarianism and other Essays* (Oxford: Oxford University Press, 2015), pp. 409, 421.
10. Olive Banks, *Faces of Feminism: A study of feminism as a social movement* (Oxford: Martin Robertson, 1981), p. 41.
11. Margaret A. Nash, *Women's Education in the United States 1780–1840* (New York: Palgrave Macmillan, 2005), pp. 20–23, 113.
12. Banks, *Faces of Feminism*, pp. 44–45.
13. www.educationengland.org.uk, *Schools Inquiry Commission Report*, vol. 1, ch. 6 (1867–68), reprinted as Chapter 1 in D. Beale, Principal of the Ladies' College Cheltenham, *Reports Issued by the Schools Inquiry Commission on the Education of Girls* (London: David North, 1870), p. 3.
14. Dorothy Page, 'Dalrymple, Learmonth White', from the *Dictionary of New Zealand Biography*: https://teara.govt.nz/en/biographies/1d2/dalrymple-learmonth-white
15. Ibid.
16. One possible reason for this was the lack of money from the goldfields, from which both Dunedin and Christchurch had benefited.
17. Samuel Edger, 'A Contribution towards Elucidating the Ideal Education', Lecture IV in *Autobiographical Notes and Lectures* (London: William Isbister, 1886), pp. 230, 231, 235, 238, 240.

18. Olive Trotter, 'Richardson, John Larkins Cheese', *Dictionary of New Zealand Biography*: https://teara.govt.nz/en/biographies/1r8/richardson-john-larkins-cheese

19. J.L.C. Richardson, *Thoughts on Female Education, with special reference to the Otago Educational Movement, a lecture delivered by the Hon. Major Richardson at Knox College, Dunedin, Tuesday October 11, 1870* (Dunedin: Otago Daily Times Office, 1870), University of Auckland Special Collections NZ LS 1506.N45R5, New Zealand Glass Case, pp. 6, 9, 10, 14, 15.

20. 'Inauguration of the Otago University', *Otago Witness*, 15 July 1871, p. 4.

21. W.J. Gardner, *Colonial Cap and Gown: Studies in the mid-Victorian universities of Australasia* (Christchurch: University of Canterbury, 1979), p. 75. Stout's article appeared in the *Southern League* on 5 July 1871.

22. 'The Otago University', *Otago Witness*, 19 August 1871, p. 17. The petition text was reproduced in the newspaper on 19 August, but the petition had been presented at a special council meeting on the 8th.

23. University of Otago Council Minutes, 8 August 1871, Hocken Library, Dunedin, cited in Gardner, *Colonial Cap and Gown*, p. 77, fn 21.

24. Gardner, *Colonial Cap and Gown*, p. 78.

25. 'Higher Education of Women', *Otago Witness*, 8 June 1872, p. 2.

26. Learmonth Dalrymple, *A Few Thoughts on the Higher Education of Women* (Dunedin: Fergusson & Mitchell, 1872), Hocken Collections, University of Otago Library, HOC 5/1/1, pp. 6–8.

27. 'Foundation of the Girls' High School', *Evening Star*, 4 April 1896, p. 6. This was one of several extracts of letters from Richardson to Dalrymple, sent to the paper by the latter over 20 years later. The letter cited was dated 14 May 1872 and headed Willowmead, Clutha.

28. Dalrymple, 'A Few Thoughts on the Higher Education of Women' p. 7.

29. Gardner, *Colonial Cap and Gown*, p. 80.

30. Ibid., pp. 80–81.

31. Kay Morris Matthews makes this suggestion in *In Their Own Right: Women and higher education in New Zealand before 1945* (Wellington: NCER Press, 2008), p. 126.

32. University of Auckland Historical Collection part 1, MSS and Archives, E8, Box 2, Folder 2, Special Collections, n.p.

33. 'New Zealand University: A lady admitted to the Degree of Bachelor of Arts', *New Zealand Herald*, 12 July 1877, p. 3.

34. *Auckland Star*, 29 March 1877, p. 2.

35. 'Our Home Letter', *New Zealand Herald*, 11 April 1877, p. 2. The editor of the *Herald* at this time, and the likely author of this piece, was William Berry.

36. Ibid.

37. See www.gutenberg.org/files/791/791-h for a full online version of the poem.

38. 'New Zealand University: A lady admitted …'.

39. *New Zealand Herald*, 11 July 1877, p. 2.

40. 'Presentation of the Degree of Bachelor of Arts to Miss Edger', *Auckland Star*, 12 July 1877, p. 3.

41. *Auckland Star*, 12 May 1891, p. 4.

42. 'New Zealand University: A lady admitted …'.

43. Ibid.

44. *Auckland Star*, 12 May 1891, p. 4.

45. 'Makers of Auckland', *New Zealand Herald*, 13 August 1929, p. 6.

46. 'First Woman Graduate, Pioneer Auckland Student', *New Zealand Herald*, 11 July 1931, p. 12.

47. *Official Handbook*, 1890: www3.stats.govt.nz/historic-publications/1890-official handbook

48. See Gina Rippon's entertaining *The Gendered Brain* (London: Penguin, 2019) re ongoing scientific claims about women's inferior brains.

CHAPTER 3 'EMINENT SUCCESS IN HER PROFESSION'

1. Although the first newspaper reference in 1877 referred to Canterbury College Girls' High School, Christchurch Girls' High School was more commonly used from 1877 onwards, and a Christchurch High School Old Girls' Association was formed in 1900.

2. Kay Morris Matthews, *In Their Own Right: Women and higher education in New Zealand before 1945* (Wellington: NCER Press, 2008), p. 12.

3. Ibid., p. 19.

4. Ibid., p. 12.

5. Lilian scored 531 from a possible 640 marks. The next highest mark, by David Norrie of Papakura and Onehunga, was 419. *Daily Southern Cross*, 29 March, 1875, p. 3.

6. University of Auckland Historical Collection part 1, MSS and Archives E8, Box 2, Folder 2, Special Collections, n.p.

7. 'Presentation of Degree of Bachelor of Arts to Miss Edger', *Auckland Star*, 12 July 1877, p. 3.

8. A situation for a 'thoroughly competent Commercial Master' for the Boys' High School in Dunedin was advertised in 1877 at the same salary as Kate's. *Otago Witness*, 31 January 1877, p. 1. By way of comparison, Lyttelton's Harbour Board secretary and treasurer, a senior local government official, received £400 per annum. *Lyttelton Times*, 21 February 1877, p. 1.

9. Raewyn Dalziel, 'The Colonial Helpmeet: Women's role and the vote in nineteenth-century New Zealand', *New Zealand Journal of History*, 11, 2, 1977, pp. 118; Jane Tolerton, 'Household services – Servants in the 19th century', Te Ara – the Encyclopedia of New Zealand: www. TeAra.govt.nz/en/household-services/page-1. See also evidence of sock-knitter 'Miss H', 'Sweating Commission. Report of the Royal Commission appointed to inquire into certain relations between the employers of certain kinds of labour and the persons employed therein', *Appendix to the Journals of the House of Representatives [AJHR]*, 1890, H–5, p. 14.

10. Population Summary at successive Census periods, 1878 Census, item 6: www3.stats.govt.nz/ historicpublications/1878 Census results

11. Geoffrey Rice, *Christchurch Changing: An illustrated history* (Christchurch: Canterbury University Press, 2008), pp. 38–41, 45.

12. Barbara Peddie, *Christchurch Girls' High School* (Christchurch: Christchurch High School Old Girls' Association, 1977), pp. 17, 18, 20–21.

13. W.J. Gardner, 'Women in the Lecture Room', *New Zealand Listener*, 10 July 1976, p. 8. This article was the text of an address entitled 'Early New Zealand Women Graduates', Macmillan Brown Lectures, 1975.

14. Morris Matthews, *In Their Own Right*, p. 91.

15. Mrs. W.A. Evans, First Assistant, September 1877–December 1882, 'Early Months: Aims and difficulties', *Canterbury College Girls' High School Christchurch Jubilee Record 1877–1927*, Girls' High School, Christchurch, New Zealand, Jubilee Committee, Old Girls' Association 1928, p. 11.

16. Evans, 'Early Months', p. 12.

17. Ibid.
18. Ibid., pp. 12–13.
19. Ibid., p. 13.
20. See Samuel Edger, 'A Contribution towards Elucidating the Ideal Education', Lecture IV in *Autobiographical Notes and Lectures* (London: William Isbister, 1886), pp. 227–42.
21. Quoted on Christchurch Girls' High School website: www.cghs.school.nz
22. Edith Searle Grossmann, *The Life of Helen Macmillan Brown, the First Woman to Graduate with Honours in a British University* (Christchurch: Whitcombe & Tombs, 1905), pp. 24, 48.
23. Edith Searle Grossmann, 'In Memoriam', *Canterbury College Girls' High School Christchurch, Jubilee Record 1877–1927*, p. 18.
24. Margaret Lovell-Smith, *Easily the Best: The life of Helen Connon, 1857–1903* (Christchurch: Canterbury University Press, 2004), p. 46.
25. Margaret Lorimer, cited in *Canterbury College Girls' High School Christchurch, Jubilee Record 1877–1927*, p. 23.
26. Elizabeth Whyte, cited in *Canterbury College Girls' High School Christchurch, Jubilee Record 1877–1927*, p. 21.
27. Quoted in Morris Matthews, *In Their Own Right*, p. 92.
28. *AJHR* 1881, Session I, E–4, 'Education: The Canterbury College', p. 3; *AJHR* 1883, Session I, E–7, 'Education: The Canterbury College', p. 3.
29. Mrs. K.W. Evans, 'The First Girl Graduates', *Lyttelton Times*, 12 May 1923, p.16. The initials, of course, should have been K.M. This article appeared in a special supplement related to the history of Canterbury College. My thanks to Margaret Lovell-Smith, who kindly sent me a photocopy of this document.
30. Elizabeth Whyte, cited in *Canterbury College Girls' High School Christchurch, Jubilee Record 1877–1927*, p. 20.
31. *New Zealand Herald*, 22 May 1878, p. 2.
32. 'Our Christchurch Letter', *Observer*, 11 February 1882, p. 344.
33. Evans, 'The First Girl Graduates'.
34. Grossmann, *The Life of Helen Macmillan Brown*, p. 25.
35. Lovell-Smith, *Easily the Best*, p. 33.
36. Edith Searle Grossmann, 'Student Life in the Eighties', *Lyttelton Times*, 12 May 1923, p. 18.
37. Lovell-Smith, *Easily the Best*, p. 36.
38. R.M. Burdon, *Scholar Errant: A biography of Professor A.W. Bickerton* (Christchurch: Pegasus Press, 1956), p. 17.
39. Evans, 'The First Girl Graduates', *Lyttelton Times*, 12 May 1923, p. 16.
40. Ibid.
41. W.J. Gardner, *Colonial Cap and Gown: Studies in the mid-Victorian universities of Australasia* (Christchurch: University of Canterbury, 1979), p. 64.
42. Ref. 122330, Correspondence from Edger, Kate, to Brown, John Macmillan, MB118/8, Macmillan Brown Papers, University of Canterbury.
43. John Macmillan Brown, *The Memoirs of John Macmillan Brown* (Christchurch: Published for the University of Canterbury by Whitcombe & Tombs, 1974).
44. Professor John Macmillan Brown, 'Canterbury College', *Star,* 15 March 1878, p. 3.
45. Charles Chiltern, *An Early History of the Canterbury College Dialectic Society: An address delivered to the Society on 19 March 1904* (Christchurch: Whitcombe & Tombs, 1923), p. 9.
46. Ibid., pp. 16–17.

47. Ibid., pp. 14, 18.
48. H.F. von Haast, 'Study in the Post-Pioneering Days', supplement, *Press*, 12 May 1923, p. iii.
49. Chiltern, *An Early History*, pp. 19, 27.
50. Lady Principal re salaries of teachers, Girls' High School, 21 October 1881, Canterbury College Inwards Correspondence, cited in Lovell-Smith, *Easily the Best*, p. 47.
51. *Nelson Evening Mail*, 15 July 1882, p. 2.
52. See Lovell-Smith, *Easily the Best*, Chapter 4.
53. *New Zealand Herald*, 23 September 1880, p. 4; 24 September 1880, p. 5.
54. The house may have been Motu Rakau, at 10 Arthur Street, with the garden fronting Ponsonby Road. Geraldine Hemus later described it as 'standing high in spacious grounds in the best part of Ponsonby and commanding exquisite views in all directions'. According to her, it was initially occupied by Frederick and Marion Judson and later by Lilian, who set up a college there in 1886 (see Chapter 5). In 1898 the Hemus family moved into the house, and in 1902 a new building called Whareora was built on the front of the property, facing Ponsonby Road. See Geraldine Hemus, *Theosophy in New Zealand, Golden Jubilee Number of the New Zealand Section 1896–1946*, April–June 1946, New Series Vol. 7, No. 2, Auckland Libraries serial 212T39, pp. 49–50, and Dora Judson, letter to Amy Causley, 13 November 1898, and June 1902 letter from Irene Hemus to Amy headed 'Motu Rakau': 'You will notice a great difference in Motu Rakau when you come again, with buildings in front. We have named them Whareora and everybody thinks they are a great improvement to Ponsonby Road', Amy Causley Papers, AWMM 87/61.
55. Edger, *Autobiographical Notes*, pp. 113, 114.
56. 'Death of the Rev. Samuel Edger', *New Zealand Herald*, 6 October 1882, p. 5; 9 October 1882, p. 6. Death certificate religious classification courtesy ancestry.com.
57. 'New Zealand University – Distribution of Diplomas', *Lyttelton Times*, 30 August 1882, p. 6.
58. Henrietta O. Barnett, 'Women as Philanthropists', in Theodore Stanton (ed.), *The Woman Question in Europe: A series of original essays* (New York: G.P. Putnam's Sons, 1884, p. 109), quoted in Linda L. Clark, *Women and Achievement in Nineteenth-Century Europe* (Cambridge: Cambridge University Press, 2008), p. 176.
59. Nancy Swarbrick, 'Primary and secondary education – Teachers', Te Ara – the Encyclopedia of New Zealand: www.TeAra.govt.nz/en/primary-and-secondary-education/page-8
60. Morris Matthews, *In their Own Right*, p. 30.
61. J. Rhoda Barr, *Within the Sound of the Bell*, Whitcombe & Tombs, 1953, p. 7, cited in Margaret Tennant, 'Matrons with a Mission: Women's organisations in New Zealand, 1893–1915', MA thesis in history, Massey University, 1976, p. 5.
62. Annual Report of Department of Education, *AJHR*, 1909, S2, E1, pp. 5–6. Girls' leaving age was 13 (Standard 4) but many advanced through the standards more quickly than the boys, which also altered their average leaving age, p. 8.

CHAPTER 4 **FOUNDING HEADMISTRESS**

1. 'Prize Day at the Girls' College', *Nelson Evening Mail*, 20 December 1887, p. 2.
2. *Nelson Evening Mail*, 25 May 1882, p. 2.
3. Lois C. Voller, *Sentinel at the Gates: Nelson College for Girls, 1883–1983* (Nelson: Nelson College for Girls for Nelson Old Girls' Association, 1982), p. 15.

4. Letterbook 1882–4, 12 November 1882, p. 49, Nelson College Collection [NCC], Nelson Provincial Museum [NPM], A4435.1, AG82, B1.7.

5. Voller, *Sentinel at the Gate*, pp. 4–5.

6. Lucy Bland, *Banishing the Beast: Sexuality and the early feminists* (New York: The New Press, 1995), p. 51.

7. Frances Porter, *Born to New Zealand: A biography of Jane Maria Atkinson* (Wellington: Bridget Williams Books, 1995), p. 275.

8. J.G. McKay (compiler), 'The Inception of Nelson College for Girls', Annual Report of Council of Governors, Nelson College, 1872, p. 1; NCC, NPM, AG 82, Box 11, Folder 2.

9. Voller, *Sentinel at the Gates*, p. 29.

10. McKay, Annual Report of Council of Governors, 1883, pp. 2–3, NCC, NPM, AG 82, Box 11, Folder 2.

11. Letter, Lilian to Eva Edger, 4 February 1883, quoted in Voller, *Sentinel at the Gates*, pp. 21–22.

12. *Nelson Evening Mail*, 2 February 1883, p. 2. The figure of 67 seems to have excluded some 13 or so boarders.

13. The prospectus had specific charges for pupils under and over 12, *Nelson Evening Mail*, 5 October 1882, p. 2.

14. Quoted in Voller, *Sentinel at the Gates*, pp. 21–22.

15. Letter from John Macmillan Brown to James Sclanders, 21 October 1882, NCC, NPM, AG82, Box 11, Folder 2. Sclanders and Co. were Nelson wholesale agents.

16. The identity of Lilian's betrothed is not known, but a likely candidate could be Thomas P. Arnold, a grandson of Thomas Arnold of Rugby, who taught at Christchurch Boys' High School in the early 1880s. Information from Bruce Harding, Curator/Archivist, Christchurch Boys' High School, December 2018.

17. W.J. Gardner, *Colonial Cap and Gown: Studies in the mid-Victorian universities of Australasia* (Christchurch: University of Canterbury, 1979), p. 98.

18. Samuel Edger's *Autobiographical Notes and Lectures* and his *The Problem of Life Considered* were published in London in 1886 and 1887 respectively by William Isbister. His essay on the ideal education appears in the *Autobiographical Notes*, pp. 227–41.

19. 'Nelson Girls' College', *Colonist*, 29 December 1887, p.1 (Supplement).

20. Ibid., and see www.theprow.org.nz/yourstory/kate-edger/#.XzSpa-gzayI, which states that merit certificates continue to be awarded at Nelson Girls' College for worthy recipients 'for excellent work and overall behaviour in class'.

21. Ruth Fry, '"Don't Let Down the Side": Physical education in the curriculum for New Zealand schoolgirls, 1900–1945', in Barbara Brookes, Charlotte Macdonald and Margaret Tennant (eds), *Women in History: Essays on European women in New Zealand* (Wellington: Allen & Unwin/ Port Nicholson Press, 1986), p. 101.

22. 'The Girls' College Tennis Tournament', *Colonist,* 21 April 1887, p. 5.

23. Quarterly Report, 1886, NCC, NPM, AG 82, Box 11, Folder 7, Letters/Memorandum. Indian clubs, which originated on the Indian sub-continent, were a popular component of the fitness movement in the Victorian era. Made of wood in various sizes, and shaped like a bowling pin, they were swung in various patterns, the aim being to develop strength and mobility. Kate herself taught club swinging, on the gravel in front of the college.

24. Nancy Swarbrick, 'Primary and secondary education – Curriculum changes', Te Ara – the Encyclopedia of New Zealand: www.TeAra.govt.nz/en/primary-and-secondary-education/ page-5

25. 'Nelson Girls' College', *Colonist*, 29 December 1887, p. 5.
26. Board of Governors Minute Book, January 1881–December 1887, A1.3, p. 171, NPM.
27. *Nelson Evening Mail*, 3 December 1883, p. 3.
28. *Nelson Evening Mail*, 17 December 1884, p. 3.
29. 'Girls' College, Distribution of Certificates', *Nelson Evening Mail*, 1 March 1884, p. 2.
30. Ibid.
31. 'The University Senate', *New Zealand Herald*, 1 March 1884, p. 5.
32. 'Girls College, Distribution of Certificates'.
33. Cecilia Summerhayes, letter to Governors, September 10, 1883, NCC, NPM, AG82, Box 11, Folder 3, Letters/Memorandum 1883.
34. Draft and final letters from Governors to Miss Bell, NCC, NPM, AG 82, Box 11, Folder 5, Documents 1884–1893 including staff appointments. Nelson Boys' College later hired Bell as a matron, but again, her employment there ended on a sour note.
35. 'Nelson Girls' College', *Nelson Evening Mail*, 9 July 1883, p. 2.
36. Voller, *Sentinel at the Gates*, p. 25.
37. Lady Principal to Secretary, Council of Governors, letters of 28 June 1889 and 17 July 1889, NGC, NPM, AG 82, Box 11, Folder 9, Letters 1889.
38. Letters, Memorandums 1886, Lady Principal Report for 1886, NGC, NPM, AG82, Box 11, Folder 7, n.p.
39. Jane Maria Atkinson to Anne E. Richmond, Nelson, 4 December 1885, in Guy Scholefield (ed.), *The Richmond Atkinson Papers*, vol. 2 (Wellington: Government Printer, 1960), p. 531.
40. Voller, *Sentinel at the Gates*, p. 26.
41. Secretary Oswald Curtis to Lady Principal, 5 September 1885, p. 351, NCC, NPM, AG82, B1.8 Letterbook, 1884–1886.
42. NCC, NPM, Ag 82, Box 11, A1.3 Minute Book, January 1881–December 1887, p. 254.
43. Oswald Curtis, Secretary to Lady Principal, 3 December 1885, p. 351, NCC NPM, ag82, Letterbook B1.8, 1884–1886.
44. Ibid.
45. NCC, NPM, Ag 82, Box 11, Folder 7, Quarterly Report, October 1886.
46. Kate Edger to Katie Thompson, 15 February 1886, NCC NPM, AG 82, Box 11, Folder 7, Letters/Memorandum 1886.
47. 'Teachers Association', *Colonist,* 17 May 1887, p. 3.
48. 'New Zealand Educational Conference', *New Zealand Herald*, 25 January 1888, p. 6.
49. 'Prize Day at the Girls College', *Nelson Evening Mail*, 20 December 1887, p. 2.
50. Kate M. Edger, 'Our Famous Women', *Colonist*, 28 April 1885, p. 3.
51. 'Girls' College', *Colonist*, 2 January 1886, p. 5.
52. 'Nelson Girls' College', *Colonist,* 29 December 1888, p. 5.
53. 'Prize Day at the Colleges, Girls' College', *Nelson Evening Mail*, 19 December 1889, p. 2.
54. Ibid.

CHAPTER 5 A REFORMING PARTNERSHIP – THE FORWARD MOVEMENT

1. Hugh Price Hughes, *Social Christianity: Sermons delivered in St. James's Hall, London* (London: Hodder & Stoughton, 1889), p. xiii, cited in Rupert Dawes, A. Raymond George and Gordon

Rupp (eds), *A History of the Methodist Church in Great Britain*, vol. 3 (London: Epworth Press, 1983), p. 310.

2. 'The Diamond Jubilee', Papers relating to the Forward Movement, MS-Papers-11535-022, ATL, n.p.

3. 'Fashionable Marriages', *Observer*, 11 January 1890, p. 11.

4. See Margaret Cole and Barbara Drake (eds), Beatrice Webb, *Our Partnership* (London: Longmans, Green & Co., 1948) and Laurence Thompson, *The Enthusiasts: A biography of John and Katharine Bruce Glasier* (London: Victor Gollancz, 1971).

5. Miss G.M. Hemus, 'Early Days of the Theosophical Society in Auckland', *Theosophy in New Zealand, Golden Jubilee Number of the New Zealand Section, 1896–1946*, April–June 1946, p. 50. Marion taught music from the Ponsonby College premises for years.

6. 'All Sorts of People', *Freelance*, 22 September 1900, p. 3.

7. 'A Local Ben Adhem, The Late Rev. W.A. Evans', *Evening Post*, 14 November 1921, p. 8.

8. 'The Rev. William Albert Evans', *The Cyclopedia of New Zealand*, Wellington Provincial District, p. 407: http://nzetc.victoria.ac.nz/tm/scholarly/tei

9. Gareth Stedman Jones, *Outcast London: A study in the relationship between classes in Victorian society* (London: Penguin, 1971), p. 7; and see Paul Harris and John Morrow (eds), *T.H. Green: Lectures on the principles of political obligation and other writings* (Cambridge: Cambridge University Press, 1986).

10. *Nelson Evening Mail*, 2 January 1890, p. 2.

11. *Nelson Evening Mail*, 9 August 1892, p. 3.

12. Andrew Mearns, *The Bitter Cry of Outcast London: An inquiry into the condition of the abject poor*, 1883: https://attackingthedevil.co.uk

13. Nigel Scotland, *Squires in the Slums: Settlements and missions in late Victorian London* (London: I.B. Tauris, 2007), pp. 36–42.

14. Scotland, *Squires in the Slums*, p. 52.

15. Jean Bethke Elshtain, *Jane Addams and the Dream of American Democracy: A life* (New York: Basic Books, 2002), p. 157.

16. Don Wright, *Mantle of Christ: A history of the Sydney Central Methodist Mission* (St Lucia, Queensland: University of Queensland Press), 1984, p. 10.

17. Hughes, *Social Christianity*, cited in Dawes et al., *A History of the Methodist Church*, p. 310.

18. 'The Voice of the Past to the Men of the Present Concerning Wealth', *Nelson Evening Mail,* 10 September 1890, p. 4.

19. 'Congregational Church', *Colonist*, 1 October 1890, p. 5.

20. 'Sweating Commission. Report of the Royal Commission appointed to inquire into certain relations between the employers of certain kinds of labour and the persons employed therein', *AJHR*, 1890, H–5, p. vi.

21. *Auckland Star*, 1 February 1893, p. 3; *Colonist*, 26 January 1893, p. 3.

22. *Evening Post*, 3 May 1893, p. 2.

23. 'Sunday Lecture', *New Zealand Times*, 19 June 1893, p. 2.

24. Papers relating to the Forward Movement.

25. Minute Book for Organisations, including The Forward Movement, MS-Papers 11535-023, ATL. The first management committee formed on 28 August 1893 comprised 'Mesdames Atkinson, Fell and Pringle and Miss Richmond; and Messrs Atkinson, Beaglehole, Briggs, Campbell, Darke, Edwards, Gain, Lankshear, Pringle, Russell, Richmond and Slater.'

26. Papers relating to the Forward Movement.

27. Mount Victoria Historical Society, Kate Edger: http://mtvictoria.history.org.nz

28. The Riwaka Valley is spelled Dehra Doon, but the Evans house and school were frequently spelled Dehra Dhoon.

29. Advertisement, *Evening Post*, 22 July 1896, p. 1.

30. Advertisement, *Evening Post*, 22 March 1897, p. 2.

31. Dorice Williams Elliott, *The Angel out of the House: Philanthropy and gender in nineteenth-century England* (Richmond VA: University of Virginia Press, 2002), p. 122.

32. See Noel Harrison, *The School that Riley Built: The story of the Wellington Technical College from 1886* (Wellington: Wellington Technical College, 1961).

33. Forward Movement Programme of Work for 1895, Papers relating to the Forward Movement.

34. Michael King, *The Penguin History of New Zealand* (Auckland: Penguin, 2003), p. 246.

35. *The Citizen*, 1, 2, Temperance Work, p. 36; Mutual Help Society, p. 37; Literary Society, pp. 35–36.

36. *Evening Post*, 6 June 1895, p. 2.

37. See Tim Beaglehole, *A Life of J.C. Beaglehole, New Zealand Scholar* (Wellington: Victoria University Press, 2006), pp. 33–34.

38. Louisa Blake, 'On the Labour Question', *The Citizen*, 1, 4, December 1895, pp. 195–202; Basil Stocker, 'Co-operative Housekeeping', pp. 165–72; Anna Stout, 'The New Woman', pp. 158–59; Lilian Edger, 'Theosophy and Social Reform', p. 253. Theosophy, a religious movement that incorporated eastern occult beliefs, was founded in 1875 by Helena Blavatsky and Henry Steel Olcott.

39. George Fowlds, 'The Ethics of the Land Question', *The Citizen*, 1, 7, March 1896, pp. 381–92, and Dr Findlay, 'The Decline of the Orthodox School of Political Economy', 1, 1, September 1895, and Part 2, 1, 2, October 1895, quotes p. 51.

40. Robert Stout, 'The Political Outlook', *The Citizen*, 1, 1, September 1895, pp. 20–26, and 'The Colony and Banking', 1, 3, pp. 89–94; J.H. Helliwell, 'Civic Duty', 1, 1, September 1895, p. 31; A.R. Atkinson, 'Christianity and the Liquor Traffic', 1, 5, January 1896 and Dr Chapple, 'The Extension of Technology in Education', 1, 7, March 1896, pp. 410–19; quotes pp. 413, 419.

41. W.A. Evans, 'Christian Citizenship', *The Citizen*, 1, 7, March 1896, pp. 421–22.

42. See Herbert Roth, *George Hogben: A biography* (Wellington: New Zealand Council for Educational Research, 1952), and Herbert Roth. 'Hogben, George', *Dictionary of New Zealand Biography*, first published in 1993. Te Ara – the Encyclopedia of New Zealand: https://teara.govt.nz/en/biographies/2h44/hogben-george

43. David McKenzie, Gregory Lee and Howard Lee, *The Transformation of the New Zealand Technical High School*, Delta Research Monograph No. 10 (Dunedin: University of Otago, 1990), p. 4.

44. In 1903 William Evans was chairman of the governing board of Wellington's Technical School (formerly Wellington College of Design). In 1914 the Social Democratic Party, later amalgamated into the Labour Party, would condemn secondary schools for fostering snobbery and promoting class distinction: McKenzie at al., *The Transformation of the New Zealand Technical High School*, p. 19.

45. 'The Diamond Jubilee', Papers relating to the Forward Movement.

46. The Hospitals and Charitable Institutions Act of 1885 created numerous local hospital and charitable aid boards that had considerable discretionary powers and overlapping jurisdictions. The new legislation aimed to reduce central government expenditure on poor relief and to discourage all but the most desperate poor from seeking assistance. See Margaret Tennant,

'Indigence and Charitable Aid in New Zealand 1885–1920', PhD thesis in history, 1981, Massey University, pp. 11–12.

47. Papers of John Cawte Beaglehole and his family, MS-Papers-11535-141, ATL; Papers relating to the Forward Movement. Ruskin actually wrote 'forever interwoven'.

48. 'Pars about People', *Observer*, 9 November 1895, p. 5.

49. Papers Relating to the Forward Movement.

50. Megan Cook, 'Domestic Workers' Unions 1890–1942': https://nzhistory.govt.nz/women-together/domestic-workers-unions

51. 'Domestic Workers' Union, The Inaugural "Social"', *Evening Post*, 17 June 1898, p. 2.

52. *Press*, 29 June 1898, p. 6.

53. 'Domestic Workers' Union, The Open Column', *New Zealand Times*, 12 October 1899, p. 7.

54. Cook, 'Domestic Workers' Unions'.

55. Harris Weinstock, 'Report on the Labour Laws and Labour Conditions of Foreign Countries in Relation to Strikes and Lockouts', Sacramento, 1910, p. 119, cited in Herbert Roth, *Trade Unions in New Zealand Past and Present* (Wellington: Reed Education, 1973), p. 21. The 1890 Maritime Strike was a dispute over pay and conditions that originated in Australia's Mercantile Marine Officers' Association in mid-August and spread to New Zealand, where watersiders, miners and seamen unions struck in support.

56. 'An Unemployment Settlement in Wellington', *Evening Post*, 3 March 1895, p. 3.

57. 'Clerics and State Farms', *Press*, 16 June 1899, p. 5.

58. Tom Brooking, *Richard Seddon, King of God's Own: The life and times of New Zealand's longest-serving prime minister* (Auckland: Penguin, 2014), pp. 176–78.

59. William, a foundation member of the College Council, served as chairman (the role that from 1957 became chancellor) from 1902 to 1904, and was a long-standing member, along with Stout, of the New Zealand University Senate; Stout, chairman from 1900 to 1902, was a Victoria College Council member until 1915. William was also a member, and in 1903 chairman, of the Technical Education Board. He actively opposed any encroachment on secularism in New Zealand schools, believing that attempts to erode that tradition were opening the door to unwanted denominationalism.

60. 'Citizens' Union', *New Zealand Times*, 31 March 1898, p. 3.

61. *Evening Post*, 31 March 1898, p. 4.

62. See *Evening Post*, 22 April 1898, p. 2; 10 May 1898, p. 5; 19 May 1898, p. 2; 29 June 1898, p. 2; 25 August 1898, p. 5.

63. 'Pars about People', *Observer*, 22 November 1902, p. 8.

64. Dora Judson to Amy Causley, letter of 9 July 1911, Amy Causley Papers, 87/61, AWMM 1626, n.p.

65. R.H. Tawney on Christian Socialism, from *Religion and the Rise of Capitalism* (1926), p. 285, quoted in Bernard Murchland, *The Dream of Christian Socialism: An essay on its European origins* (Washington and London: American Enterprise Institute for Public Policy Research, 1982), p. 35.

CHAPTER 6 SUFFRAGE AND THE DEMON DRINK

1. Lilian signed too while both sisters were teaching at Ponsonby College, sheet 403: https://nzhistory.govt.nz/politics/womens-suffrage/petition

2. Phillida Bunkle, 'The Origins of the Women's Movement in New Zealand: The Women's Christian Temperance Union 1885–1895', in Phillida Bunkle and Beryl Hughes (eds), *Women in New Zealand Society* (Auckland: Allen & Unwin, 1980), p. 71.

3. Jock Phillips, 'Alcohol', Te Ara – the Encyclopedia of New Zealand: www.TeAra.govt.nz/en/alcohol/page2

4. Beryl Hughes. 'Edger, Kate Milligan', *Dictionary of New Zealand Biography*, first published in 1993. Te Ara – the Encyclopedia of New Zealand: https://teara.govt.nz/en/biographies/2e3/edger-kate-milligan

5. Barbara Brookes, 'The Power of the Word', in Bronwyn Labrum (ed.), *Women Now: The legacy of female suffrage* (Wellington: Te Papa Press, 2018), p. 25.

6. The motto was originally 'For God, Home and Native Land' but 'Native Land' later changed to 'Every Land' and then to 'Humanity'. The WCTU's watchwords were 'Agitate, Educate, Legislate' and its platform 'Peace, Purity and Prohibition'; see Ian Dougherty, *Without Compromise: A brief history of the New Zealand Women's Christian Temperance Union* (Auckland: New Zealand Women's Christian Temperance Union, 2013), p. 4.

7. See Charlotte Macdonald, 'The "Social Evil": Prostitution and the passage of the Contagious Diseases Act (1869)', in Barbara Brookes, Charlotte Macdonald and Margaret Tennant (eds), *Women in History: Essays on European women in New Zealand* (Wellington: Allen & Unwin/Port Nicholson Press, 1986), pp. 13–33.

8. Megan Cook, 'Women's movement', Te Ara – the Encyclopedia of New Zealand: www.TeAra.govt.nz/en/womens-movement/print

9. Women's Pledge of Purity cited in Bunkle, 'Origins of the Women's Movement', in Bunkle and Hughes (eds), *Women in New Zealand Society*, p. 71.

10. Macdonald, 'The "Social Evil"', in Brookes et al., *Women in History*, p. 21.

11. A.R. Grigg, 'Prohibition and Women: The preservation of an ideal and a myth', *NZJH*, 17, 2, 1983, Table I, p. 153.

12. *Leader*, 3 May 1889, p. 14, cited in Patricia Grimshaw, *Women's Suffrage in New Zealand* (Auckland: Auckland University Press; Oxford: Oxford University Press, 1987), p. 31.

13. 'Women's Suffrage Meeting', *Nelson Evening Mail*, 11 March 1891, p. 2.

14. *New Zealand Herald*, 3 June 1892, p. 4.

15. Grimshaw, *Women's Suffrage*, p. 84.

16. Julia Bush, *Women Against the Vote: Female anti-suffragism in Britain* (Oxford: Oxford University Press, 2007), pp. 45–46. Some of the prominent signatories to the 1889 'Appeal Against Women's Suffrage' included Mary Ward, Louise Creighton, Charlotte Green, Charlotte Toynbee, Ethel Harrison and Lucy Soulsby, along with 11 students and staff from Lady Margaret Hall, Oxford. By 1910 the Oxford branch of the Women's National Anti-Suffrage League boasted over 300 female members and associates and was still headed by several university wives.

17. 'Evangelistic Department', *White Ribbon*, 1 May 1895, p. 4.

18. Kate Sheppard writing her regular column as 'Penelope' in *The Prohibitionist*, 2 January 1892, p. 3, cited in Laurie Guy, *Shaping Godzone: Public issues and church voices in New Zealand 1840–2000* (Wellington: Victoria University Press, 2011), p. 181, fn 20. Guy makes the point that despite this victory for non-sectarian tolerance, the evangelical Christianity of the WCTU remained strong and fundamental to its various operations; all meetings opened and closed with a scripture reading and prayer, p. 182.

19. Roberta Nicholls, *The Women's Parliament: The National Council of the Women of New Zealand 1896–1920* (Wellington: Victoria University Press, 1996), pp. 30–31.
20. 'The Southern Cross Society', *Evening Post*, 10 August 1895, p. 2.
21. 'Southern Cross Society, Paper by Lady Stout', *Evening Post*, 23 August 1895, p. 4.
22. 'Charitable Aid: Mrs. Evans points out where in her opinion reforms are necessary', *New Zealand Times*, 28 July 1896, p. 2; 'The Social Question', *Evening Post*, 28 September 1897, p. 5.
23. *Evening Post*, 18 February 1892, p. 2.
24. Kate Sheppard, 'The Responsibilities of Women as Citizens', *White Ribbon*, 1 April 1899, pp. 8–9.
25. Nicholls, *The Women's Parliament*, pp. 51–52, 73–75, 80.
26. Mrs. W.A. Evans quoted in 'Evening Session, Dominion Convention of WCTU', *Colonist,* 11 March 1913, p. 6.
27. Marion Judson, 'Some General Principles of Good Citizenship', *White Ribbon*, 18 July 1913, p. 10.
28. 'Of sixty-nine people who were listed in 1910 as vice-presidents of the N.Z. Alliance … only three (4.3%) were women.' Grigg, 'Prohibition and Women', p. 152.
29. Julie Melnyk, *Victorian Religion: Faith and life in Britain* (London: Praeger, 2008), pp. 92–93. The League of the Cross, founded in London in 1873 by Cardinal Henry Edward Manning, promoted total abstinence among Catholics throughout Britain. Later in the century James Cullen took up the cause again in Ireland, founding the Pioneer Total Abstinence Association in 1898.
30. Reverend Samuel Edger, 'Annual Sermon on Intemperance', *New Zealand Liberator*, No. 20, 22 July 1876, p. 5.
31. Paul Frederick McKimmey, 'The Temperance Movement in New Zealand, 1835–1894', MA thesis in history, University of Auckland, 1968, p. 159. The figure of 37 percent is from the 1891 census, see fn 83.
32. See Grigg, 'Prohibition and Women'.
33. Kate Sheppard, New Zealand Franchise Superintendent, speaking at the NZWCTU 1894 annual convention, quoted in 'How the Women of New Zealand Won the Vote', *Southern Cross*, 3 March 1894, p. 8.
34. Lily Kirk, 'The Moral and Social Aspects of Temperance', *White Ribbon*, 1 July 1897, pp. 1–2.
35. Guy, *Shaping Godzone*, pp. 144–45.
36. *New Zealand Observer*, 14 July 1906, p. 3.
37. Grigg, 'Prohibition and Women', pp. 157–58.
38. *White Ribbon*, 18 December 1914, p. 19.
39. G.R. Searle, 'The Politics of National Efficiency and of War, 1900–1918', in Chris Wrigley (ed.), *A Companion to Early Twentieth-Century Britain* (Oxford: Blackwell Publishing, 2003), p. 58.
40. *AJHR*, 1917, H-43, p. 1, cited in Steven Loveridge and James Watson, *The Home Front: New Zealand society and the war effort, 1914–1919* (Auckland: Massey University Press, 2019), p. 276.
41. *Dominion*, 22 July 1916, p. 4.
42. *Evening Post,* 7 April 1916, p. 9.
43. Kate M. Evans, 'The 1919 Convention', *White Ribbon*, 18 February 1919, p. 11.
44. Kate Evans, 'Stop: Look out for the Bogey!', *White Ribbon*, 18 March 1919, p. 11.
45. 'After the Battle', *White Ribbon*, 19 April 1919, p. 9.
46. Paul Christoffel, 'Prohibition and the Myth of 1919', *NZJH*, 42, 2, 2008, p. 154.

47. A decrease in the prohibition vote in 1928 was due largely to the Alliance, which failed to invest in its usual advertising campaign, see Christoffel, 'Prohibition and the Myth of 1919', p. 164.
48. 'Decline', from A.H. McLintock (ed.), *An Encyclopedia of New Zealand* (Wellington: Government Printer, 1966): www.TeAra.govt.nz

CHAPTER 7 **PROTECTION AND REDEMPTION**

1. Kate Sheppard, 'Responsibilities', *White Ribbon*, 1 October 1896, p. 7.
2. Hon. Thomas Kelly, *New Zealand Parliamentary Debates [NZPD]*, 5 September 1900, p. 476.
3. 'Mrs. Kate M. Evans, Obituary', *Evening Post*, 11 May 1935, p. 18.
4. Barbara Brookes, 'A Weakness for Strong Subjects: The women's movement and sexuality', *NZJH*, 27, 2, 1993, p. 140.
5. Margaret Tennant, *The Fabric of Welfare: Voluntary organisations, government and welfare in New Zealand 1840–2005* (Wellington: Bridget Williams Books, 2007), p. 64.
6. See Raewyn Dalziel, 'Wilding, Henry', *Dictionary of New Zealand Biography*, first published in 1996. Te Ara – the Encyclopedia of New Zealand: https://teara.govt.nz/en/biographies/3w16/wilding-henry. Now called Home and Family Counselling, the organisation Wilding founded is New Zealand's oldest charity.
7. Margaret McClure, *A Civilised Community: A history of social security in New Zealand 1898–1998* (Auckland: Auckland University Press/Historical Branch, Internal Affairs, 1998), pp. 12–13.
8. Margaret Tennant, '"Brazen-Faced Beggars of the Female Sex": Women and the charitable aid system, 1880–1920', in Barbara Brookes, Charlotte Macdonald and Margaret Tennant (eds), *Women in History: Essays on European women in New Zealand* (Wellington: Allen & Unwin/Port Nicholson Press, 1986), p. 36.
9. 'Charitable Aid', *Star*, 12 October 1897, p. 1.
10. 'Charitable Aid: What the supervisor thinks of the Benevolent Institution', *New Zealand Times*, 28 March 1896, p. 3; 'The Report of Mr. Evans', *New Zealand Times*, 1 April 1896, p. 3, and *Evening Post*, 19 December 1899, p. 6. In 1898, Arthur Atkinson, one of the Wellington SPWC's greatest supporters, wrote a long diatribe about the new old-age pension, which he saw as unwarranted charitable largesse, claiming that Dickens's Bill Sykes would have qualified for the scheme had he lived in New Zealand long enough. See 'Old Age Pensions', *Evening Star*, 20 August 1898, p. 1. Robert Humphrey's *Poor Relief and Charity 1869–1945: The London Charity Organization Society* (Houndsmills and New York: Palgrave, 2001) examines the beliefs that motivated members of the English COS.
11. 'Charitable Aid: Mrs. Evans points out where in her opinion reforms are necessary', *New Zealand Times*, 28 July 1896, p. 2.
12. 'Quiet, Active Kindness', *Evening Post*, 17 October 1906, p. 2.
13. 'The Juvenile Depravity Question', *Evening Post*, 30 September 1897, p. 2.
14. Society for Protection of Women and Children, Wellington Branch Annual Reports, 1897–1919, MSX-3292, ATL, p. 1. Annie Williams was married to major landowner Thomas C. Williams; Margaret Fell to Dr Walter Fell.
15. After arriving in the city in 1899, Mother Aubert and her Sisters of Compassion did much to assist the health and well-being of Wellington's poor. They established St Joseph's Home for Incurables in Buckle Street, and Our Lady's Home of Compassion in Island Bay for

disadvantaged children of all kinds. See Margaret Tennant, 'Aubert, Mary Joseph', Dictionary of New Zealand Biography, first published in 1993. Te Ara – the Encyclopedia of New Zealand: https://teara.govt.nz/en/biographies/2a18/aubert-mary-joseph

16. SPWC, Wellington Branch Annual Reports, 1898, p. 3

17. SPWC, Wellington Branch Annual Reports, 1900, pp. 8–9.

18. SPWC, Wellington Branch Annual Reports, 1900, p. 7.

19. 'Protection of Women and Children', *Evening Post*, 18 October 1899, p. 2; 'Protection of Women and Children', 24 October 1900, p. 2. Uchter Knox, the fifth Earl of Ranfurly, was governor of New Zealand from 1897 to 1904. His predecessor, the Earl of Glasgow, had been the SPCW's inaugural patron.

20. SPWC, Wellington Branch Annual Report, 1898, pp. 3–4.

21. 'Protection Society', *New Zealand Times*, 18 October 1899, p. 3. The committee members were listed as Mesdames O.H. Izard, J. Brown, Ewart, Hoby, Fell, Lukin, Kirkcaldie, Paterson, Mackenzie, Oliver, Wallis, Sister Bird, Adjutant Spargo and Miss Glasgow. Adjutant Spargo was a member of the Salvation Army.

22. SPWC Wellington Branch Annual Reports, 1900, pp. 4, 8.

23. Tennant, *The Fabric of Welfare*, p. 76.

24. SPWC, Wellington Branch Annual Reports, 1900, pp. 7, 9, and SPWC, Wellington Branch, Minute Book, 1912–1915, qMS-1564, ATL, 13 12/12.

25. 'Protection of Women and Children', *Evening Post*, 7 October 1903, p. 2.

26. SPWC, Wellington Branch, Minute Book, 1897–1901, qMS-1560, ATL, p. 86.

27. Hon. T. Kelly, *NZPD*, 5 September 1900, p. 476.

28. Mrs. Kate Milligan Evans, *New Zealand Legislative Council, Journals and Appendix No. 6, 1899–1900*, Young Person's Protection Bill, 13 September 1899, p. 20.

29. Hon. Mr. W.C. Walker, *NZPD*, vol. 116, July 1901, p. 459.

30. Mr. Wilford, *NZPD*, vol. 117, July–August 1901, p. 399.

31. Mr. Fisher, *NZPD*, vol. 117, July–August 1901, p. 405.

32. Mr. Hall-Jones, *NZPD*, vol. 117, July–August 1901, p. 411.

33. 'Inspectors of Morality', *Hawke's Bay Herald*, 9 October 1899, p. 4.

34. Premier Seddon, *NZPD*, vol. 123, June–July 1903, p. 763.

35. Polly Plum, 'A Scandal to Our Province: The women's department of the gaol', *Daily Southern Cross*, 6 December 1871, p. 3; see Jenny Coleman, *Polly Plum: A firm and earnest woman's advocate, Mary Ann Colclough 1836–1885* (Dunedin: Otago University Press, 2017), pp. 88–89.

36. Samuel Edger, *The Folly and Evil of Hanging Men: An argument against capital punishment, given in the City Hall, on Sunday evening, Aug. 3, 1873, on the occasion of the execution of Eppwright, in the Mount Eden Gaol, Auckland* (Auckland: William Atkin, 1873), pp. 3–11.

37. Wounding of adult males took place at the rate of 11.6 per 100,000, while in England the rate was 7.1. The homicide rate in New Zealand was 5.1 per 100,000 and 1.9 in England: John Pratt, *Punishment in a Perfect Society: The New Zealand penal system 1840–1939* (Wellington: Victoria University Press, 1992), pp. 151–52.

38. Mrs. W.A. Evans, 'The Treatment of the Criminal', paper presented to the National Council of Women, April 27th 1898; Third Session, Bellamys, Parliament Buildings, April 20–28th, 1898; Auckland University Special Collections NZGC 301.41200927p1899.

39. Lombroso has been described as 'the single most important figure in accounts of the founding of criminology and the study of aberrant behaviour in the human sciences'; Paul Knepper and P.J. Ystehede (eds), *The Cesare Lombroso Handbook* (London and New York: Routledge, 2013),

p. 5. For a more critical examination of his legacy, see Mary Gibson's *Born to Crime: Cesare Lombroso and the origins of biological criminality* (London: Praeger, 2002), which focuses on Lombroso's views about the biological determinism of habitual criminals rather than his advocacy of humane and liberal prison reform. Elmira Reformatory and its superintendent, Zebulon Reed Brockway, encountered troubled waters in the late 1890s. Brockway was made to retire in 1900, aged 72, following accusations of disciplinary excesses.

40. Evans, 'The Treatment of the Criminal', pp. 44, 47. Elmira was founded in 1875.
41. Ibid., p. 39
42. Ibid.
43. 'Treatment of the Criminal', *Evening Post*, 28 April 1898, p. 2.
44. Elizabeth Fry, 'Observations on the Visiting, Superintendence and Government of Female Prisoners', London, 1827, p. 2, cited in Anne Isba, *The Excellent Mrs Fry: Unlikely heroine* (London, New York: Continuum, 2010), p. 205.
45. 'Prison Reform – Lecture by Mrs Cunnington', *Star*, 23 August 1897, p. 6.
46. National Council of the Women of New Zealand Minutes 1897, MS-Papers 1376, ATL, p. 3.
47. 'Women's Work', *Dominion*, 1 November 1916, p. 3.
48. See www.police.govt.nz/about-us/history-and-museum/75-years-women-police
49. Debates on this legislation in the New Zealand Parliament did not, as in Europe and England, focus on degenerationist fears; rather the arguments focused more on the protection of society, deterrence and/or rehabilitation. Lombroso's views about 'born criminals' were not invoked, nor were fears of society being overrun by the 'dangerous classes'. For a discussion of such views in England with regard to habitual criminals, see David Taylor, *Crime, Policing and Punishment in England 1750–1914* (Basingstoke: Macmillan, 1998), pp. 57–58.
50. *White Ribbon*, 15 August 1904, p. 9.
51. *NZPD*, 1906, vol. 156, pp. 175–76.
52. 'Quiet Active Kindness', *Evening Post*, 17 October 1906, p. 2.
53. Geoffrey G. Hall, 'Findlay, John George', *Dictionary of New Zealand Biography*: https://teara.govt.nz/en/biographies/3f7/findlay-john-george
54. *NZPD*, 1910, vol. 15, p. 348.
55. *NZPD*, 1909, vol. 148, p. 1035.
56. Department of Justice, 'A Scheme for the Reorganisation of the Prison System of New Zealand', *AJHR*, 1910, H20b, Wellington.
57. Pratt, *Punishment in a Perfect Society*, pp. 213–14.
58. J.G. Findlay, Crimes Act Amendment Act 1910, Legislative Council, *NZPD*, vol. 150, p. 349.
59. *New Zealand Times*, 17 March 1910, p. 6; *Evening Post*, 10 August 1910, p. 3. The *Otago Daily Times* was also complimentary: 'Prison Reform', 18 March 1910, p. 4.
60. *NZPD*, 1910, vol. 151, p. 359.
61. K.A. Sheppard, *Woman Suffrage in New Zealand* (London: International Woman Suffrage Alliance, 1907), p. 11.
62. Tennant, *The Fabric of Welfare*, p. 81.
63. Bronwyn Dalley, *Family Matters: Child welfare in twentieth-century New Zealand* (Auckland: Auckland University Press/Historical Branch, Department of Internal Affairs, 1998), p. 9.

CHAPTER 8 **COMPULSORY DOMESTICITY**

1. 'Society for the Promotion of the Health of Women and Children', Address by Dr. F.C. Batchelor, University of Auckland Special Collections, New Zealand Pamphlets, 83–99, p. 4.

2. 'Sketch of the Movement for Higher Education of Girls', *White Ribbon*, 18 August 1914, p. 14.

3. 'Regulations, Manual and Technical Instruction', *New Zealand Gazette*, 1917, vol. 2, p. 3030, and *AJHR*, 1917, E–1, p. 42.

4. G.R. Searle, *The Quest for National Efficiency: A study in British politics and British political thought 1899–1914* (Oxford: Blackwell, 1971), p. 11, 60–67, 238.

5. James Belich, *Paradise Reforged: A history of the New Zealanders from the 1880s to the year 2000* (Auckland: Penguin, 2001, p. 181) suggests a tendency to stop having children earlier in married life as one reason for the decline, combined with a trend towards less marriage, and less sex in late marriage: see pp. 182–83. Margaret Tennant argues that there was a *perception* that families were willfully limiting their size, causing 'pessimistic eugenists' to worry that the wrong people, i.e. the middle classes, were doing so; see Margaret Tennant, 'Natural Directions: The New Zealand movement for sexual differentiation in education during the early twentieth century', in Barbara Brookes, Charlotte Macdonald and Margaret Tennant (eds), *Women in History: Essays on European women in New Zealand* (Wellington: Allen & Unwin/Port Nicholson Press, 1986), p. 89.

6. 'Women, Work, and Wages', *NZ Truth*, 29 January 1910, p. 1.

7. Linda Bryder, *A Voice for Mothers: The Plunket Society and infant welfare, 1907–2000* (Auckland: Auckland University Press, 2003), p. 19.

8. 'Health of Women and Children', *Dominion*, 22 October 1907, p. 3.

9. 'Saving the Babies', *Dominion*, 17 March 1908, p. 3.

10. Anna Stout, *Woman Suffrage in New Zealand* (London: The Woman's Press, 1911), p. 8.

11. 'Society for the Promotion of the Health of Women and Children, Address by Dr. F.C. Batchelor', University of Auckland Special Collections, New Zealand Pamphlets, 83–99, p. 4; 'An endorsement by Dr. King', p. 11.

12. *Dominion*, 25 May 1909, p. 8.

13. Ruth Fry, *It's Different for Daughters: A history of the curriculum for girls in New Zealand schools 1900–1975* (Wellington: New Zealand Council for Educational Research, 1985), p. 86.

14. WCTU National Convention Minutes, 27 March 1911, MS-79-057-09/10, ATL, n.p.

15. 'Report of the Education Commission, together with Minutes and Proceedings of Evidence', *AJHR*, 1912, E-12, p. 739: https:atojs.natlib.govt.nz/cgi.bin. And see www.parliament.nz/en/pb/library-research-papers/research-papers/the-government-s-changing-role-in-the-governance-of-new-zealand-s-schools-since-1847/#_Toc26873347

16. 'Women and Children. Society's Annual Meeting', *Evening Post*, 26 October 1910, p. 9.

17. Heath McDonald, 'Boys-Smith, Winifred Lily', *Dictionary of New Zealand Biography*, first published in 1996. Te Ara – the Encyclopedia of New Zealand: https://teara.govt.nz/en/biographies/3b41/boys-smith-winifred-lily

18. Tennant, 'Natural Directions', pp. 92–93.

19. Melanie Nolan, *Breadwinning: New Zealand women and the state* (Christchurch: Canterbury University Press, 2000), p. 124.

20. 'Report and Evidence of the Royal Commission on Cost of Living in New Zealand', *AJHR*, 1912, H-18, p. lxii: https://atojs.natlib.govt.nz.

21. 'Women in Print', *Evening Post*, 18 June 1913, p. 9.

22. 'Science of the Home and Macarthy Fund', *Dominion*, 26 June 1913, p. 6.

23. Fry, *It's Different for Daughters*, p. 51.

24. 'Sketch of the Movement for Higher Education of Girls', *White Ribbon*, 18 August 1914, p. 14.

25. Tennant, 'Natural Directions', p. 94.

26. 'Educational Progress. Memorandum by the minister dealing with some phases of educational progress and reviewing existing conditions in the light of national requirements', *AJHR*, 1916, E-1A, pp. 8-9: https://atojs.natlib.govt.nz

27. Nolan, *Breadwinning*, p. 106.

28. 'Mothers' Thought Guild', *Auckland Star*, 18 April 1917, p. 8; 'Mothers' Thought Guild', *Auckland Star*, 10 July 1918, p. 3.

29. 'Girls' Education', *New Zealand Times*, 14 September 1916, p. 2.

30. Cited in Angela Wanhalla, 'To "Better the Breed of Men": Women and eugenics in New Zealand 1900–1935', *Women's History Review*, 16, 2, April 2007, p. 165.

31. Anne Kerr, Tom Shakespeare and Suzy Varty, *Genetic Politics: From eugenics to genome* (Cheltenham: New Clarion Press, 2002), pp. 8–14.

32. Philip J. Fleming, 'Eugenics in New Zealand, 1900–1946', MA thesis in history, Massey University, 1981, p. 73.

33. Ibid., pp. 73–76.

34. Wanhalla, 'To "Better the Breed of Men"', p. 166.

35. Fleming, 'Eugenics', p. 10; *Otago Daily Times*, 31 May 1911, p. 5.

36. 'Feeble-Minded Girls', *New Zealand Herald*, 6 October 1911, p. 3.

37. Fleming, 'Eugenics', p. 76.

38. *Evening Star*, 17 February 1911, p. 9.

39. *Herald*, 6 October 1911, p. 3.

40. Truby King, 'The Feeding of Plants and Animals', Wellington 1905, cited in Erik Olssen, 'Truby King and the Plunket Society: An analysis of a prescriptive ideology', *NZJH*, 1981, 15, 1, p. 6.

41. 'The Control of the Feeble-Minded: Home for girls needed', *New Zealand Times*, 25 March 1911, p. 1.

42. Lily Atkinson was the founding president.

43. 'Education of Girls', *Dominion*, 20 November 1916, p. 2. This was a letter summarising the motions carried at the October meeting and sent to the minister of education by the Women's Social Investigation League.

44. *Evening Post*, 28 October 1916, p. 6.

45. 'Training of Girls', *Dominion*, 5 July 1917, p. 7.

46. Editorial, 'Differentiation in the Education of Girls', *White Ribbon*, 18 June 1917, p. 9.

47. Kate Evans letter, entitled 'Sex Differentiation in Education', *White Ribbon*, 18 July 1917, p. 1.

48. Editor's response, *White Ribbon*, 18 July 1917. pp. 1–2.

49. Beryl Hughes, 'Coad, Nellie Euphemia', *Dictionary of New Zealand Biography*: https://teara.govt.nz/en/biographies/3c23/coad-nellie-euphemia

50. Chaplin invoked this quote by C.A. Stewart, a male teacher who used it when responding critically to a paper she had delivered over a year earlier to the Otago Educational Institute on the subject of educational differentiation. Wielding his own words against him, she asked, 'Why, then, all these objections to differentiation?' Arguing that women teachers 'earnestly desire that girls shall have no inferior education. It must be in complete harmony with their needs, mental, moral and physical,' she concluded her reply to Stewart by noting that 'it is sheer hypocrisy to

applaud equality for girls and boys at school if one is unprepared to apply that principle to men and women working side by side in the teaching profession'. See 'Educational Adjustment: A reply', *Evening Star,* 15 August 1918, p. 7. Stewart's paper, 'A Defence of Co-Education', appeared in the *Evening Star* on 12 July 1918, p. 6.

51. A comprehensive account of the historiographical aspects of the debate over compulsory domestic science is found in 'The Domestic Education Debate', Chapter 4 of Nolan, *Breadwinning,* pp. 103–36. Historians who emphasise the negative repercussions of the regulation and the 'cult of domesticity' include Ruth Fry and Erik Olssen. Nolan takes the differing view; see p. 122.

52. Nolan, *Breadwinning,* p. 124.

53. 'Girls' High School', *Press,* 14 December 1917, p. 9.

CHAPTER 9 WAR, SOCIAL PURITY AND MORAL FIBRE

1. Hon. Mr. Russell, *NZPD,* 1916, vol. 177, p. 214.

2. WCTU Convention Minutes, 1913–1918, 79-057-09/11, ATL, 18 March 1918.

3. See https://teara.govt.nz/en/biographies/2s24/sievwright-margaret-home and https://teara.govt.nz/en/biographies/2d2/daldy-amey

4. Roberta Nicholls, *The Women's Parliament: The National Council of the Women of New Zealand 1896–1920* (Wellington: Victoria University Press, 1996), p. 73.

5. Deborah Montgomerie, 'New Women and Not-So-New-Men: Discussions about marriage in New Zealand 1890–1914', *NZJH,* 51, 1, 2017, p. 41.

6. NCW resolution passed at 1897 National Convention, quoted in Megan Hutching, 'Mothers of the World: Women, peace and arbitration in early twentieth-century New Zealand', *NZJH,* 27, 2, 1993, p. 7.

7. Hutching, 'Mothers of the World', pp. 176–77.

8. 'Women in Print', *Evening Post,* 17 October 1914, p. 9. Equal pay for equal work was a long time coming. Differentiation between female and male teachers' salaries remained until the Government Service Equal Pay Act of 1960.

9. *AJHR,* H14, 'Report of the Public Service Commissioner', 1 January 1914, Education Department List of Examiners, E8, 1916 and 1917.

10. *New Zealand Times,* 17 January 1910, p. 7.

11. Geraldine Hemus, 'Early Days of the Theosophy Society in Auckland', *Theosophy in New Zealand,* New Series, 7, 2, April–June 1946, p. 50, Auckland Libraries, serial 212T39, p. 49.

12. *New Zealand Times,* 17 January 1910, p. 7. For an insight into Frank Edger's professional career see Richard Boast, 'The Lost Jurisprudence of the Native Land Court: The Liberal Era, 1891–1912', *New Zealand Journal of Public and International Law,* vol. 12, 2014, pp. 81–102.

13. 'Guild of Service', *New Zealand Times,* 12 August 1914, p. 6; *Evening Post,* 5 June 1916, p. 9; 'Women's Work in Shops and Offices: Minister explains the position', *Evening Post,* 1 June 1916, p. 4.

14. Nicholls, *Women's Parliament,* p. 101.

15. 'Organise! An appeal to women: "You Don't Realise Your Power!"', *Evening Post,* 29 September 1914, p. 8.

16. Philip Fleming, 'Fighting the Red Plague', *NZJH,* 22, 1, 1988, p. 58.

17. Barbara Brookes, *A History of New Zealand Women* (Wellington: Bridget Williams Books, 2016), p. 156.

18. Philip J. Fleming, 'Shadow over New Zealand: The response to venereal disease in New Zealand 1910–1945', PhD in history, Massey University, 1989, p. 107.
19. Fleming, 'Shadow over New Zealand', pp. 21–24.
20. Minutes of 27 March 1917, WCTU Convention Minutes 1913–1918, ATL, 79-057-09/11. The 24 March article in the *Auckland Star* (p. 10), entitled 'Ravages of Venereal', warned the subject had 'no right to be tabooed' and advised that 'the nation needs to wake up and tackle this great problem'.
21. 'Women Police: A deputation's request', *Evening Post*, 3 August 1917, p. 9.
22. 'Social Hygiene – Government's Proposals Discussed by Meeting of Women', *Evening Post*, 8 October 1917, p. 4.
23. 'Social Hygiene: Women discuss bill protest against inequitable provisions', *New Zealand Times*, 11 October 1917, p. 2.
24. 'Social Hygiene: Bringing the new act into operation', *Press*, 10 November 1917, p. 13; *Colonist*, 16 July 1919, p. 3.
25. Jane Tolerton, *Ettie Rout: New Zealand's safer sex pioneer* (Auckland: Penguin Books, 2015), pp. 22, 34.
26. Ettie A. Rout, 'Venereal Disease – Alarming Spread – Infection Among New Zealand Soldiers', *New Zealand Times*, 24 October 1917, p. 3.
27. *New Zealand Times*, 31 December 1917, p. 8.
28. A series of sensational articles written by the English journalist W.T. Stead in 1885 prompted a widespread moral panic about the 'white slave trade'. The furore the articles evoked resulted in a push by feminists to raise the age of consent and tighten up on 'procurement'. Concerns about this issue recurred intermittently in ensuing decades.
29. Tolerton, *Ettie Rout*, p. 34.
30. WCTU Convention Minutes, 1913–1918, 79-057-09/11, ATL, 24 March 1914, n.p.
31. WCTU Convention Minutes, 18 March 1918, n.p.
32. *Evening Post*, 22 April 1918, p. 4.
33. *Evening Post*, 2 April 1918, p. 9.
34. Nicholls, *Women's Parliament*, p. 104.
35. Katherine Sanders, '"The Sensational Scandal which has Worried Wellington": The Kelburn raid, sex and the law in First World War New Zealand', *NZJH*, 48, 2, 2014, pp. 91–92.
36. Sanders, '"The Sensational Scandal"', p. 93.
37. *NZ Truth*, 'A Police Raid', 4 May 1918, p. 5.
38. *NZ Truth*, 'A 'Touching' Tale of Upliftment', 5 April 1919, p. 5, cited in Sanders, '"The Sensational Scandal"', p. 93, fn. 14.
39. 'Cops Catch at Cultured Kelburn', *NZ Truth*, 11 May 1918, p. 5.
40. 'Women and Justice', *Evening Post*, 10 June 1918, p. 6.
41. 'Equal Treatment Women and the War Regulations: Demand for reforms', *Dominion*, 10 June 1918, p. 3.
42. *Dominion*, 10 June 1918, p. 3.
43. 'Social Morality: Large women's meeting, a lively gathering', *New Zealand Times*, 10 June 1918, p. 6.
44. 'Manslaughter', *Star*, 11 June 1915, p. 3.
45. 'A Plea for Alice Parkinson', *Maoriland Worker*, 28 July 1915, p. 4.
46. 'Lynch Law', *Auckland Star*, 29 July 1916, p. 6.
47. 'Women's Meeting', *Evening Post*, 10 June 1918, p. 2.

48. 'The Protest Meeting', letter from Anna Stout, *New Zealand Times*, 15 June 1918, p. 10.

49. 'Sassiety Spice' by 'Lady Dot', *NZ Truth*, 22 June 1918, p. 2.

50. Mrs. Isabel Hulbert, 'Warfare of Wild and Whirling Words', *NZ Truth*, 22 June 1918, p. 2.

51. Richard J. Evans, *Comrades and Sisters: Feminism, socialism and pacifism in Europe 1870–1945* (Sussex: Wheatsheaf Books, 1987), p. 31; Clara Zetkin, *Selected Writings*, Philip S. Foner (ed.), (New York: International Publishers, 1984), p. 77.

52. New Zealand Women's Christian Temperance Union Convention Minutes, 1913–1918, 3 March 1913, 23 March 1917, n.p.

CHAPTER 10 A JUST COMMUNITY IN A HAPPY FAMILY OF NATIONS

1. 'Social Gatherings', *Auckland Star*, 8 February 1930, p. 13.

2. Cited in Malcolm McKinnon, *Independence and Foreign Policy: New Zealand in the world since 1935* (Auckland: Auckland University Press, 1993), p. 15.

3. James' knee problem, which pre-dated the war, became problematic in August, shortly after his arrival in England. For the remainder of his service abroad he was moved around various hospitals and camps. See Edger James Evans, WW1 48478, Duplicate Personnel File, R 20547281, Archives New Zealand.

4. 'Enthusiastic Celebrations', *Hawera and Normanby Star*, 13 November 1918, p. 4.

5. Barbara Brookes, *A History of New Zealand Women* (Wellington: Bridget Williams Books, 2016), p. 187; 'Deaths', *New Zealand Herald*, 21 November 1918, p. 1.

6. Melanie Nolan, *Breadwinning: New Zealand women and the state* (Christchurch: Canterbury University Press, 2000), p. 150.

7. Society for the Protection of Women and Children, Wellington Branch Minutes, qMS-1565, ATL, 13 December 1918.

8. Brookes, *History of New Zealand Women*, p. 221.

9. Ibid., p. 195.

10. Letter from Kate Evans to Myrtle Bell, 21 January 1921, Jill Smith Collection.

11. Author conversation with Jill Smith, May 2017.

12. 'Obituary, Lily May Atkinson', *Evening Post*, 20 July 1921, p. 6.

13. Frances Porter, 'Atkinson, Lily May', *Dictionary of New Zealand Biography*: https://teara.govt.nz/en/biographies/2a17/atkinson-lily-may

14. Author conversation with Jill Smith, May 2017.

15. 'The Rev. W.A. Evans', *Evening Post*, 7 November 1921, p. 7.

16. 'A Local Ben Adhem: The late Rev. W.A. Evans', *Evening Post*, 14 November 1921, p. 8.

17. *NZ Truth*, 26 November 1921, p. 1.

18. 'Bereavement Notices: Thanks', *Evening Post*, 8 November 1921, p. 1.

19. This reference to the horse-drawn cortège is mentioned in a personal letter among family papers, Jill Smith Collection.

20. Lord Robert Cecil, quoted in the *New York Times* of 28 December 1918, cited in Martyn Housden, *The League of Nations and the Organization of Peace* (Harlow: Longman, 2012), p. 9.

21. LNU Pamphlet, 'The League of Nations Union', London, 1919, p. 3, cited in Donald S. Birn, *The League of Nations Union 1918–1945* (Oxford: Clarendon Press, 1981), p. 11.

22. Frank McDonough, *Neville Chamberlain: Appeasement and the road to war* (New York: Manchester University Press, 1998), p. 11.

23. B.J. Ellis, 'The League of Nations Union and History Teaching in England: A study in benevolent bias', *History of Education,* 1977, 6, 2, p. 131.

24. 'League of Nations Union: The movement in Wellington', *Evening Post*, 8 April 1922, p. 6.

25. Bain Attwood, 'Apostles of Peace: The New Zealand League of Nations Union', MA thesis in history, University of Auckland, 1979, pp. 14–15.

26. League of Nations Union Executive Minutes 1922–39, 8 August 1924, 10 June 1924 and 11 May 1928, MSX-2569, ATL, n.p. The Executive Committee of the Wellington branch decided to amalgamate with the Dominion Executive in August 1922, because many were members of both and it meant duplicating the work. See August 1922 Minutes.

27. 'League of Nations Union Annual Meeting', *Press,* 12 June 1930, p. 9

28. Attwood, 'Apostles of Peace', p. 32.

29. *Evening Post*, 1 May 1925, p. 5.

30. League of Nations Union Executive Minutes, 25 March 1926.

31. League of Nations Union Executive Minutes, 25 March 1926 and 4 June 1946. Middleton commanded a flotilla of ships engaged in minesweeping operations in the Dardanelles during World War I. In 1926 he was secretary of the Auckland Navy League and commander of the New Zealand Naval Reserve. *Evening Post*, 2 June 1926, p. 10.

32. 'League of Nations Union Annual Conference', *Otago Daily Times*, 23 April 1926, p. 7.

33. League of Nations Union Wellington Branch Minutes, 4 September 1926.

34. 'Information for Women: Address by Sir James Allen,' *Evening Post*, 23 September 1926, p. 13.

35. 'World Friendship Badge', *Evening Post*, 23 March 1931, p. 11.

36. 'To Prevent War, Honolulu Conference, Pacific Problems, Professor Condliffe Returns', *Press*, 4 August 1925, p. 8.

37. 'Pacific Relations', *Evening Star*, 8 October 1927, p. 6.

38. *New Zealand Worker*, 16 November 1927, cited in Keith Sinclair, *Walter Nash* (Auckland: Auckland University Press/Oxford University Press), p. 82.

39. Sinclair, *Nash*, p. 83.

40. J.B. Condliffe, *Problems of the Pacific: Proceedings of the Second Conference of the Institute of Pacific Relations, Honolulu, Hawaii, July 15–29, 1927* (Chicago: University of Chicago Press, 1928), p. vi.

41. Tomoko Akami, *Internationalizing the Pacific: The United States, Japan and the Institute of Pacific Relations in war and peace, 1919–45* (London: Routledge, 2002), pp. 4–5.

42. 'WCTU. Convention', *Evening Post*, 24 September 1927, p. 13.

43. 'Social Gatherings', *Auckland Star*, 8 February 1930, p. 14.

44. 'Pan-Pacific Conference', *New Zealand Herald*, 22 June 1925, p. 8.

45. See Samuel Edger, 'Anti-Chinese Agitation: A better way', *New Zealand Herald*, 13 September 1879, p. 5.

46. League of Nations Wellington Branch Minutebook, 1922–1933, MSX2572, ATL, 10 June 1931 records that in May there had been some criticism among members of Kate's performance as secretary. She submitted a letter of resignation on 7 June but was asked to stay longer and told that a sub-committee would be formed to look after the subscriptions and keep them up to date. On 9 July the minutes record that Kate had also resigned the dominion secretaryship and it was imperative to find a replacement. An item in the press later attributed her resignation to 'ill-health', 'Tribute to Mrs. Evans', *New Zealand Herald*, 2 September 1931, p. 4.

47. 'Tribute to Mrs. Evans', *New Zealand Herald*, 2 September 1931, p. 4.

48. E.P. Malone, 'The *New Zealand School Journal* and the Imperial Ideology', *NZJH*, 7, 1, 1973, pp. 23–24.

49. J.B. Condliffe, *A Short History of New Zealand* (Christchurch: I.M. Isitt, 1925), p. 207.

50. Elsie Locke, *Peace People: A history of peace activities in New Zealand* (Christchurch: Hazard Press, 1992) p. 77.

51. Cited in Malcolm McKinnon, *The Broken Decade: Prosperity, depression and recovery in New Zealand, 1928–1939* (Dunedin: Otago University Press, 2016), p. 15.

52. Sinclair, *Nash*, p. 18; his election manifesto is quoted p. 112. Nash expressed the admiring views on Robert Owen in the House while speaking on the financial statement for 1937, *NZPD*, vol. 248, p. 1107, cited in Sinclair, *Nash*, p. 112; his views on socialism and conservatism in 1943 are from his *New Zealand: A working democracy* (New York: Duell, Sloan & Pearce, 1943), p. 265, cited in Sinclair, *Nash*, pp. 112–13, fn. 13.

53. Cited in Fred Northedge, *The League of Nations: Its life and times, 1920–1946* (Leicester: Leicester University Press, 1986), p. viii.

54. Leonard Woolf, *The War for Peace* (New York: Garland Publishing, 1972, 1st published 1940), p. 116.

CHAPTER 11 **LAST YEARS**

1. 'Jubilee Celebrations', *Nelson Evening Mail*, 17 April 1933, p. 2.

2. 'Women the World Over', specially written for the *Press* by 'Atalanta', *Press*, 1 June 1935, p. 2.

3. Malcolm McKinnon, *The Broken Decade: Prosperity, depression and recovery in New Zealand, 1928–1939* (Dunedin: Otago University Press, 2016), p. 14.

4. 'No Sex in Citizenship', *White Ribbon*, 18 August 1932, p. 1.

5. See Barbara Brookes, *A History of New Zealand Women* (Wellington: Bridget Williams Books, 2016), p. 247. Over a third of the Canterbury Education Board's married female teachers were widows, separated or deserted.

6. Auckland Insolvency files, R24404866, 138/1930, Box 9, Archives New Zealand, Auckland.

7. 'Land for Soldiers', *New Zealand Herald*, 30 August 1918, p. 4.

8. 'Soldier Settlement: Fighting the gorse on Pakaraka', *Auckland Star*, 6 December 1921, p. 7. This piece noted the rapid growth of gorse on the land and observed: 'Outside of a few sections, Pakaraka has little to commend it as a soldier settlement …'

9. Discharged Bankrupts, 'Mother's Heavy Loss', *Auckland Star*, 27 March 1931, p. 3.

10. Probate, Kate Milligan Evans, Box 481, Record 14748, Dunedin Probate and Letters of Administration Files (I), 1907–1950, Archives New Zealand, Dunedin.

11. See for example *New Zealand Herald*, 11 August 1920, p. 4, announcing Lilian's talk 'World's Peace' at the Remuera WCTU monthly meeting.

12. Jessie Mackay, 'Obituary', [Edith Searle Grossmann], *Evening Post*, 28 February 1931, p. 11.

13. 'Obituary', [W.F. Judson], *New Zealand Herald*, 17 September 1931, p. 14.

14. Lois C. Voller, *Sentinel at the Gates: Nelson College for Girls, 1883–1983* (Nelson: Nelson College for Girls for Nelson Old Girls' Association, 1982), p. 110.

15. 'Girls' College Jubilee', *New Zealand Herald*, 18 April 1933, p. 3.

16. 'Jubilee Celebrations', *Nelson Evening Mail*, 17 April 1933, p. 2.

17. 'Pioneer's Death', *Auckland Star*, 20 April 1935, p. 15.

18. Dora Judson to Amy Causley, letter of 5 June 1935, Amy Causley Papers, AWMM 87/61.

19. Right Honourable Sir Frederick Ponsonby, Treasurer of the King and Keeper of the Privy Purse to Governor General of New Zealand, telegram of 3 September 1932; Honours and Awards, General, King's Silver Jubilee Medal, 28/1/4, pt 1, 1934–1937, (R21681736), Archives New Zealand.

20. 'Mrs. Kate M. Evans, Obituary', *Evening Post*, 11 May 1935, p. 18.

21. 'Women the World Over', *Press*, 1 June 1935, p. 3.

22. 'Message from Minister of Education', *Press*, 12 December 1935, p. 4.

EPILOGUE

1. W.J. Gardner, 'Women in the Lecture Room', *New Zealand Listener*, 10 July 1976, p. 8. This was the text of a talk broadcast by the Concert Programme on 'Early New Zealand Graduates', an address in the Macmillan Brown Lectures, 1975.

2. Vryn's youngest daughter, she was born after Kate's death.

3. Nelson Girls' College principal Cathy Ewing, email to author, 24 November 2018.

4. Margaret Tennant, *The Fabric of Welfare: Voluntary organisations, government and welfare in New Zealand 1840–2005* (Wellington: Bridget Williams Books, 2007), p. 221.

5. See https://nzfvc.org.nz/news/nzfvc-data-summaries-2017-family-violence-reports-reach-record-high; www.rnz.co.nz/news/national/365452/violence-against-women-is-a-national-crisis-helen-clark; www.orangatamariki.govt.nz/assets/Uploads/About-us/Report-and-releases/Annual-Report/Oranga-Tamariki-Annual-Report-2018.pdf

Select Bibliography

PRIMARY SOURCES

Alexander Turnbull Library
League of Nations Union Executive Minutes 1922–39, MSX-2569
League of Nations Union Wellington Branch Minutes 1922–33, MSX-2572
Minute Book for Organisations, including The Forward Movement, MS-Papers 11535-023
National Council of the Women of New Zealand Minutes 1897, MS-Papers 1376
Papers relating to the Forward Movement, MS-Papers-11535-022
Samuel Edger Letters, 1862–63, MS-0711, B1507
Society for the Protection of Women and Children, MS Group 0180, Annual Reports MSX-3292
    and Minute Books, 1897–1923, qMS-1560–qMS1566
Women's Christian Temperance Union Papers, 709-057

Archives New Zealand
Edger James Evans WWI 48478-DPF (R20547281) [digital]
Honours and Awards, General, King's Silver Jubilee Medal, 28/1/4, pt. 1, 1934–1937 (R21681736)

Auckland War Memorial Museum
Amy Causley Papers, 1626.
Auckland Institute and Museum Minute Book IV, 1878–1883, MUS-1995-1-4

University of Auckland Special Collections
University of Auckland Historical Collection part 1, MSS and Archives E8, Box 2, Folder 2, Special
    Collections

University of Canterbury Macmillan Brown Library
Macmillan Brown Papers, MB118/8

Nelson Provincial Museum
Nelson College Collection

SECONDARY SOURCES

Published Books and Articles

Banks, Olive, *Faces of Feminism: A study of feminism as a social movement* (Oxford: Martin Robertson, 1981)

Beaglehole, Tim, *A Life of J.C. Beaglehole, New Zealand Scholar* (Wellington: Victoria University Press, 2006)

Birn, Donald S., *The League of Nations Union 1918–1945* (Oxford: Clarendon Press, 1981)

Bland, Lucy, *Banishing the Beast: Sexuality and the early feminists* (New York: The New Press, 1995)

Bradley, Ian, *The Call to Seriousness: The evangelical impact on the Victorians* (London: Jonathan Cape, 1976)

Brett, Sir Henry and Henry Hook, *The Albertlanders: Brave pioneers of the 'sixties* (Christchurch: Capper Press, 1979, original edn 1927)

Brookes, Barbara, 'A Weakness for Strong Subjects: The women's movement and sexuality', *New Zealand Journal of History*, 27, 2, 1993, pp. 140–56

Brookes, Barbara, *A History of New Zealand Women* (Wellington: Bridget Williams Books, 2016)

Brookes, Barbara, Charlotte Macdonald and Margaret Tennant (eds), *Women in History: Essays on European women in New Zealand* (Wellington: Allen & Unwin/Port Nicholson Press, 1986)

Brooking, Tom, *Richard Seddon, King of God's Own: The life and times of New Zealand's longest-serving prime minister* (Auckland: Penguin, 2014)

Brown, John Macmillan, *The Memoirs of John Macmillan Brown* (Christchurch: Whitcombe & Tombs, 1974)

Bryder, Linda, *A Voice for Mothers: The Plunket Society and infant welfare, 1907–2000* (Auckland: Auckland University Press, 2003)

Bunkle, Phillida and Beryl Hughes (eds), *Women in New Zealand Society* (Auckland: Allen & Unwin, 1980)

Burdon, R.M., *Scholar Errant: A biography of Professor A.W. Bickerton* (Christchurch: Pegasus Press, 1956)

Bush, Julia, *Women Against the Vote: Female anti-suffragism in Britain* (Oxford, New York: Oxford University Press, 2007)

Clark, Linda L., *Women and Achievement in Nineteenth-Century Europe* (Cambridge: Cambridge University Press, 2008)

Cole, Margaret and Barbara Drake (eds), Beatrice Webb, *Our Partnership* (London: Longmans, Green & Co., 1948)

Coleman, Jenny, *Polly Plum, a firm and earnest woman's advocate: Mary Ann Colclough 1836–1885* (Dunedin: Otago University Press, 2017)

Condliffe, J.B., *A Short History of New Zealand* (Christchurch: I.M. Isitt, 1925)

Condliffe, J.B., *Problems of the Pacific: Proceedings of the Second Conference of the Institute of Pacific Relations, Honolulu, Hawaii, July 15–29, 1927* (Chicago: University of Chicago Press, 1928)

Cristoffel, Paul, 'Prohibition and the Myth of 1919', *New Zealand Journal of History*, 42, 2, 2008, pp. 154–75

Daggers, Jenny and Diana Neal (eds), *Sex, Gender and Religion: Josephine Butler revisited* (New York: Peter Lang, 2006)

Dalley, Bronwyn, *Family Matters: Child welfare in twentieth-century New Zealand* (Auckland: Auckland University Press and Historical Branch, Department of Internal Affairs, 1998)

Dougherty, Ian, *Without Compromise: A brief history of the New Zealand Women's Christian Temperance Union* (Auckland: New Zealand Women's Christian Temperance Union, 2013)

Edger, Samuel, *Autobiographical Notes and Lectures* (London: William Isbister, 1886)

Elliott, Dorice Williams, *The Angel Out of the House: Philanthropy and gender in nineteenth-century England* (Richmond, VA: University of Virginia Press, 2002)

Ellwood, Robert S., *Islands of the Dawn: The story of alternative spirituality in New Zealand* (Hawai`i: University of Hawai`i Press, 1993)

Evans, Mrs. W.A. [Kate], 'Early Months: Aims and difficulties', *Canterbury College Girls' High School Christchurch Jubilee Record 1877–1927* (Girls' High School, Christchurch New Zealand, Jubilee Committee, Old Girls' Association 1928)

Evans, Kate M., 'The 1919 Convention', *White Ribbon*, 18 February 1919

Evans, W.A., 'Christian Citizenship', *The Citizen*, 1, 7, March 1896

Evans, Richard J., *Comrades and Sisters: Feminism, socialism and pacifism in Europe 1870–1945* (Sussex: Wheatsheaf Books, 1987)

Fleming, Philip, 'Fighting the Red Plague', *New Zealand Journal of History*, 1988, 22, 1, pp. 56–64

Ford, Katrina, *Unpretending Excellence: A life of Kate Edger* (Auckland: The Kate Edger Educational Charitable Trust, 2017)

Gardner, W.J., *Colonial Cap and Gown: Studies in the mid-Victorian universities of Australasia* (Christchurch: University of Canterbury, 1979)

Grigg, A.R., 'Prohibition and Women: The preservation of an ideal and a myth', *New Zealand Journal of History*, 17, 2, 1983, pp. 144–65

Grossmann, Edith Searle, *The Life of Helen Macmillan Brown, the First Woman to Graduate with Honours in a British University* (Christchurch: Whitcombe & Tombs, 1905)

Guy, Laurie, *Shaping Godzone: Public issues and church voices in New Zealand, 1840–2000,* (Wellington: Victoria University Press, 2011)

Harrison, Brian, *Drink and the Victorians* (Staffordshire: Keele University Press, 1994, 2nd edn)

Harrison, Noel, *The School that Riley Built: The story of the Wellington Technical College from 1886* (Wellington: Wellington Technical College, 1961)

Hemus, Geraldine, 'Early Days of the Theosophy Society in Auckland', *Theosophy in New Zealand*, New Series, 7, 2, April–June 1946

Isba, Anne, *The Excellent Mrs. Fry: Unlikely heroine* (London, New York: Continuum, 2010)

Humphrey, Robert, *Poor Relief and Charity 1869–1945: The London Charity Organization Society* (Houndsmills and New York: Palgrave, 2001)

Kerr, Anne, Tom Shakespeare and Suzy Varty, *Genetic Politics: From eugenics to genome* (Cheltenham: New Clarion Press, 2002)

Labrum, Bronwyn (ed.), *Women Now: The legacy of female suffrage,* (Wellington: Te Papa Press, 2019)

Locke, Elsie, *Peace People: A history of peace activities in New Zealand* (Christchurch: Hazard Press, 1992)

Lovell-Smith, Margaret, *Easily the Best: The life of Helen Connon, 1857–1903* (Christchurch: Canterbury University Press, 2004)

Malone, E.P., 'The *New Zealand School Journal* and the Imperial Ideology', *New Zealand Journal of History*, 7, 1, 1973, pp. 12–27

McClure, Margaret, *A Civilised Community: A history of social security in New Zealand 1898–1998* (Auckland: Auckland University Press in association with the Historical Branch, Internal Affairs, 1998)

McKinnon, Malcolm, *Independence and Foreign Policy: New Zealand in the world since 1935* (Auckland: Auckland University Press, 1993)

McKinnon, Malcolm, *The Broken Decade: Prosperity, depression and recovery in New Zealand, 1928–1939* (Dunedin: Otago University Press, 2016)

Melnyk, Julie, *Victorian Religion, Faith and Life in Britain* (London: Praeger, 2008)

Mill, John Stuart, *On Liberty, Utilitarianism and other Essays* (Oxford: Oxford University Press, 2015)

Millar, Grace, 'Women's Lives, Feminism and the *New Zealand Journal of History*', *New Zealand Journal of History* 52, 2, 2018, pp. 134–52

Montgomerie, Deborah, 'New Women and Not-So-New-Men: Discussions about marriage in New Zealand 1890–1914', *NZJH* 2017, 51, 1, 2017, pp. 36–64

Morris Matthews, Kay, *In Their Own Right: Women and higher education in New Zealand before 1945* (Wellington: NCER Press, 2008)

Nicholls, Roberta, *The Women's Parliament: The National Council of the Women of New Zealand 1896–1920* (Wellington: Victoria University Press, 1996)

Nolan, Melanie, *Breadwinning: New Zealand women and the state* (Christchurch: Canterbury University Press, 2000)

Norman, Edward R., *The Victorian Christian Socialists* (Cambridge, New York: Cambridge University Press, 1987)

O'Connor, P.J., 'Keeping New Zealand White, 1908–1920', *New Zealand Journal of History*, 2, 1, 1968, pp. 41–65

Olssen, Erik, 'Truby King and the Plunket Society: An analysis of a prescriptive ideology', *New Zealand Journal of History* 15, 1, 1981, pp. 3–23

Peddie, Barbara, *Christchurch Girls' High School* (Christchurch: Christchurch High School Old Girls' Association, 1977)

Phillips, Jock and Terry Hearn, *Settlers: New Zealand immigrants from England, Ireland and Scotland 1800–1945* (Auckland: Auckland University Press, 2008)

Porter, Frances, *Born to New Zealand: A biography of Jane Maria Atkinson* (Wellington: Bridget Williams Books, 1995)

Pratt, John, *Punishment in a Perfect Society: The New Zealand penal system 1840–1939* (Wellington: Victoria University Press, 1992)

Rice, Geoffrey, *Christchurch Changing: An illustrated history* (Christchurch: Canterbury University Press, 2008)

Roth, Herbert, *George Hogben: A biography* (Wellington: New Zealand Council for Educational Research, 1952)

Ruskin, John, *Sesame and Lilies* (London: George Allen, 1905)

Sanders, Katherine, '"The Sensational Scandal which has Worried Wellington": The Kelburn raid, sex and the law in First World War New Zealand', *New Zealand Journal of History*, 48, 2, 2014, pp. 91–118

Scotland, Nigel, *Squires in the Slums: Settlements and missions in late Victorian London* (London: I.B. Tauris, 2007)

Sheppard, K.A., *Woman Suffrage in New Zealand* (London: International Woman Suffrage Alliance, 1907)

Sinclair, Keith, *Walter Nash* (Auckland: Auckland University Press/Oxford University Press, 1976)

'Sketch of the Movement for Higher Education of Girls', *White Ribbon*, 18 August 1914

Somerville, Jennifer, *Feminism and the Family: Politics and society in the UK and USA* (New York: St Martin's Press, 2000)

Stedman Jones, Gareth, *Outcast London: A study in the relationship between classes in Victorian society* (London: Penguin, 1971)

Steinbach, Susie, *Women in England 1760–1914: A social history* (New York: Palgrave Macmillan, 2004)

Stenhouse, John, 'God's Own Silence: Secular nationalism, Christianity and the writing of New Zealand history', *New Zealand Journal of History*, 38, 1, 2004, pp. 52–71

Tennant, Margaret, *The Fabric of Welfare: Voluntary organisations, government and welfare in New Zealand 1840–2005* (Wellington: Bridget Williams Books, 2007)

Thompson, Laurence, *The Enthusiasts: A biography of John and Katharine Bruce Glasier* (London: Victor Gollancz, 1971)

Tolerton, Jane, *Ettie Rout: New Zealand's safer sex pioneer* (Auckland: Penguin Books, 2015)

Tosh, John, *A Man's Place: Masculinity and the middle-class home in Victorian England* (New Haven and London: Yale University Press, 1999)

Voller, Lois C., *Sentinel at the Gates: Nelson College for Girls, 1883–1983* (Nelson: Nelson College for Girls for Nelson Old Girls' Association, 1982)

Walkowitz, Judith, *City of Dreadful Delight: Narratives of sexual danger in late Victorian London* (London: Virago, 1992)

Wanhalla, Angela, 'To "Better the Breed of Men": Women and eugenics in New Zealand 1900–1935', *Women's History Review*, 16, 2, April 2007, pp. 163–82

Watts, Michael, *The Dissenters, Volume II: The expansion of evangelical nonconformity* (Oxford: Clarendon Press, 1995)

Theses

Attwood, Bain, 'Apostles of Peace: The New Zealand League of Nations Union', MA in history, University of Auckland, 1979

Fleming, Philip J., 'Eugenics in New Zealand, 1900–1946', MA in history, Massey University, 1981

Fleming, Philip, 'Shadow Over New Zealand: The response to venereal disease in New Zealand 1910-1945', PhD in history, Massey, 1989

McKimmey, Paul Frederick, 'The Temperance Movement in New Zealand, 1835–1894', MA in history, University of Auckland, 1968

Tennant, Margaret, 'Matrons with a Mission: Women's organisations in New Zealand', MA in history, Massey University, 1976

Tennant, Margaret, 'Indigence and Charitable Aid in New Zealand 1885–1920', PhD in history, Massey University, 1981

Index

Bold denotes illustrations